EARTHTALK

EARTHTALK

Communication Empowerment
for Environmental Action

Edited By Star A. Muir
and Thomas L. Veenendall

Praeger Series in Political Communication

Westport, Connecticut
London

Library of Congress Cataloging-in-Publication Data

Earthtalk : communication empowerment for environmental action /
   edited by Star A. Muir and Thomas L. Veenendall.
      p.   cm.—(Praeger series in political communication, ISSN
   1062–5623)
   Includes bibliographical references and index.
   ISBN 0–275–95370–X (alk. paper)
      1. Environmental sciences—Information services.   2. Mass media.
   3. Environmental policy.   I. Muir, Star A.   II. Veenendall, Thomas
   Lee.   III. Series.
   GE25.E27   1996
   363.7′0014—dc20   95–34420

British Library Cataloguing in Publication Data is available.

Library of Congress Catalog Card Number: 95–34420
ISBN: 0–275–95370–X
ISSN: 1062–5623

First published in 1996

Praeger Publishers, 88 Post Road West, Westport, CT 06881
An imprint of Greenwood Publishing Group, Inc.

Printed in the United States of America

The paper used in this book complies with the
Permanent Paper Standard issued by the National
Information Standards Organization (Z39.48–1984)

10 9 8 7 6 5 4 3 2 1

Copyright Acknowledgments

The author and publisher gratefully acknowledge permission to quote from the
following:

Excerpts from *Earth in the Balance.* Copyright © 1992 by Senator Al Gore. Reprinted by permission of Houghton Mifflin Co. All rights reserved.

The Adirondack Park by Frank Graham, Jr. Copyright © 1978 by the National
Audubon Society Inc. Reprinted by permission of Alfred A. Knopf, Inc.

Understanding Media by Marshall McLuhan. Copyright © 1964 by Corinne
McLuhan. Reprinted by permission of MIT Press.

CONTENTS

SERIES FOREWORD

THOSE OF US from the discipline of communication studies have long believed that communication is prior to all other fields of inquiry. In several other forums I have argued that the essence of politics is "talk" or human interaction.[1] Such interaction may be formal or informal, verbal or nonverbal, public or private but it is always persuasive, forcing us consciously or subconsciously to interpret, to evaluate, and to act. Communication is the vehicle for human action.

From this perspective, it is not surprising that Aristotle recognized the natural kinship of politics and communication in his writings *Politics* and *Rhetoric*. In the former, he establishes that humans are "political beings [who] alone of the animals [are] furnished with the faculty of language."[2] And in the latter, he begins his systematic analysis of discourse by proclaiming that "rhetorical study, in its strict sense, is concerned with the modes of persuasion."[3] Thus, it was recognized over 2,300 years ago that politics and communication go hand in hand because they are essential parts of human nature.

Back in 1981, Dan Nimmo and Keith Sanders proclaimed that political communication was an emerging field.[4] Although its origin, as noted, dates back centuries, a "self-consciously cross-disciplinary" focus began in the late 1950s. Thousands of books and articles later, colleges and universities offer a variety of graduate and undergraduate coursework in the area in such diverse departments as communication, mass communication, journalism, political science, and sociology.[5] In Nimmo and Sanders's early assessment, the "key areas of inquiry" included rhetorical analysis, propaganda analysis, attitude change studies, voting studies, government and the news media, functional and systems analyses, technological changes, media technologies, campaign techniques, and research techniques.[6] In a survey of the state of the field in 1984, the same authors and Lynda Kaid found additional, more specific areas of concern such as the presidency, political polls, public opinion, debates, and advertising to name a few.[7] Since the first study, they also noted a shift away from the rather strict behavioral approach.

Five years later, Dan Nimmo and David Swanson argued that "political communication has developed some identity as a more or less distinct domain of scholarly work."[8] The scope and concerns of the area have further expanded to include critical theories and cultural studies. While there is no precise definition, method, or disciplinary home of the area of inquiry, its primary domain is the role, processes, and effects of communication within the context of politics broadly defined.

The editors of *Political Communication Yearbook: 1984* noted that "more things are happening in the study, teaching, and practice of political communication than can be captured within the space limitations of the relatively few publications available."[9] In addition, they argued that the backgrounds of "those involved in the field [are] so varied and pluralist in outlook and approach, . . . it [is] a mistake to adhere slavishly to any set format in shaping the content."[10] And more recently, Nimmo and Swanson called for "ways of overcoming the unhappy consequences of fragmentation within a framework that respects, encourages, and benefits from diverse scholarly commitments, agendas, and approaches."[11]

In agreement with these assessments of the area and with gentle encouragement, Praeger established the Praeger Series in Political Communication. The series is open to all qualitative and quantitative methodologies as well as contemporary and historical studies. The key to characterizing the studies in the series is the focus on communication variables or activities within a political context or dimension. As of this writing, nearly forty volumes have been published and there are numerous impressive works forthcoming. Scholars from the disciplines of communication, history, journalism, political science, and sociology have participated in the series.

I am, without shame or modesty, a fan of the series. The joy of serving as its editor is in participating in the dialogue of the field of political communication and in reading the contributors' works. I invite you to join me.

Robert E. Denton, Jr.

NOTES

1. See Robert E. Denton, Jr., *The Symbolic Dimensions of the American Presidency* (Prospect Heights, Ill.: Waveland Press, 1982); Robert E. Denton, Jr., and Gary Woodward, *Political Communication in America* (New York: Praeger, 1985; 2nd ed., 1990); Robert E. Denton, Jr., and

Dan Hahn, *Presidential Communication* (New York: Praeger, 1986); and Robert E. Denton, Jr., *The Primetime Presidency of Ronald Reagan* (New York: Praeger, 1988).

2. Aristotle, *The Politics of Aristotle*, trans. Ernest Barker (New York: Oxford University Press, 1970), p. 5.

3. Aristotle, *Rhetoric*, trans. Rhys Roberts (New York: The Modern Library, 1954), p. 22.

4. Dan Nimmo and Keith Sanders, "Introduction: The Emergence of Political Communication as a Field," in *Handbook of Political Communication*, ed. Dan Nimmo and Keith Sanders (Beverly Hills, Calif.: Sage, 1981), pp. 11–36.

5. Ibid., p. 15.

6. Ibid., pp. 17–27.

7. Keith Sanders, Lynda Kaid, and Dan Nimmo, eds., *Political Communication Yearbook: 1984* (Carbondale: Southern Illinois University, 1985), pp. 283–308.

8. Dan Nimmo and David Swanson, "The Field of Political Communication: Beyond the Voter Persuasion Paradigm," in *New Directions in Political Communication*, ed. David Swanson and Dan Nimmo (Beverly Hills, Calif.: Sage, 1990), p. 8.

9. Sanders, Kaid, and Nimmo, *Political Communication Yearbook: 1984*, p. xiv.

10. Ibid.

11. Nimmo and Swanson, "The Field of Political Communication," p. 11.

ACKNOWLEDGMENTS

THE EDITORS WISH to thank many people whose efforts made this project possible. Thanks are due to Janette Kenner Muir for the original idea for the volume and for providing support and encouragement along the way. The associate editors, Nick Sebasto-Smith, Jonathan Lange, and Carol Corbin, all contributed to the dialogue this book represents by providing thoughtful and timely comments on all manuscripts. The support staff at Montclair State University and George Mason University are also appreciated, for their input of time, effort, and moral support that sustains any edited project. Finally, a debt should be acknowledged to the newest member of our rhetorical community— Caitlin Kenner Muir—whose innocent smile and trusting gaze bring the entire point of this book home for us all. Even as we learn to speak, we learn to construct and shape our world. It is the wonderful possibility of this world that moves us to explore the varieties of Earthtalk.

Star A. Muir
Thomas L. Veenendall

INTRODUCTION

DISCOURSE ABOUT THE environment plays a formidable role in shaping human interaction with nature. From Juvenal's satirical lamentation about the sewers of Rome, to Carson's quiet rage about DDT, Foreman's call to arms for ecotage, and Gore's "strategic environmental initiative," environmental communication has become a major political force affecting all of our lives. Perhaps the most important question facing teachers, scholars, critics, and students of environmental communication today is the appropriate and effective involvement of average citizens in issues that span local, regional, and global arenas. Aimed at exploring some of the challenges and opportunities now confronting the movement, this volume addresses the issue of environmental empowerment from a communication perspective and offers insight into the applicability and utility of a wide variety of communication theories.

ISSUES IN EMPOWERMENT

The first issue, an inescapable feature of the current political landscape, is that environmentalists now face considerably more opposition to their efforts, opposition that is vocal and becoming increasingly sophisticated at managing public appeals. Some say, for example, that the Wise Use movement has replaced communism with environmentalism as the number one enemy (Schneider, 1992, p. E3). A coalition of property owners, cattle ranchers, shrimpers, off-road-vehicle enthusiasts, and a diversity of other organizations form the core of this antienvironmental effort. The Alliance for America, the National Inholders Association, and the Multiple-Use Land Alliance have joined forces to protest the purpose and the range of environmental regulation. The movement favors opening up public lands, reducing restrictions on private development, and drilling for oil in the Arctic National Wildlife Refuge. Its organizers have been able to tap into deep resentment of the federal government (Murphy, 1995). Many of the environmental movement's tactics, including lobbying campaigns and lawsuits, have been adopted by the "wise users" (Alexander, 1992, p. 51). The incorporation of environmental values into the current administration, or at least a perception of the validation of environmental regulation, has increased the strength of the antienvironmental movement by providing the focal point for negative identification that the environmentalists have lost. Chuck Cushman, director of Battle Ground, a Washington-based association, claims that "Bill Clinton is [doing] for me what Jim Watt did for the Sierra Club" ("Grass Roots," 1993, p. 1). To date, The Bellevue, a group led by Ron Arnold, a founder of the Wise Use movement, has experienced a 40 percent rise in fundraising ("Grass Roots," 1993, p. 1). Ron Tipton, of the Wilderness Society, agrees that one value of having a Democratic White House is that "the wise-use movement is going to be bigger and meaner and better financed," since "they have a bogyman in the White House" (Knickerbocker, 1993, p. 11).

With recent Supreme Court decisions allowing the compensation of coal companies for profits lost because of environmental protections, the private property coalition has gained considerable strength. Erik Meyers, general counsel for the Environmental Law Institute, argues that the "property rights backlash is the most important challenge to the modern environmental movement that has appeared in years," and he further observes that "the environmental groups have done almost nothing to counter it" (Schneider, 1992, p. E3). The 1994 midterm elections ushered in a Republican-controlled Congress, thereby increasing the power and support for those opposing environmental protection. The end result is an escalating rhetorical conflict over future directions in public policy. Bruce Babbitt, head of the Interior Department, observes that this resurgence of opposition has frustrated many environmental activists since, after many years of clear sailing, the "tides are changing, [and] the water is real choppy" (Hebert, 1995, p. A16).

A second issue concerning environmental empowerment is the polarization that characterizes so much of this rhetorical conflict. The recent home-rule movement, with local officials publicly thwarting federal policies governing federal lands, illustrates some of the vehemence, fanned by property rights concerns and access issues, that constitutes much of the public "dialogue" on the environment. The language of war is also prominent in environmental responses to the Republican Contract with America. The use of "covert" legislation to "dismantle" environmental legislation is an "assault" that recalls a "scorched earth" policy (see, e.g., Emery, 1995). Defending against perceptions of radicalism, environmental organizations are now countering with charges about conservative "extremists." The effect of all of this is an extremely charged debate over the different sections of the proposed Contract and a rejuvenated environmental fundraising effort by organizations with an enemy to focus on.

A necessary outcome of this trend toward polarization is concern for a cooperative framework to ease some of the more obvious pitfalls of a polarized framework for discussion. An inability to resolve conflicts is one of the major features of a polarized environment for discussion. Efforts to foster a cooperative discussion become, in this light, increasingly important for sustained environmental progress.

A second outcome of increasing polarization is the development of tremendous pressure for compromise and for centrist policies. With the focus on issues set by the Republican agenda, Mathews observes that there is a shift in "the boundaries of legitimate debate, and that automatically shifts the center" (1994, p. C7). The effects of such a move toward the "hegemony of the center" remain to be seen, but Easter's analysis of the prevalence and implications of "neither/norism" in this volume illustrates some of the hidden power of this cultural mythology. It is worth noting that environmental implications of the current political situation are not limited to the United States alone. The first follow-up conference held by the United Nations after Rio, an effort to bring about action to reduce the risk of global warming, has likewise fallen prey to the pressures of compromise. One clear reason, argues the *Washington Post*, is the swing in U.S. politics ("Cooling Down," 1995, p. C6).

A third issue in empowering action on the environment is the need to increase the diversity of environmental activism. Foreman, Manes, Limbaugh, and others from across the political spectrum have decried the advent of slick and well-paid environmental lobbyists. While many conservative groups try to erase public images of shoestring grass-roots organizations valiantly defending the environment, many of the grass-roots organizations charge the larger national organizations with selling out and compromising on environmental issues. Lobbyists for environmental organizations, some charge, "roam Gucci Gulch with the rest of the Capitol Hill special-interest crowd," while the organizations put 20 to 25 percent of the money received back into fundraising and pay the presidents six-figure salaries (Begley & King, 1992, p. 78). Cockburn (1995) even points to specific events, such as the failure of the amendment to stop the recent Republican forest "salvage" act, as an outcome of larger environmental groups forsaking grass-roots power for an "inside-the-beltway lobbying presence" (p. B9).

It is hard to deny that larger organizations are less "in touch" with people by the very fact of their size. One of the key criticisms of the major environmental organizations is that they are largely white and middle class oriented. In addressing the weaknesses of the current environmental organizations, activist Solangel Rodriguez is clear about the lack of minority representation in the environmental movement: "[P]eople have been shut out. I don't think the environmental groups have sought out people of color to belong to their organizations. . . . These are organizations that are supposedly there to protect the environment for us all. Yet they're out of touch with the issues of the inner cities" ("Activist," 1993, p. 2). Snow has argued that part of the problem with these organizations has been concern with funding. This has impacted on the scope and the function of their efforts in the community:

> [M]anaging for the bottom line has allowed the leaders of many large, prestigious conservation groups to become virtually divorced from their own memberships. . . . Practically none of the mainstream conservation-environmental groups in the United States—regardless of location, scope, or size—works effectively with or deliberately tries to include people of color, the rural poor, the politically and economically disenfranchised. (Knickerbocker, 1993, p. 1)

Shabecoff's (1993) historical review of the environmental movement, *A Fierce Green Fire*, ultimately concludes that some major changes must occur in the movement for it to be effective. National organizations must tap the diversity and determination of grass-roots groups, and the national environmental agenda must address social, economic, and racial inequities in society.

Strategies to diversify the movement are numerous and include environmental justice rallies, efforts by children's environmental organizations, and the proliferation of grass-roots networks willing to assist local groups in framing and influencing environmental issues. Much more, of course, needs to be done. An understanding of the varieties and richness of Earthtalk may, in this regard, become increasingly important as we move to confront the environmental challenges of the twenty-first century.

CHALLENGES FOR EARTHTALK

The task of environmental empowerment, then, involves a curious mixture of national and local politics, of abstract principles and concrete actions, and of ethical frameworks and political expediency. Public support for the environment is still high, as a recent *Newsweek* poll reveals that 73 percent of Americans would be upset if cutting back government weakened or eliminated environmental protections. Another poll, conducted by the Peter D. Hart organization, found that only 8 percent of Americans would agree that enough has been done for the environment already ("Television Offensive," 1995, p. 1). The question remaining, for 1996 and beyond, is whether this interest can translate to sustained environmental action. The contributors to this volume provide an array of different perspectives on how to go about this task and on how Earthtalk continues to shape and frame human perceptions and actions on environmental issues.

The first section explores the specific strategies that corporations, individuals, and grass-roots organizations use to create particular perspectives on environmental issues. Identifying some of the larger tactics and appeals used in environmental discourse, Michael Spangle and David Knapp analyze how different groups opt for different strategies in reconstructing an idealized Other within a polarized communication context. Outlining and explaining a particular typology of environmental appeals, they offer specific suggestions for overcoming this polarization and for making a proactive effort to establish cooperative discussion. This cooperative perspective becomes more important in Laura Belsten's work on risk communication and community collaboration. Briefly summarizing the evolution of risk communication, Belsten identifies particular areas where risk communication has encountered severe obstacles. This analysis then moves toward the support of a collaborative model, outlining a case study that illustrates successful community collaboration.

Focusing more specifically on the power of media as a means of empowering environmental action, the next section offers a specific textual reading of audience interpretations of environmental meanings, a general philosophical treatment of the possibilities of media empowerment, and an empirical case study in video activism. David Easter's work on audience interpretations of mediated environmental constructions delves into cultural constructions of environmental reality. Addressing the process by which extremes are marginalized in favor of "moderatist" positions, the chapter closely examines the means by which seemingly polysemic meanings are closed down in favor of hegemonic constructions. A close reading of an episode of *L.A. Law* offers insight into how opposing positions are constructed to resolve in favor of a moderatism that itself embodies a hegemonic portrayal of environmental activists. Kevin DeLuca's approach to the pervasiveness of mediated realities draws on Ihde and McLuhan to illustrate how the cultural environment is constituted by a continuous interaction among pluralities of media. In empowering individuals to respond to this continuous interaction, Angus's concept of judgment offers hope in reconstructing a meaningful world. Image tactics of environmental groups are one way this judgment can destabilize the ideograph of "nature" and make possible the rearticulation of alternative points of view. Rod Carveth and Roger Desmond take this rearticulation into the educational system and into specific media techniques whereby young students construct and gain knowledge from videos about recycling. Targeting specific objectives of knowledge gain and attitude change, this program provides schools with an effective means of meeting environmental challenges.

Shifting focus from how Earthtalk works in media to the resources of language, the third section provides specific case studies in the power and varieties of language use on environmental issues. Susan Senecah's extended analysis of metaphors in the controversy over the use and development of the Adirondack Park lends credence to a general thesis about the power of Earthtalk. Isolating the conceptual development of metaphors about the cartographic Blue Line defining the park's boundaries and about the "invisibility" of the residents of the park, Senecah's close reading of the interaction of political, economic, and environmental values identifies several possibilities for reframing the social construction of the conflict. Warren Sandmann's critical assessment of Al Gore's *Earth in the Balance* further articulates the symbolic nature of our environmental predicament. The metaphors of addiction and dysfunction figure large in the economic and political depiction of the environment, and they reframe a human understanding of how symbolism deeply construes humanity's relationship to nature. The battle over the environment, Sandmann argues, is first and foremost a battle for the power to name. Thomas Flynn extends this point in a different direction, examining in detail the preservationist construction of an environmental past. Through a critical analysis of Frank Graham's *The Adirondack Park: A Political History*, Flynn underscores the potential of historical discourse to contribute to a deeper public understanding of those cultural forces that are at the heart of our current environmental crisis.

Concluding the volume is a section appropriately addressing the nature and viability of alternative rhetorics, of alternative visions of human existence and of human interaction. John Delicath's essay argues for a reconceptualization of utopian rhetorics and constructs a theory of utopian rhetorics en route to such a reconceptualization. Representing a discursive strategy that transcends choices of form, content, and function, utopian rhetorics are a necessary component of any attempts to transform society. Utopian rhetorics open up possibilities, embrace the potential for change, and provide a sense of hope for the future. Susan Mallon Ross grounds her discussion of responsible care in the communicative ethics and interactions of the Mohawk Indians. Ranging from topics of risk communication, Habermas's communicative action, and Mohawk environmental ethics, Ross uses two case studies on siting environmental hazards near a Mohawk reservation to underscore the liabilities of restrictive discursive practices. Correcting Habermas's abstract framework for communicative action with an alternative ethical philosophy of responsible care, she argues, offers the best hope for a just and lasting peace with the earth. Finally, Trudy Milburn highlights the differences between a technological worldview and a perspective that embraces a Goddess spirituality. The social construction of identity can bridge the dualistic premises of the technological society in a therapeutic framework of narrative and myth. The "magic" of human symbolism, a magic that obviates some of the more pernicious features of technological society, reconstitutes power and control within a sacred sense of self.

These differing perspectives on Earthtalk, ranging from general tactics and strategies, to the power of media, to resources in language, and to alternative rhetorics, all share a common assumption about the power of symbolism in shaping human attitudes and actions toward the natural world. On the basis of this common assumption, the project of exploring the complexities and implications of human symbolic constructions remains at the forefront of empowering human responses to environmental challenges.

PART I
STRATEGIES AND TACTICS OF EARTHTALK

CHAPTER ONE

Ways We Talk about the Earth:
An Exploration of Persuasive Tactics and Appeals
in Environmental Discourse

Michael Spangle and David Knapp

IN AN EDITORIAL published a few weeks before the 1992 presidential election, the senior editor of the *Denver Post* raised the question, "Is good environmentalism good economics too?" (Hornsby, 1992, p. 6B). This is a frequently asked question in an era of multimillion-dollar pollution-prevention programs, multifaceted legislative acts, and multileveled media battles. Often, the answer to this complicated question is determined by which individual or group is asked.

Radical environmental activists argue that the economy, like everything else, is fundamentally dependent upon the planet's ecosystem. Radical pro-industry and agriculture groups counter that excessive environmental regulation is detrimental to the nation's economy and that people must be put ahead of plants and animals. Moderates from both groups advocate compromises that incorporate the concerns of industry and agriculture with the concerns of the environmentalists.

Because the environment has become one of the leading political issues of the 1990s, it is imperative that communication specialists analyze the persuasive tactics and appeals of these competing perspectives to help clarify the issue and, more important, make suggestions for future persuasive strategies that will bring these diverse groups together, rather than drive them further apart. To that end, this chapter explores three major perspectives on the environment through an analysis of the specific persuasive tactics and appeals employed in the discourse of their followers. It begins with a discussion of the theoretical foundation for the study, provides a detailed description of the method, chronicles the persuasive tactics and appeals of the three main perspectives on the environment, offers specific suggestions for empowerment for environmental action through persuasive tactics and appeals that promote collaboration while minimizing polarized and divisive communication, and concludes with a discussion of the immediate future of environmental discourse given the changing political landscape.

THEORETICAL FOUNDATION

Because "the general public is the force that tips the balance, assesses the arguments, tests them against its diverse experiences of contemporary existence, and becomes the ultimate 'decision-maker' in the political process as we know it" (Killingsworth & Palmer, 1992, p. 25), members of industry, agriculture, and environmental groups all attempt to win public support in America through the use of specific persuasive tactics and appeals. These tactics and appeals are carefully designed to shift public opinion and influence the way citizens think about the environment by altering how the information or knowledge is organized and subsequently understood. The existence of a culture's general system of organizing knowledge (commonly referred to as an "episteme" or "discursive formation") was first discussed by Socrates; however, it was Michel Foucault who extended the concept and discussed its impact on contemporary discourse.

To understand what constitutes knowledge in a particular period of history, Michel Foucault examined the nature of discourse that societies valued. Foucault concluded that knowledge was largely a result of "the total set of relations that unite, at a given period, the discursive practices that give rise to epistemological figures, sciences, and possible formalized systems" (Foucault, 1972, p. 38). He termed this set of relations the "episteme" or "discursive formation" of the era (Foucault, 1970, p. xx; Foucault, 1972, pp. 39, 191). Foss, Foss, and Trapp (1991) explain that the episteme

is a cultural code, characteristic system, structure, network, or ground of thought that governs the language, perception, values, and practices of an age. It is a kind of period style for the organization of knowledge that functions automatically in that age. Only one episteme can dominate at any one time because the structure governing the episteme is so fundamental that in the age of one episteme, to think by means of another is impossible. (pp. 216–217)

In his book *The Archaeology of Knowledge* (1972), Foucault replaced the label "episteme" with "discursive formation." While the reason for the change is not crucial to this analysis, the replacement illustrates Foucault's belief in the strong relationship between a society's knowledge and its discursive practices. As Foss, Foss, and Trapp (1991) note: "For Foucault, knowledge and discursive practices are inseparable. Everything about which we can speak in a discursive formation is knowledge; knowledge is generated by discursive practice. . . . Only a particular kind of knowledge is allowed by particular discursive formations, and nothing else receives support in the discourse" (p. 217). It was this notion that a society's dominant discursive formation determines what is acceptable and unacceptable in the society that led Foucault to examine the concepts of societal exclusion and inclusion.

As Fink-Eitel (1992, pp. 31–34) notes, two of Foucault's major works (*Madness and Civilization* and *The Order of Things*) form two complementary parts of a single entry based on the societal structures responsible for the notions of societal exclusion (or "the Other") and societal inclusion ("the Same"). Foucault defines these concepts in the preface to *The Order of Things*: "the Other—of that which, for a given culture, is at once interior and foreign, therefore to be excluded (so as to exorcise the interior danger) but by being shut away (in order to reduce its otherness); whereas . . . the Same—of that which, for a given culture, is both dispersed and related, therefore to be distinguished by kinds and to be collected together into identities" (p. xxiv). Granted, Foucault was dealing with individuals when discussing the Same and the Other, not the society as a whole; however, it is possible that any society or culture can be waging the same internal battle on a larger scale. In other words, the society is subject to a battle between those positions or perspectives that are considered related and worthy of being collected into societal attitudes, beliefs, and values (the Same) and those positions that are considered foreign and deserving of being excluded (the Other)—an "us" versus "them" paradigm. The paradigm can be combined with the notion of knowledge as the human encoding and decoding of discursive practices and applied directly to the environmental debate.

As long as the subjective process of human encoding and decoding of discourse is the basis of knowledge, the opportunity exists for persuasion or manipulation—an observation not lost on the various groups engaged in the battle for public support of their environmental positions. Each side uses persuasive tactics and appeals to define the others as negative and worthy of societal exclusion (of being the Other). Each side then uses these tactics and appeals to establish itself as the Same—that which is worthy of being accepted as the keeper of "correct" cultural attitudes, beliefs, and values. This approach places great emphasis on the development of the Other in any group's discussion, and it is alluded to by Killingsworth and Palmer (1992), who argue that the first question of environmental discourse analysis should be: "Who is the person described in the discourse as the opponent, the challenger, the other?" (p. 23).

In summarizing Foucault's philosophical tenets, Fink-Eitel (1992, p. 31) observes that they constitute at a basic level, an ethnographic view of one's own culture and society where an individual tries to act as a disinterested observer looking inward from without—not an easy task! Unfortunately, communication scholars are faced with the same difficulty when attempting to analyze discourse in their own society. If the dominant episteme or discursive practice is indeed so inclusive that it makes other ways of thinking impossible, our analysis might be tainted by the same shortcomings from which our data suffers. Nevertheless, the remainder of the chapter attempts to examine environmental discourse in America from the perspective of its attempt to change public opinion based on the notion of the Other versus the Same. We begin with a brief discussion of our methods of analysis.

METHODS OF ANALYSIS

The data for our analysis was collected from a review of current articles (1990–1995) in national news, environmental, and business magazines; newspaper accounts in the *New York Times* and *Washington Post* for the same time period; and recently published books on the environment. The method of analysis was a cluster analysis based on the four main perspectives on the environment (radical functionalism, resource functionalism, resource environmentalism, and radical environmentalism). Before any further discussion of the cluster analysis can be given, the rationale behind looking at these four perspectives should be presented.

The attempt to classify perspectives on the environment is not unique to this study. O'Riordan (1981) offered a polarized classification system concerning the ideological themes of environmentalism: ecocentrism and technocentrism. One pole emphasizes biocentrism and the elimination of industry from environmental influence; the other affirms industrial moderation and technological fixes to environmental problems. While this classification is helpful, it is overly simplistic in its explanation and classification of the philosophical tenets of the middle-ground environmentalists and omits the position of mainline business and industry. Similar shortcomings are noted by Norton (1991), who argued that the classification of environmentalists into conservationists and preservationists is no longer realistic. As we demonstrate shortly, however, both of these classifications are helpful in developing the categories of resource and radical environmentalism.

Killingsworth and Palmer (1992) propose a continuum that includes a pro-industry category. In their model, attitudes toward the natural world form three points along a continuum: nature as object, nature as resource, and nature as spirit. While this continuum provides different information concerning environmental attitudes, it has limited value for explaining how all three perspectives use the data of science—which treats nature as object—as rationale for their knowledge of the environment.

A more useful model for communication scholars is one that addresses how rhetors view knowledge, the central issues, and opponents in its discourse. Thus, we developed our own labels based on these models (as well as others reviewed in Bookchin, 1980; W. Fox, 1990; Merchant, 1992; and Pepper, 1990).

The belief that scientific and industrial advancements are more impo⸳ than any environmental damage that may result from progress or production characterizes the radical functionalism perspective. Proponents of this perspective create knowledge about the environment in terms of technological progress, human need, and economic development because they believe the environment functions as a resource for human development and management. As we will see in the analysis section, their tactics and appeals are grounded in this idea of environmental functionalism.

The second perspective, resource functionalism, agrees that technological progress for human benefit should continue, but it recognizes that this progress puts a strain on our natural resources. This perspective argues that knowledge about the environment must include components that assess damage and need for repair; advocates of this perspective might therefore agree to compromise with environmentalists if a risk assessment shows potential environmental damage, even if the damage might fall within acceptable legal guidelines. This is in contrast with the radical functionalist perspective, which only begrudgingly works within the legal guidelines.

The resource environmentalism perspective is more holistic in that it views knowledge about the environment from both nonhuman and human perspectives. The needs and interests of animals, plants, and natural resources are equated with human needs and interests. Proponents of this perspective promote the judicious use of our natural resources and agree that science and technology may reveal data about the environment, but that some facts concerning damage extend beyond quantifiable data. However, like the resource functionalists, this group is willing to compromise on certain issues because they recognize and accept the existence of other worldviews.

This willingness to accept the functionalist worldview—and even compromise with it—separates the resource environmentalism perspective from the radical environmentalism perspective. This view personifies Nature as a sacred entity that demands to be revered and respected as much as humans. Scientific data serves only one function—to demonstrate the terrible wounds humans have inflicted on the sacred nature. If science and its data disagree with environmental protection, it is rejected as a tool of industrial and agricultural special interests. Proponents of this view demand the protection of all the earth's species, human and nonhuman, as well as of the earth's natural resources. They argue that all human activities should be judged in terms of their impact on our fellow earth dwellers and that any activity that even remotely damages another species should be altered or eliminated.

While we believe the literature and data support this separation into four perspectives, for the purposes of our study we followed the approach of Crowfoot and Wondolleck (1990), who separate parties involved in environmental discussion into three groups: business, environmentalists, and radical environmentalists. They contend that "[t]hese three categories are known by different names, depending on whether one links their views to political ideologies or to sociological theories as the source of information to describe and interpret these perspectives" (p. 10). Though we identify four strategic orientations to environmental issues, the discourse tactics for influencing public opinion appear to fall most comfortably into Crowfoot and Wondolleck's three categories, with resource functionalism and resource environmentalism being combined into one perspective due to their willingness to compromise.

Using our three categories, the data was examined using a cluster analysis. Cluster criticism was originally developed by Kenneth Burke to help the critic discover a communicator's worldview (S. Foss, 1989, p. 367). Krippendorf (1980) explains: "Clustering seeks to group or to lump together objects or variables that share some observed qualities or, alternatively, to partition or to divide a set of objects or variables into mutually exclusive classes whose boundaries reflect differences in the observed qualities of their members" (p. 115). Foss describes the clustering process as one involving four steps: (1) identifying key terms or symbols in the artifact; (2) charting terms that cluster around the key terms; (3) discovering patterns of clusters around the key terms to determine meanings of the key terms; and (4) naming the communicator's motive on the basis of the meanings of the key terms (pp. 367–368).

This study followed this procedure with a few modifications. After gathering the data, the researchers went through each piece looking for examples of the persuasive tactics or appeals used by proponents of the three groups. To be as thorough as possible, we first went through the data looking for the appeals of the radical functionalist view, then for the combined views of the resource functionalist and resource environmentalist, before ending with a search for tactics and appeals of the radical environmentalist.

When we encountered a specific tactic or appeal, the example was recorded on a master list. This is a slight variation of clustering technique as described by Burke and Foss because we were not focusing on key terms; rather, we looked for illustrations and examples of broad tactics and appeals. After each group's appeals and tactics had been recorded, the lists were subjected to a second clustering process in which the appeals and tactics were grouped by overall theme. We found this to be an easy process, because each group relied on similar tactics and appeals over and over again. It is this second clustering of appeals that is reported in the results section.

RESULTS

Tactics and Appeals of Radical Functionalists

The radical functionalist worldview places a high value on anthropocentric community interests (such as profit, development, or comfort), on unrestricted technological progress, and on free development of the market economy. In order to achieve goals based on their worldview, proponents of this view the additional task of protecting their public image and their market potential. It may be excusable for radical environmental activists to spike trees or sabotage logging machinery to combat industry opponents, but such tactics by industry or agriculture would damage image and profits. Our review of the data uncovered four persuasive tactics and appeals most frequently employed by radical functionalists in environmental discourse: (1) appeal to economic self-interest; (2) demonstrate adjustment and capitulation; (3) downplay risk; and (4) promote polarization and contrast. This list is not exhaustive, but it does include the most commonly used tactics and appeals.

Economic Self-Interest

Economic self-interest has been a primary component in industry and agriculture discourse. This appeal flows consistently from a worldview that values market interests and human needs. Examples of this tactic are abundant. In the Pacific Northwest, the logging industry told communities that environmental concern for the northern spotted owl could cost one hundred thousand jobs if protests were successful (Lamonick, 1991). In Lovell, Wyoming, the president of Crown Mines, David Rovig, proposed the digging of three "world class" ore deposit mines in north central Wyoming. In response to environmentalists, Rovig promised that the project would employ 130 people, produce tax revenues, and boost the economy ("Foes of Gold," 1991, p. I6). In scenic Clear Creek Canyon on the eastern slope of the Rocky Mountains, mining industry officials assured community planners that a $25 million mining operation would provide gravel for roads and buildings, create jobs, and "return the site to its natural state after the mining is complete in 35 years" ("Jeffco Quarry," 1991, p. I7). Richard di Pretoro, a hydrogeologist who operates an independent consulting business in Morgantown, West Virginia, summarizes the power of economic-interest rhetoric in the East: "Coal states are willing to ignore the long-term problems because of short-term benefits: jobs, money, taxes, votes" (Raskin, 1990, p. 20).

Radical functionalists define the environmentalists as the Other by questioning the economic self-interests of some environmental groups. They note that some environmental groups have accepted large donations from corporations which they oppose. For example, in 1987, Waste Management, Inc. (WMI)—the nation's third-largest operator of toxic waste dumps—gave thousands of dollars to the National Wildlife Federation (NWF). Soon, WMI's chief executive officer (CEO), Dean Buntrock, was elected to NWF's governing board. Pell (1991) reported that waste disposal policies favorable to WMI were formulated after NWF set up a "cozy breakfast meeting" between representatives of the Environmental Protection Agency and WMI. Environmentalist Philip Chabot commented, tongue in cheek, about this tactic at a northeast Washington Earth Day celebration: "Money is money. I'm sure Al Capone gave to the church and the church didn't mind" (D. Cohn, 1990, p. C3).

Adjustment and Capitulation

A second tactic, demonstrating adjustment and capitulation, has recently become popular among radical functionalists. Bowers, Ochs, and Jensen (1993) describe this tactic as surrendering power voluntarily or demonstrating that agitator demands have been adopted. In terms of industry and agriculture, this approach is reflected in persuasion that displays environmental priority in industry agenda. Wald (1990) claims that "many corporations have dropped their old arguments pitting pollution against jobs and, sensing competitive advantages, are scrambling instead to demonstrate how 'green' they are" (p. 1). A similar motive may be behind Du Pont chairman and CEO Edgar Woolard's claim that he is "born again" on environmental matters and a "chief environmental officer." Friends of the Earth writer Jack Doyle (1991) investigated Du Pont's new orientation and found that "Du Pont's feel-good advertising is a distortion of environmental fact. Using seal pups and dolphins to obscure its real record is disingenuous and misleading" (p. 5). Despite Doyle's conclusion, industry marketing strategists have found this tactic effective. During 1991, Coca Cola ran a promotion in cooperation with the National Parks and Conservation Association chapter in Washington State. Minute Maid Orange Juice advertised: "The makers of Minute Maid In-The-Box Help Keep America Growing and Beautiful. Get a tree planted at a National Park in your name." Elliot Gruber, director of development for the National Parks and Conservation Association, expressed concern in his observation that a "lot of companies are saying the environment is hot now and see it as a way of increasing their sales" (Meier, 1991, p. 136). This technique demonstrates an understanding on the part of radical functionalists that if being "green" contributes to public acceptance, they must appear to be "green."

Downplaying of Risk

The radical functionalists' worldview, based on classical science, portrays nature as the object of human observation and design. Further, this perspective characterizes nature in mechanistic terms as a "sophisticated machine whose behavior is not random but is a knowable and predictable outcome of its structure" (Pepper, 1990, p. 38). Damage to nature is the product of predictable forces which may be quantifiable, controllable, and reversible. If risk is not quantifiable and exceeds agreed-upon thresholds, restrictions in environmental policy lack rational justification. Patrick Michaels (1992), state climatologist for the commonwealth of Virginia, illustrates this perspective in his call for "[t]he new vision: Verification by the data" (p. 111). Based on a lack of verifiable historical trends and observable consequences, Michaels argues against apocalyptic predictions of global warming, since "[a]ll of the contentions for major warming or cooling on continent or global scales were based on incomplete models and unrealistic assumptions that ran counter to observations" (p. 148).

Similarly, Lawrence Summers, chief economist for the World Bank, argues that the "computer model has no validity . . . [it] is only feeding back the author's prior views. The conclusions are built in" ("Report Warns," 1992, p. A8).

The late Washington governor Dixie Ray (1990) complained that Americans have been subject to a litany of catastrophic proclamations, predictions of impending disaster, and dire warnings. Ray concluded that "[d]espite all the evidence of our physical well-being beyond all the dreams of all previous generations, we seem to have become a nation of easily frightened people—the healthiest hypochondriacs in the world!" (p. 8).

Polarization and Contrast

Bowers, Ochs, and Jensen (1993) argue that almost every movement makes deliberate attempts, once it attracts a substantial following, to adopt the tactic of polarization. Polarization focuses on a contrast between movement followers and opponents but also on the contrast between movement ideology and opponent ideology. The discourse of many radical functionalist proponents demonstrates this tactic, which is the ultimate in defining the Other. For example, T. S. Ary, the head of the United States Bureau of Mines, describes environmentalists as "a bunch of nuts. . . . I don't believe in endangered species. I think the only ones are sitting here in this room" ("Interior Official," 1991, p. I6). Arnold (1980) describes environmentalists as "misguided plain folks and faddish hangers-on" (p. 53). Polarization of those who back industry claims and those who view risk from the perspective of environmentalists occurs in Claus and Bolander's (1977) assertion that "[o]ne reading of *Silent Spring* is enough to throw any psychologically balanced layman into a seesaw syndrome of deep depression and hypochondriacal anxiety" (p. 7). Dick Baldwin (1993), CEO of the Springfield Group, which operates plywood and veneer mills in Oregon, specifically contrasts perspectives based on strategies of choice in his assessment: "Destructive participation can be a tree spiker on Mary's Peak or a fire setter in South Africa. Contrastingly, constructive participation fosters innovative, creative solutions. . . . Transitory popular opinion, whether proclaimed or scientific, must not be allowed to tamper with forest plans" (p. 15).

The implication in each statement is that the traditional episteme on which industry objectives and progress are built is the most competent way to view environmental issues and measure environmental risk. In other words, the radical functionalist view is the Same, while the radical environmentalist view is the negative Other.

Tactics and Appeals of Resource Functionalists and Environmentalists

Bowers, Ochs, and Jensen (1993) distinguish between vertical deviance, where "agitators accept the value system of the establishment but dispute the distribution of benefits of power within that value system," and lateral deviance, where "agitators dispute the value system itself" (pp. 7–8). Vertical deviance tactics tend to be direct and easily understood ideologically, while lateral deviance, which rejects the values of the status quo, tends to be viewed as aberrant behavior that is difficult to understand. Because tenets of worldview or ideology in resource functionalism and resource environmentalism overlap, the tactical choices appear less defiant.

A review of the data uncovered four rhetorical tactics frequently used by proponents of these two perspectives: (1) Project a persona as defender of public interests; (2) Invest in efforts to make corporations more environmentally responsible; (3) Promote pragmatic prescriptions and agendas for solutions to environmental problems; and (4) Involve well-known television and movie celebrities in ethos appeals.

Persona as Defender of Public Interests

Projecting a persona as defender of public interests is as important to resource functionalists and environmentalists as the positive community image is for radical functionalists. These two groups believe that they are close to the mainstream of America, the ideological center, and shape their persuasive approach to protect that credibility. McCloskey, former executive director of the Sierra Club, characterizes the Sierra Club's membership as "those who care the most, those who believe deeply in a good cause" (Mitchell, 1970, p. 12). Whalen (1993), executive director of the American Council on Science and Health, observes that "environmental groups . . . often style themselves as defenders of the public interest, crusaders who protect the American public from the greed and callousness of American industry" (p. 432). Even the names of environmental groups support the persona of defender of the public good: Common Cause, Public Citizen, and Consumer Federation of America. Environmentalists must maintain moderate, low-confrontational strategies in order to protect their persona as guardians of the environment who are objective, rational, and benevolent to all. The wording of risk assessments and prescriptive solutions published by resource functionalists and environmentalists needs to reflect a worldview that places high value on the community's long-term interests.

This perspective's moderate approach is further demonstrated by its willingness to work within the established political system while maintaining the persona as the defender of the public. In *The Politics of Regulatory Change* (1989), Richard Harris and Sidney Milkis summarize the resource environmentalists' posturing: "As such they [environmentalists] found it necessary to operate incrementally rather than holistically . . . to moderate their anti-establishment rhetoric, to make serious economic arguments about market efficiency, and to spend much more time in the corridors of the Capitol than in the streets" (p. 235). Environmentalists have become "Washington insiders" who have learned to speak the language of politicians, lawyers, and some industries.

Promoting the Greening of Corporations

Both resource functionalists and environmentalists spend ;
amount of energy on efforts to make corporations more en'
responsible. Environmentalists call this the "greening of corporations." David
Brower, former executive director of the Sierra Club, summarizes this point:
"We have to green the corporate movement. We have to green all businesses
that operate without ecological conscience" (Chiras, 1990, p. 101). In a recent
speech, Brower further claimed that environmentalists must be the conscience
for corporate America since "they [corporations] have the rights of a person,
but not the conscience." Environmentalists must "help them do what they'd
like to do in their hearts but can't" (1995a). An example of successful corporate conscience raising occurred when environmentalists convinced Dow
Chemical to install corrosion-resistant pipes, work with its chemical suppliers
to obtain purer raw materials, and remove chloralethelene from its K2R spot
lifter (Kleiner, 1991).

A more significant effort at greening corporate policy occurred in September
1989, when resource functionalist and resource environmentalist groups united
in Boston to form the Coalition for Environmentally Responsible Economies
(CERES). CERES described itself "as a unique collaboration of worldwide
environmental organizations working with companies and individuals critically involved in responsible investing" (Russell & deLong, 1991, p. 35). CERES
drafted ten recommendations for corporate conduct, which they called the
Valdez Principles. This set of recommendations, a kind of environmental ethic
for corporations, calls on businesses to minimize and eliminate pollution,
conduct annual assessments and audits, market safe products and services,
practice sustainable resource use, use energy efficiently, reduce risk to workers
and the public, and repair damage caused to the environment. CERES leadership now boasts that they represent $150 billion in invested assets and 10 million
people. They further note that eighty companies, including General Motors,
endorse their proenvironmental principles. The organization's success can be
directly attributed to its aggressiveness in the business community. As Judith
Kuszewski (the coalition's director) points out, "the group is dedicated to
moving companies toward environmentally responsible practices" ("Companies Go Green," 1995, p. 36A).

Personalizing Environmental Problems

This approach follows gracefully from a worldview that highly values the
present social system, centers on human need, and affirms the possibility of
human and technological solutions for environmental problems. Examples of
human-choice solutions abound. In *50 Simple Things You Can Do to Save the
Earth* by EarthWorks (1990), readers are encouraged to stop junk mail, snip
six-pack plastic rings, aerate home faucets, recharge batteries, stamp out Styro-

foam, recycle motor oil, use cloth diapers, and eat low on the food chain. In *The Green Consumer*, Elkington, Hailes, and Makower (1990) encourage readers to drive fuel-efficient cars, choose organic baby food, and buy "green gifts." Jon Naar (1990) takes a similar approach in *Design for a Livable Planet*. He lists ways to recycle trash (the "Zen of recycling"), provides thirty-three answers to what individuals can do about acid rain, and suggests eight tips on how to plant healthy trees.

Rhetorically, both resource environmentalists and resource functionalists are required to maintain the perception that individual actions can make a difference in reducing danger to the earth's ecosystem. Educating an audience about motor oil's impact on groundwater supplies creates a daily awareness that supports requests for policy change when oil spills occur off Alaska's coast. Harris (1990) argues that "[w]e need to resurrect our sense of responsibility to the earth if we are going to have any chance of solving the environmental crisis" (p. xiv). Proponents of the middle ground tend to focus on strategies and tactics to solve immediate problems rather than long-term goals. Thus, they must maintain the perception that individual responsibility and efforts will have a significant impact.

Legitimization

A highly visible tactic that heightens public awareness concerning environmental issues is the use of celebrities to demonstrate legitimization. The audience is asked to support an environmental policy based on the credibility and ethos of the celebrity. Bowers, Ochs, and Jensen (1993) point out that every movement seeks out legitimizers, "individuals within the establishment who endorse some parts of the agitator's ideology" (p. 22). Brower (1995b) further characterizes this tactic as an attempt to find a "sympathetic celebrity to provide them glitz and charismatic leadership" (p. 181). Such an appeal was aired by the American Wildlife Foundation (AWF) during 1988. The appeal was in the form of a radio advertisement featuring the narration of movie star Jimmy Stewart. In Stewart's unique, raspy speaking style, he urged Americans to support efforts to stop the slaughter of elephants by not buying products made from ivory. The AWF believed that Stewart's long career in American Westerns and value-oriented films would translate into credibility concerning environmental issues. At a 1989 "Don't Bungle the Jungle" fundraiser in New York City, pop icon Madonna asked her audience to support policies that prevent further deforestation: "Every second, an area the size of a football field is gone—forever. At this rate, the entire rain forest will be gone in fifty years—forever. The forests gave us life; we've got to find a way to preserve them" (Piasecki & Asmus, 1990, p. 161).

It is obvious that the moderate tactics of resource functionalists and resource environmentalists focus less on the defining of the opposition as the Other. This is in direct contrast to the tactics and appeals of the radical functionalists and the radical environmentalists.

Tactics and Appeals of Radical Environmentalists

Radical environmentalists propose an extreme new way to view the ment through the promotion of radical functionalists as the Other. Mc ....l environmentalists share a worldview that rejects anthropocentrism in favor of biospheric egalitarianism, rejects ideology that distinguishes humans from animals in the global ecosystem, and discounts industry and moderate environmental rhetoric that promotes technological fixes for environmental problems. Dobson (1990) points out the importance of ways of knowing and thinking about the environment and ecological ideology in his assessment that "[c]entral to the theoretical canon of Green politics is the belief that our social, political, and economic problems are substantially caused by our intellectual relationship with the world" (p. 37). M. Lewis (1992) adds that "many eco-radicals hope that a massive ideological campaign can transform popular perceptions, leading both to a fundamental change in lifestyles and to a large-scale social reconstruction" (p. 11). Radical environmentalists view Nature as a sacred entity with an integrity of its own that should be revered and respected.

The revolutionary ideology of this perspective, which defends a personified nature, promotes agitator tactics based on lateral deviance: "The agitators' ideology and demands may be difficult for the establishment to understand because the agitators are likely to display symbols, engineer events, and behave in unusual ways which illustrate their rejection of society" (Bowers, Ochs, & Jensen, 1993, p. 8). Viewing themselves as nature's warriors, some radical environmentalists glorify violence as a rhetorical tactic and condemn compromise as a policy choice.

The most common persuasive tactics and appeals used by radical environmentalists to paint themselves as the Same and functionalists and resource environmentalists as the Other include (1) demonstrating urgency through fear appeals; (2) including the environment as an actor in the world drama; (3) employing language tactics that contrast and polarize; (4) approaching risk with a no-threshold perspective; and (5) blending scientific interpretation with ideology.

Fear Appeals

During the past two decades, radical environmental groups have employed many different tactics, but are probably best known for their fear appeals. John Broughton (1982) claims that "[a] new crop of doomsayers are making a very good living by frightening people to death with their best sellers, their well-paid lectures, and their . . . scientific half truths" (pp. 78–79). Impending doom is prophesied in comments like Scarce's (1990) prediction that "[o]nly by dramatically changing the way industrialized societies operate will Homo Sapiens and other species be able to survive and thrive beyond the next few decades" (p. 7). Paul Ehrlich (1968) forecasted that the "battle to feed all of humanity is over.

In the 1970s the world will undergo famines—hundreds of millions of people are going to starve to death" (p. xi).

Julian Simon (1980) explains that the regular use of this appeal targets those people who view the past and future idealistically and those individuals and institutions who want to make things better. The power of this tactic is its ability to "create negative expectancies in the minds of the readers and listeners, expectancies that would come about unless a change was instituted or stifled" (Stewart, Smith, & Denton, 1984, p. 167).

Dramatic Appeals

A second persuasive tactic, one that provides values that are alternative values to those of high-tech society, approaches environmental issues from the perspective of a world drama. A personified nature becomes a character in the human drama. Bowers, Ochs, and Jensen (1993) explain that in the rhetoric of agitation it is important to stage newsworthy events that are unusual or involve conflict so that "when the media cover conflict they also expose the agitators' message to the public" (p. 23). Philip Lowe and David Morrison (1984, p. 79) identify the following dramas enacted in radical environmental rhetoric:

the people	vs.	the bulldozers
the community	vs.	the planners
a rare species	vs.	speculators
local beauty spot	vs.	the juggernauts
unspoiled nature	vs.	pollution
the national heritage	vs.	agribusiness
our birthright	vs.	vandalism

Americans are drawn into a drama where they become actors who must fight against the evils and villains of modern industrial society (the Other) and their damaging acts against nature.

A planned dramatistic appeal is exemplified in the tactics of environmentalists associated with a radical group called the Sea Shepherds. One of the group's leaders, Paul Watson, explains: "When you do an action, it goes through the camera and into the minds of millions of people. The things that were previously out of sight and out of mind now become commonplace. Therefore, you use the media as a weapon. . . . The more dramatistic you can make it, the more controversial it is, the more publicity you will get. . . . [T]he drama translates into exposure" (Scarce, 1990, p. 104). David Morris (1995), who traveled with Watson, points out that Paul "crafts all his public campaigns for maximum electronic impact" with the goal of inducing "an inherently conservative mass media—simply by following visual logic, hunger for novelty, and capitalistic principle—to disseminate a historical and revolutionary message" (pp. 73–74).

In an age dominated by television reporting, groups can strategically include dramatic elements in the form of short vignettes or emotion-laden images that can be sensationalized for dramatistic presentation in the media. In a study of every environmental risk story (564 of them) aired by CBS, ABC, and NBC during the two-year period from January 1984 through February 1986, Greenberg, Sachsman, Sandman, and Salomone (1989) concluded that "[i]n their coverage of environmental risk, the networks are guided more by traditional determinants of news and the availability of dramatic visual images than by the scientific degree of risk of the situation involved" (p. 275). These carefully constructed vignettes, which may be cautiously called "ecobites," may function for environmentalists much as soundbites do for politicians (Spangle & Germann, 1994). Scarce (1990) describes an animal-liberation protest at Trafalgar Square in London:

> We had a demonstration there which involved 9,000 people. We had a slogan, "Every Six Seconds an Animal Dies in a British Laboratory." At the base of the plinth of Nelson's column we made a mock laboratory. We got a tape loop playing that struck a bell every six seconds and a sign with big numbers on it that turned over every time the bell struck. Two people dressed as scientists took people from the audience at the demonstration and symbolically killed them. They would lie on the ground. At the end of the hour we had 600 people lying down. (p. 257)

These carefully staged dramatic events are designed as visual appeals that trigger emotions of anger and guilt within audiences. Ecobites serve as arguments for change and are better remembered by audiences than are volumes of statistics. Dramatic acts and made-for-television ecobites converge in a strategy of "nonviolent" unlawful confrontation. Because there exists a prominent axiom within the worldview of radical environmentalism that human values and institutions are the root sources of problems, followers of this perspective are more inclined to openly challenge the status quo. Radical environmentalists have spiked trees to prevent cutting, sat in front of bulldozers to prevent them from moving earth, parachuted from helicopters to form a human blockade in front of a fleet of Japanese whaling ships, blowtorched a utility tower in the desert west of Phoenix, or climbed trees to prevent foresters from chainsawing.

Though this tactic lies within the limits of their worldview, they run the danger of alienating the audience they wish to influence if they are perceived by the general public as being the dangerous or extreme Other. But for a radical group such as Earth First!, the risk is within sustainable limits. Central in their worldview is the slogan "No compromise in the defense of Mother Earth!" (Gabriel, 1990, p. 59).

guage Tactics That Contrast and Polarize

Language steeped in emotion-laden imagery often serves to create an air of urgency or a rationale for consequences of policy decisions. For example, Davenport (1970) employs emotional imagery to focus on urgency as rationale for action in his conclusion that the present state of the global environment is "an intolerable situation close to Hell" (p. 116). Similarly, an environmental report captures a mood of urgency, arguing that "[a]s earth stands on the brink of a global temperature increase . . . [there is] a new sense of urgency fueled in part by disquieting surprise in the stratosphere" (Kerr, 1988, p. 23). Max Ways focuses on the dire consequences of industrial growth in his assessment that "snails, along with all other species are poisoned, choked, or pushed around" (1970, p. 98) as a result of environmental abuses.

Scarce (1990) highlights a rhetoric of contrast between "us" and "them" in his opinion that characterizes industry as an "Ecowall" as damaging to human freedom as the Berlin Wall. Contrast lies at the root of Ways's (1970) assessment that the environment has "been ambushed by its misbegotten children, the unintended by-blows of the modern lust to know and to do" (pp. 98–99). Radical environmentalists foster an orientation of the Same versus the Other with imagery that depicts technology and scientists as "brazen reductionists who attack the unity of nature by carving it up into isolated bits that they can proceed arrogantly to manipulate for their own satisfaction" (M. Lewis, 1992, p. 124). A vivid example of radical environmentalist defiance is the professional protest group B.E.I.R.U.T. (Boisterous Extremists for Insurrection Against Republicans and Other Unprincipled Thugs), who handed out "Smash the summit" brochures at a presidential summit meeting on the environment ("Birds and the Trees," 1993, p. 53). Radical environmentalists describe with disdain the capitulation of public opinion and resource environmentalists in metaphors such as "a fire sale of marked-down concessions and lowered standards" and "dealmakers [who] were busy selling the lifeboats" ("Year of the Deal," 1991, p. 33).

No-Threshold Appeals

In the evaluation of scientific data to determine environmental risk, the discourse of many radical environmentalists reflects a one-molecule or no-threshold perspective. Since carcinogens, toxic waste, and ozone depletion have differing effects on people and since those actual effects are difficult to measure, radical environmentalists regard any effect as significant. Dr. Umberto Saffiotti of the National Cancer Institute illustrates this perspective in his conclusion that "[a]nything proven carcinogenic in any animal must be assumed to be carcinogenic for some human somewhere at even the lowest level" (Fumento, 1993, p. 52). A letter, signed by eleven EPA scientists and published in *Science* in 1991, demonstrates a similar perspective: "When the current data do not resolve the issue, EPA assessments employ the assumption basic to all toxicological evaluation that effects observed in animals may occur in humans and the effects observed at high doses may occur at low doses, albeit to a lesser extent" (Marshall, 1989, p. 21). The message is that one molecule of damage that exists in one animal or human is sufficient grounds to err on the side of caution in terms of decision making. This is a shift from a more traditional perspective that seeks data that identifies levels of exposure that predict harm.

Blending Science and Environmental Ideology

All groups who argue public policy on environmental issues use scientific data to support their conclusions. But it appears that in the discourse of radical environmentalists, there is a greater tendency to blend science and ideology as a persuasive tactic. For example, in response to pro-industry critics of environmental statements concerning the spraying of red apples with the chemical Alar, Dr. Edward Groth of Consumers Union readily affirms that "[t]he scientific facts are just part of what the public knows about Alar. The policy choices—both the personal and the public kind—depend on far more than facts. . . . [they are] heavily influenced by moral dimensions of the risk" (Null, 1990, p. 125).

Historically, science has served as a central component in an industrial American worldview, but in the past two decades radical environmentalists have proposed a way of knowing based on a blend of science and "ethical shoulds." Scarce (1990) describes radical environmentalism as a "subversive science" that extends beyond traditional limitations "to overcome the disasters created by the other sciences and the mindset that exalts them . . . with a healthy infusion of intuition from a re-sensitized public unafraid to follow its heart while making major decisions" (p. 34). Merchant (1992) summarizes the radical environmentalist conclusion that we are nearing the end of a period which views science as the primary factor in assessing the environment: "The clock-like machine model of nature and society that dominated the past three centuries of western thought may be winding down. . . . [A new paradigm is emerging.] . . . Each being is a subject that is interrelated with its environment, not something that can be studied in isolation" (pp. 94, 97).

The major impact of radical environmentalism's perspective is its emphasis on the unity of humans and nature as the Same and a human-based perspective as the Other. M. Lewis (1992) summarizes the radical environmentalists' two-fold agenda as denouncement of harmful technologies and denouncement of the scientific worldview causing an "intellectual rift that has torn humanity away from nature" (p. 124). Ideology and science converge in an interpretation of scientific data that focuses on how harmful technology impacts the earth's ecosystem and the future of nonhuman entities.

RECOMMENDATIONS FOR EMPOWERMENT

Two goals guided this research. The first goal was to examine the strategies and tactics that constitute the discourse of the three perspectives on environmental issues: radical functionalism, resource functionalism and environmentalism, and radical environmentalism. The tendency to polarize participants in environmental discussions, or to engage in emotional and often counterproductive debate concerning solutions, leads to the second goal of this paper: fashioning a set of principles that empower environmental discussion toward more constructive ends. Here empowerment means a process that moves parties toward common ground, that promotes a constructive, problem-solving approach, that provides greater participation by community members impacted by environmental decisions, and that reduces persuasive tactics that diminish the likelihood of collaborative or conciliatory behavior. The goal of these principles is to reduce the kind of frustration expressed by Joe Parkinson, executive director of the Vermont Ski Areas Association, who laments: "I have the feeling there is a cultural fault line running right through this country. Instead of being strengthened by our differences, we've allowed ourselves to become embattled by them. At a time when we should have developed a deeper appreciation for the interdependence of our human resources, we have allowed them to become adversaries" (Campbell, 1994, p. 7).

Empowerment occurs by design, not accident, and involves a proactive effort to establish collaborative discussion. In an effort to minimize divisive and polarizing communication on environmental issues and promote empowerment, the authors provide the following four principles for consideration: (1) reduce moral positioning; (2) focus on common ground; (3) downplay dramatistic approaches; and (4) create a new model for data disputes.

Reduce Moral Positioning

A tactic common to parties on the polarized edges of environmental discussion is the use of moral argument to support ideology. Adopting the moral high ground often prevents discussion of substantive issues and reduces movement toward solutions. The first principle is to promote an amoral view of conflict where all parties suspend moral judgments or assignment of blame and focus greater energy on addressing interests. Bacon and Wheeler (1984) believe that the goal must be to "recognize that there are no right answers—only compromise worked out on intermediate positions. Instead of creating the illusion of truth, bargaining embraces the accommodation of competing interests. Moreover, the process of compromise forces each side to acknowledge the legitimacy of claims of the opposition" (p. 364).

Empowerment begins by reducing the perception of absolute truth positions and moving toward respect for concerns and interests. Louis Fernandez, chairman of the board of Monsanto Corporation, affirms that business and environmentalists must "discard old, combative ways of thinking and acting. . . . [C]ooperation must become the theme of this country's environmental efforts" (Amy, 1987, p. 3). This approach does not minimize the importance of a moral component in environmental discussions but asks parties to withhold statements that polarize and reduce collaborative efforts. Political scientist Douglas Amy (1987) proposes that "promoting an amoral view of the dispute is an important part in laying the conceptual groundwork necessary to encourage and legitimate compromise. If disputes are seen in moral terms, where one party is right and the other is wrong, the attractiveness of compromise is minimized" (p. 178).

Perhaps it is naive to believe that moral judgments will not be made in discussions of environmental issues, but the first principle proposes that a greater empowerment will occur if parties are made aware of the divisiveness of assigning blame and of the counterproductive discussion that occurs when disputants focus on the opposition as the Other instead of focusing on common interests and concerns.

Focus on Common Ground

At times, selective attention characterizes parties involved in environmental discussions. Participants from any of the perspectives may focus on emotionally charged aspects of an issue or gravitate to nonnegotiable issues. Often, selective attention artificially narrows an issue and diverts energy away from consideration of issues that may provide common ground. Therefore, a second principle of empowerment is to facilitate awareness of counterproductive diversions that emphasize nonnegotiable issues and to promote discussion of negotiable issues that provide substance for common ground.

Achieving common ground may occur in one of three domains: philosophy, policy, or regulation. The first of these domains, philosophy, presents the greatest challenge to achieving common ground because of the myriad of values inherent in environmental philosophies. Arguments focus on choices between technological fixes and changes in cultural behavior, limits to growth or unlimited growth, human interests or nonhuman interests, or biocentric or anthropocentric approaches. Philosophic common ground is most achievable by resource environmentalists and resource functionalists, the great center of environmental perspectives. For parties sufficiently different in perspective, philosophic discussion runs the risk of further polarization. Empowerment in this domain must center on promoting respect for opposing philosophies and on emphasizing negotiable philosophic tenets.

Though often out of the realm of community discussion, the second area where common ground might be achieved is in the domain of policy. A successful example of policy discussion is the National Coal Policy Project, which involved 105 participants. Environmentalists, utility representatives, and coal company officials came together for a series of policy discussion meetings. The five-year project utilized plenary sessions and task force meetings that addressed two hundred different issues. Murray and Curran (1983) concluded that "the most frequently cited accomplishment of the National Coal Policy Project was that it demonstrated a new process whereby individuals of opposing viewpoints could rationally discuss the issues until some agreement could be reached" (p. 31).

Success in policy discussions such as the National Coal Policy Project occur when focused, interpersonal communication breaks down historical polarizations. Crowfoot and Wondolleck (1990) find that as stereotypes are dispelled and alliances are reduced, "adversarial relationships may evolve into cooperative ones as formerly opposed groups find new awareness for mutual cooperation" (p. 256). Old emotional wounds may be healed and a new forum for ongoing discussion established through this rejection of the Same and the Other orientations. In addition, though state or federal agencies determine most policies, community members, through participatory discussions, at least have input into how those policies are administered. Bingham (1986) proposes that empowerment which promotes dialogue in policy discussions begins with parties who share common objectives: conciliatory behavior by participants, sharing information, clarifying issues, and generating alternatives on controversial proposals (p. 84).

The third domain in which common ground may be reached in environmental discussions is regulatory negotiation. This area of discussion involves a proactive attempt by conflicting parties to design environmental regulations prior to litigation. Regulatory negotiation is the newest domain of discussion and offers the greatest opportunity for community involvement and a balance between industry interests and community concerns. The Common Ground Consensus Project exemplifies regulatory discussion by community, environmental, and agricultural groups (Crowfoot and Wondolleck, 1990). From September 1982 to September 1983, representatives of fourteen organizations discussed soil erosion issues at the University of Illinois. Early in the process, farmers and environmentalists stereotyped the perspectives of the other. Throughout the first few meetings, poor communication, mistrust from past discussions, and lack of technical information needed to be dealt with before collaborative common ground could be achieved. In the end, the group agreed on a strategy for wetland protection and soil conservation which was partially adopted by the state legislature. These discussions exemplify the local-level empowerment of groups that are impacted by environmental regulations by giving them a participatory voice in the process.

Downplay or Refashion the Drama

A familiar component of environmental discussion is the tendency to over-simplify complex issues through dramatic characterizations of the Other versus the Same. Disputants portray bulldozers in opposition to trees, owls against jobs, the health of the ecosystem placed against human survival, or agriculture and industry as villains of wilderness protection. Within the drama, groups depersonalize opponents with demeaning caricatures. Radical environmentalists cast industrialists as "Darth Vaders" or "environmental rapists." Industry spokespeople reciprocate with descriptions of environmentalists as "nature nazis" or "forest faggots." Many of the characterizations provide good reading in monthly periodicals or great quotes for television newscasts, but they are counterproductive to constructive discussion. Amy (1987) points out that stereotypes "fuel adversarial approaches by exaggerating the differences between parties and increasing polarization. . . . [W]ithout some kind of basic trust between the parties, no voluntary agreement is possible and stereotypes make trust seem irrational" (p. 48).

A key principle for empowerment is the facilitation of awareness in community groups and disputant parties concerning the power of overly simplistic dramatizations. Joe Parkinson affirms that in environmental dialogue "[w]e must build more bridges and fewer walls" (Campbell, 1994, p. 10). Focusing upon characteristics of the opponent distracts parties from discussion of substantive issues. Some disputants may actually use dramatization as a tactic to create diversion, stall progress, or disrupt discussion. As we move to the twenty-first century, if a new respect and personalization of the Other as a necessary part of the Same emerges, it can be applied to opponents in environmental discussions. Empowerment begins by downplaying simplistic characterizations and focusing more energy on problem solving.

If dramatizations are forever going to be a part of environmental discussions, then it might be helpful to fashion a new drama, one that is free of the blaming and "villainizing" that currently occur. Piasecki and Asmus (1990) point out that as we engage in global dialogue, we discover that the desire to protect the environment cuts across all societal divisions and that there is a universal concern for the environmental health and safety of the earth (p. 170).

Create a New Model for Data Disputes

As long as scientific data provides ambiguous evidence concerning the earth's ozone layer, climatic warming, the extinction of animal species, the renewability of natural resources, or the long-term impact of carcinogens on humans, unity will be difficult to achieve in global environmental discussions. Solution-producing discussions are often inhibited by disagreements over data. Bingham (1986) points out that many environmental conflicts arise because of a lack of access to information or because of a dispute over information (p. 86). Empowerment in terms of facilitating dialogue among antagonists in environmental discussions must at some point deal with differences of opinion regarding data.

For example, many conclusions in environmental debates are based on computer simulations such as the General Circulation Model. These models project how the climate should change based on assembled data. The difficulty with these forecasts is that they are based on assumptions about the physics and chemistry of the atmosphere that are incomplete. The cause-and-effect relationship is at best unclear and at worst unreliable. Climatologist Patrick Michaels (1992) affirms, "We obviously cannot reliably simulate the current climate from first principles, so the question of 'how much do we expect the climate to change from what it was' becomes impossible to answer" (p. 35).

Computer simulations are limited by our ability to isolate the factors that have a direct cause-and-effect relationship on long-term climatic behavior. Conclusions based on interpretations of data or computer simulations range from catastrophic decline of the earth's ecosystem (see Meadows, 1972, or Ehrlich & Ehrlich, 1991) to unlimited potential for renewable resources (Bailey, 1993). Discussions where antagonists fail to achieve common ground because of failure to agree on interpretations of data or levels of acceptable risk may present a formidable challenge for reaching consensus. But where there is openness to negotiation regarding methodology for gathering data, a new model might have usefulness.

THE FUTURE OF ENVIRONMENTAL DISCOURSE

A new, significant era of environmental discourse lies ahead after the landslide Republican victory in the 1994 midterm elections. Many environmentalists fear a legislative movement (beginning with the adoption of the GOP's Contract with America) that will promote business and development, while repealing much of the proenvironmental legislation enacted over the past decades. Nixon (1995) writes that "the Contract with America includes planks that scare environmental lobbyists half to death, so they've revived the old battle cries used against Ronald Reagan" (p. 35). Bill Snape, congressional lobbyist for Defenders of Wildlife, agrees, observing that "the environmental community feels shell shocked. There's confusion on how to react" ("Environmental Laws," 1994, p. 30A).

If Republicans maintain control through the next few elections (as some environmentalists expect), changes in the tactics of environmentalists are inevitable. One change already evident is the increased pressure on legislators who vote against environmental issues. In the spring of 1995, the Sierra Club began a $35,000 radio advertising campaign directed at Colorado Congressmen Dan Shaefer and Wayne Allard. Bruce Hamilton, national conservation director for the club, justifies the tactic with the explanation that they are trying to "expose and denounce a hidden war on the environment going on in Washington, D.C. This Congress is trying to roll back the clock on 25 years of environmental programs" ("Sierra Club Targets," 1995, p. 7A).

The former executive director of the Sierra Club, David Brower, affirms that environmentalists need "to be much more a part of the political discussion in this country. This was the reason I founded the League of Conservation Voters, so that we could see who was voting on the side of the Earth" (1995b, p. 183). We can expect more direct political involvement and greater pressure by moderate environmentalists who will undoubtedly attempt to portray legislators with antienvironmental voting records as being out of touch with American attitudes and values (the Other).

A second tactic that may increase is the use of messages emphasizing personal responsibility instead of governmental legislation. Nixon (1995) asserts that the lesson of the Gingrich revolution is, "Don't count on Washington. If you want a better society, build it yourself" (p. 36). This could result in the release of more environmental videos and a deliberate attempt to place more choreographed ecobites on the evening news. Whatever the medium, the goal will be the same—raising levels of community awareness and personal responsibility. As David Brower advised students in a speech at the University of Denver, "Do what you like and give it an ecological spin" (1995a).

A new tactic that may also gain popularity is the packaging of environmental appeals in terms of economic incentives. Brower (1995b) illustrates this in his argument for restoration efforts: "Once the restoration takes hold, there is big money to be made. . . . There is big money to be saved, once you understand how to solve the problem before it starts" (pp. 117–118). John Kenneth Galbraith (1994) echoed this theme in the *EPA Journal* when he observed that "we inevitably find ourselves defending environmental concerns more and more for their positive, affirmative support to economic life in the later stages of economic development" (p. 41). Even members of the Green movement are beginning to shape appeals that integrate economic goals. Brian Tokar (1992), founder of the Central Vermont Greens, admits that "in the face of mounting ecological and economic crisis, the need for new cooperative models for living and working is greater than ever" (p. 115). We can expect more rhetorical appeals crafted to integrate economic and environmental concerns.

Finally, the next few years may see an increase in the use of appeals based in radical and polarized language—at least if recent examples are any indication. In an *Audubon* editorial, Michael Robbins (1995) characterized the congressional chairs of the House and Senate Parks Committees as "ideologues" possessing ignorant and radical antigovernment perspectives because they are insensitive to environmental concerns. He further labeled them as individuals who "assault the very idea of the commonweal" (p. 6). Similarly, Hamilton (1995) used a Sierra Club bulletin to describe antienvironmental legislators as "radicals . . . [and] insidious threats . . . involved in a stealth campaign bent on wiping the entire green agenda off the map" (pp. 13–14). Carl Pope, executive director of the Sierra Club, describes the Contract with America as a "covert attack on the environment" that possesses a "radical version of risk assessment" (1995, p. 20).

The increased use of radical and polarized language might lead to the increased use of other radical and polarized tactics. However, this approach could backfire. After evaluating the use of radical tactics, Braile (1994) concluded that the tactics have lost their edge with the general public. The media looks skeptically at claims by radical environmentalists because it has become more difficult to characterize corporations as the evil Other now that so many have capitulated to basic environmental guidelines. Braile also concludes that it has become more difficult to scare people with data because the population is now desensitized to it.

If Braile's conclusions are correct, the radical environmentalists may try to reach that desensitized audience by engaging in more confrontational, threatening, and violent tactics. If they do, radical functionalists would undoubtedly respond in kind. This would make it difficult, if not impossible, for resource functionalists and resource environmentalists to help implement the recommendations for empowerment outlined in the previous section.

Instead, the participants in the environmental battle may choose to "circle the wagons and fight it out" (Brower, 1995a). If they do, future environmental discourse will cease to be a collaborative and proactive interchange of ideas; rather, it will become a divisive and destructive labeling of the opposing perspectives as the Other—with potentially disastrous consequences. Some conflict between the various perspectives is inevitable, but there is a choice between the self-destructive path of confrontation and polarization and the self-determining path of empowerment and cooperation.

CHAPTER TWO

Environmental Risk Communication and Community Collaboration

Laura A. Belsten

CLEANING UP THE nation's environment is projected to take several decades and cost billions of dollars. As of mid-1991, over 1,236 sites were listed on the National Priorities List (World Resources Institute, 1992), and one study has estimated that this number is likely to grow to 3,000 by the year 2020 (Colglazier, Cox, & Davis, 1991). An additional 31,500 potentially contaminated and dangerous sites have been identified in the nation's Comprehensive Environmental Response, Compensation, and Liability Information System (CERCLIS) (English, Gibson, Feldman, & Tonn, 1993). The costs associated with remediating these sites throughout the United States could run to as much as one trillion dollars (Russell, Colglazier, & English, 1991).

Inadequate communication with the public and a lack of stakeholder involvement in the cleanup and other environmental decisions are thought to result in public opposition, prolonged cleanup time schedules, and increased costs. A formidable obstacle to the management of hazardous wastes in the United States is a phenomenon called the "not-in-my-backyard" (NIMBY) syndrome. Federal and state laws mandate the safe handling, treatment, storage, and disposal of hazardous wastes; however, public agencies and private sector companies have found it virtually impossible to comply with these laws because of the lack of hazardous waste disposal facilities. Siting new facilities has come to a virtual standstill in the United States because of growing citizen resistance and strong public opposition. Members of the public often feel excluded from environmental decisions related to cleanup techniques and remediation technology selection; that exclusion creates feelings of disempowerment and cynicism and sometimes leads to outright hostility. In extreme cases, litigation or political initiatives to inhibit or stop remediation and facility-siting decisions may result. Resistance or outright opposition can lead to more intense regulatory review, schedule delays, and increased costs.

The human communication discipline offers hope in the form of promising risk communication and community collaboration techniques which serve to empower community members and facilitate public participation in tough policy decisions. Broad-based, inclusive, credible, open, and early stakeholder involvement and risk communication mechanisms are increasingly being utilized to overcome opposition to and build community support for selecting cleanup technologies, adopting remediation plans at contaminated locations, and siting new environmental treatment, storage, and disposal facilities.

THE EVOLUTION OF ENVIRONMENTAL RISK COMMUNICATION

Environmental risk communication is considered a fairly young field of study (Covello & Mumpower, 1985; National Research Council, 1989; Plough & Krimsky, 1987; Sandman, 1986). Prior to the early 1980s, very few articles appeared in the published literature with "risk communication" in the title. Since then, however, dozens of risk communication articles and books have been published. Numerous conferences, seminars, and workshops have been held, and research grants have been awarded from various federal and state agencies with the objective of studying procedures for better communication of environmental and health risks to the public. This explosion of activity attests to the increased attention from both governmental agencies and private sector organizations to the task of informing the public about the nature of health, safety, and environmental risks.

Covello and Mumpower (1985) trace the origins of structured risk analysis and communication to the ancient Babylonians over five thousand years ago. In fact, they maintain, much of human history is a story of communication about risks associated with natural hazards (e.g., floods, earthquakes, famine, disease) in the forms of myth, metaphor, ritual, and folk discourse.

Plough and Krimsky (1987) trace the transition from folk discourse about risk to "expert-centered communication" beginning in the late eighteenth century. They describe three conditions which needed to be present to "professionalize" the study of risk. The first condition was the rise of democracy and the assignment of the responsibility for protecting public health, safety, and welfare to the government. The second condition was the enhancement of the medical profession and the development of public health institutions. Physicians and public health departments have developed a history of determining risk and trying to communicate that risk to their patients and the public. For example, current public health policy has advanced risk communication through the use of educational campaigns to inform the public about the risks related to smoking, AIDS, substance abuse, teenage pregnancy, and unhealthy dietary practices. The third condition leading to the "expert-centered" field of risk assessment was the evolution of "decision analysis." Plough and Krimsky state:

> During World War II, the government's need for scientifically based decision methodologies gave rise to a new era of federal research support that spawned fields like operations research and systems analysis. In the late 1940s a variety of quantitative methodologies were introduced to promote understanding of chance processes and to create a rational frame-work for economic and strategic military decisions. Eventually, these models were applied to the practical problems of predicting and altering the course of risk factors in public health, medicine, and the environment. (pp. 224–225)

While these conditions were necessary to the evolution of the study of risk, another set of factors has influenced the development of environmental risk communication. First, since the end of World War II, the American public has seen a significant rise in the use of new technologies and in the manufacture of new products and chemical compounds. From 1945 to 1965 alone, the American Chemical Society registered more than four million chemicals (Rosenbaum, 1991). By the mid-1980s, between six hundred and eight hundred substances tested showed substantial evidence of carcinogenicity (Rosenbaum, 1991). Toxic and hazardous substances have a tendency to evoke fear and dread in the American public (Sandman, 1991), with cancer being one of the most widely feared results of exposure to hazardous substances. The proliferation of chemical compounds in recent decades, along with the perception on the part of the public that many of these substances are hazardous, is one of the primary factors driving the need for effective communication or risk.

A second factor which has led to the evolution of environmental risk communication is the emergence of "environmentalism" as a recognized social movement beginning in the 1960s and 1970s. The publication in 1962 of *Silent Spring* by Rachel Carson is often cited as launching the modern environmental movement. Carson's book awakened the public to the dangers of DDT, arsenic, and other pesticides which accumulate in the soil, water, our food supplies, and the human body. Her book documented increased rates of cancer among the American population and the destruction of songbirds and other wildlife through the overuse of certain chemicals (hence the title, "Silent Spring"). On the *New York Times* bestseller list for nearly two years, the book was translated into thirty-two foreign languages. Ironically, Carson died of cancer in 1964. *Silent Spring* jolted the American public into an awareness of other environmental hazards: commuters noticed their eyes smarted as a result of driving through daily smog; mothers learned that DDT was present in their breast milk and that arsenic and lead were accumulating in the bodies of their children from smelters and leaded gasoline; poultry farmers wondered why eggshells were breaking so easily; fishing enthusiasts saw their trout streams, once pure, running brown; and many watched whale hunters reduce two species of whales to extinction. The turning point, to many, was the year 1969, a year which included the Santa Barbara oil spill and the seizure of eleven tons of coho salmon in Wisconsin and Minnesota because of excessive DDT concentrations. It was the year that the Cuyahoga River in Cleveland caught on fire, and radio and TV stations in Los Angeles recommended, on behalf of the County Medical Association, that children not be allowed to play outside on smog alert days. Public concern over these issues culminated in Earth Day, 1970, and a call for new initiatives to resolve environmental problems. Widely publicized events such as Three Mile Island, Love Canal, and, later, Bhopal, Chernobyl, and the Exxon *Valdez* further sensitized the public to a myriad of environmental hazards. Congress responded with a vast outpouring of environmental protection legislation during the 1970s and 1980s. While this legislation was hailed by some in the environmental movement, the credibility of those entrusted with enforcing and complying with the legislation was called into question.

This gave rise to the third factor in the evolution of environmental risk communication: the decline in public trust and confidence in almost every major American institution. Laird (1989) terms this phenomenon "the decline of deference." He writes: "Across the board, people have lost confidence in every profession and institution associated with risk management controversies: science, government and business. Clearly, confidence has declined precipitantly [and] is much lower than the mid-1960s. For government and the press, confidence remains extremely low. The pattern is the same for other occupations" (p. 547). Laird traces the decline of public confidence in American institutions through a series of Louis Harris polls, and he reports that in 1966, 55 percent of adults had a "great deal of confidence" in business leaders, but by 1986, only 16 percent rated business leaders highly. According to the Harris polls the "great deal of confidence" figure in 1986 for federal governmental agencies was 18 percent; for Congress, 21 percent; for leaders of state government, 19 percent; and for leaders of local government, 21 percent. These figures suggest that Americans are skeptical both toward the claims of businesses and governments that they can handle complex and dangerous substances and technologies responsibly and toward the statements of government officials that they can be trusted to protect the interests of the public. With such widespread distrust, it is not surprising that many citizens do not want industries that utilize technologies perceived as risky coming into their communities. Congress has responded to the public's concerns by enacting environmental legislation that specifically requires federal agencies and industries to operate in a more open fashion.

No state in the United States is untouched by Superfund sites or by the need to site hazardous waste treatment, storage, and disposal (TSD) facilities. Citizens, however, have strongly opposed the siting of hazardous waste TSD facilities in their communities, and some communities have opposed the negative connotation associated with being designated a Superfund community. Other acronyms related to the NIMBY syndrome include LULUs (locally-unwanted-land uses), NIMTOO (not-in-my-term-of-office, referring to elected officials' opposition to LULUs), BANANA (build-almost-nothing-anytime-near-any-where), and NOPE (not-on-planet-Earth). Humor notwithstanding, the NIMBY syndrome represents a significant challenge and dilemma for those whose job it is to communicate environmental risk. One of the most important questions facing the environmental community today is how to move beyond the current gridlock created by opposition to innovative remediation techniques and technologies and the NIMBYism associated with siting hazardous waste treatment facilities. The answer is central to realizing the nation's environmental goals.

ENVIRONMENTAL RISK COMMUNICATION IN PRACTICE

Collectively, these factors are driving governmental agencies and American businesses full throttle into the field of environmental risk communication. In actual practice, however, environmental risk communication has failed miserably. Governmental agencies and private firms dealing with environmental siting and remediation decisions have traditionally excluded the public from the decision-making process, opting instead to solicit public comment after decisions have been made. This approach to environmental decision making, "decide-announce-defend" (or DAD), has paralyzed the facility-siting process in the United States. O'Hare, Bacow, and Sanderson (1983) describe the process as follows: the proponents or developers of a facility make a series of technical decisions in consultation with their engineers (regarding various hazardous waste technologies), with realtors (regarding land selection), and with their attorneys. Typically, there is no interaction at this stage with those who will be affected by the decision. The facility proponent then announces the site and technology to the public. If any alternative options are mentioned, they are presented in such a way as to appear impossible. The facility developers then begin the process of obtaining permits from local, state, and federal governments, which triggers the mandatory public hearings process. Because the public perceives that the decision has already been made, and they have no reason to believe that the facility proponent/developer will take their concerns into consideration, significant opposition is heard at the public hearings. If opponents don't stop a project at the local level, they try again at the state and finally the federal level. If they are unsuccessful in stopping the project through the permitting process, they try the court system. If the courts do not rule in their favor, they use political influence or civil disobedience. Although the proponents of a facility invest significant sums in engineering what they consider the best technology and in buying the necessary site, opponents are frequently successful in stopping the project. Risk communication as typically practiced is, in reality, an attempt to gain public acquiescence or compliance.

An alternative approach to siting hazardous waste facilities just as likely to produce political alienation has been attempted in at least twelve states. Documented by Portney (1991), the "preemptive" method entails legislative authorization for a state siting board or siting authority within state government which has no community representation. The theory behind this type of legislation is that the state should have the authority to overrule local opposition to siting hazardous waste facilities in the greater public interest of the general population of the state. In actual practice, local residents have been able to generate enough political influence to prevent siting despite the legislative authority of a siting board. As Portney documents, this approach "has proven to be no more effective than any other . . . in providing a way of siting treatment facilities" (1991, p. 57).

A related approach, which Portney refers to as "limited local input," also establishes a statewide siting board or other statewide waste management planning council, but adds an element of local participation in the decision-making process. The theory behind this approach is that local input is one of the many different interests or points of view which need to be considered in making siting decisions. It has also been met with limited success. In fact, political processes which attempt to preempt community involvement in environmental decision making and facility siting have resulted in a voter reaction akin to "throwing the bums out" in the next election.

Still another approach, that of offering economic compensation, has been considered by O'Hare, Bacow, and Sanderson (1983) and Kunreuther, Kleindorfer, Knez, and Yaksick (1987). It has also met with disappointing results. The theory behind this approach is that communities should be compensated for the risks they bear in hosting a hazardous waste facility. Economic incentives are offered to local residents to offset perceived risks. However, offering financial compensation is often perceived as attempting to "buy" community acceptance.

A variation on the economic compensation approach has also had limited success. This approach has communities submit sealed bids indicating how much compensation each would require in order to accept siting of a facility. The lowest bidder—that community requiring the least compensation—would "win" the facility. In actual practice, communities opt not to submit a bid at all because of the difficulty of designing a political process capable of defining what an acceptable bid would be.

Examples of public opposition and resistance to hazardous waste site permits and remediation decisions abound. For example, consider the case of Bloomington, Indiana, where the Environmental Protection Agency, Westinghouse Corporation, the Indiana Department of Health and Environment, the county of Monroe, and the city of Bloomington worked for almost ten years to identify a solution to the problem of the more than 650,000 cubic yards of PCB-contaminated soil left at the Westinghouse Superfund site. After many years, they reached a settlement whereby an incinerator was to be constructed to burn the contaminated soil and other materials. This agreement was entered into and approved by the federal district court (in the form of a consent decree) in 1989. However, due to community opposition, the incinerator has yet to be built. Community groups have organized to lobby elected officials and to stop the permitting and construction of the incinerator (Perrecone, 1992).

In Aspen, Colorado, the Environmental Protection Agency (EPA) made plans to clean up lead and heavy metal contamination in the soil in the vicinity of the now inactive Smuggler Mountain lead and silver mine. The EPA had listed Smuggler Mountain on the National Priorities List, or Superfund list, in 1986. The residents of this Aspen neighborhood organized in opposition to the remediation plans, and they are also now opposed to being designated a Superfund site. To date, the residents have thwarted all efforts of the EPA to remove and/or clean the contaminated soil (S. Pennock, personal communication, April 1993).

The Seabrook, New Hampshire, nuclear power plant originally proposed in the early 1970s was the subject of significant public opposition and litigation throughout the mid to late 1970s. The litigation from opponents of the facility cost the facility owners almost $15 million monthly in delays and almost succeeded in shutting the facility permanently (Rosenbaum, 1991).

While these are just a few examples, it is clear that citizen opposition to remediation decisions, technology selections, and facility siting is costly, not only in terms of the financial resources which must be committed to responding to the opposition and which are lost through project delays, but also in terms of the adverse impact which these delays may have on environmental quality. As delays occur in cleaning up PCB-contaminated soil and greatly deteriorated containers storing radioactive waste, the health of the American public and the environment itself are at risk.

Effective environmental risk communication and, more recently, community collaboration and stakeholder involvement approaches can overcome many of these problems. In the earliest years of risk communication research, a mechanistic communication paradigm emerged that drew a comparison between risk communication and the transfer of electronic signals. This model (Covello, von Winterfeldt, & Slovic, 1986b) traces the risk communication process from an information source (transmitter) through a channel (transducer) to an audience (receiver). Finally, it analyzes the message itself. Under the theory of risk communication proposed by Covello et al., risk communication problems arise from problems with the message, the source, the channel, or the receiver. For example, source problems can result from a lack of credibility in those individuals delivering the risk information, from disagreements among scientific experts, or from a lack of data. Message problems can result from highly technical risk analyses which are often unintelligible and poorly communicated to laypersons. Channel problems include biased media reporting or a poorly run public hearing. Receiver problems might include a desire (or demands) on the receiver's part for scientific certainty or a difficulty in understanding scientific, technological, or quantitative risk assessment information. This early approach to environmental risk communication emphasized the conveying or transmitting of scientific information from experts to lay audiences, usually in a one-way direction. While government officials, industry representatives, and scientists complained that the public did not accurately perceive and evaluate risk information, individual stakeholders and representatives of citizen groups were often equally frustrated, perceiving risk communicators and risk assessment experts as uninterested in their concerns and unwilling to take actions to solve health and environmental problems.

While the earliest risk communication approaches failed in part because they emphasized one-way communication of risk information and the need to create a "better" risk message, later approaches placed greater emphasis on the interactive nature of human communication and the need to involve members of a community in a meaningful fashion in the decisions which affect them. Benjamin and Belluck (1990), for example, make a strong argument that risk communication is, in reality, citizen participation, citizen empowerment, and team building. Stern considers risk communication "not information transfer, but a type of political discourse" (1991, p. 100). Interestingly, the evolution of the approaches to environmental risk communication suggest that it is increasingly being recognized that risk communication needs to focus more on the process and integrity of the communication and less on the quantitative and scientific assessments of risk.

Krimsky and Plough (1988) were among the first authors and researchers to identify social, political, and cultural factors in the risk communication process. They suggest that the term "risk communication" could have either the traditional, narrow definition or a new, broader definition. The narrow definition consists of scientists and technical "experts" intentionally conveying information about health and environmental risks to a targeted audience of "nonexperts" through designated channels. This approach suggests that risk assessment methodologies are fail-safe, that they tell decision makers how dangerous a hazard actually is, and that this assessment guides decisions about what ought to be done. If the public reacts in opposition, the job of risk communication in the conventional sense is to do a better job of explaining risk findings, so that the public accepts the judgments of the experts. This approach assumes that all risk assessments are done well and without bias, that a well-executed risk assessment will lead all honorable experts to agreement about risk, that the nontechnical concerns of the public (e.g., fairness of siting decisions, local control, property values, and other intrinsic values) are irrelevant or secondary, and that risk communication can therefore be one-directional instead of multidirectional, and technical instead of focused on values. Krimsky and Plough challenge these assumptions. They propose that risk communication be examined more broadly in the context of political and cultural factors and that it is essentially a social process. They propose a broader definition of risk communication:

The field of risk communication can be divided between those who view risk as a technical concept and those who emphasize its cultural and social dimensions. Some people talk of risk in terms of cost-effective solutions, of efficiency; others use the language of "rights," emphasizing moral issues and questions of social responsibility, justice and obligation. Some measure risks and evaluate them in statistical terms; others talk of "victims" and "real people." Some define risk as a problem which requires expert direction; others seek more participatory control. (1988, p. xiii)

Sandman (1986, 1991) also addresses the qualitative characteristics of risk. If the risk communication process is defined to a discussion of probabilities and consequences, a wide range of risk perception factors are ignored. Risk perception research evaluates how perceptions of risk are influenced by various factors, including the source of the risk information, styles of presentation, and dimensions of risk such as whether it is voluntarily assumed or involuntarily thrust upon a set of individuals and whether the risk is natural or human-created, familiar or unfamiliar, controlled by affected stakeholders or by some external decision-making authority, and so forth. An approach to risk communication which acknowledges citizen judgments about the seriousness of specific risks goes beyond communicating solely about scientific measures of the magnitude of risk and allows consideration of other dimensions or qualities of risk (what Sandman terms "outrage factors").

The most commonly cited definition of risk communication today recognizes that environmental risk communication is, most fundamentally, a communication process. The National Research Council (1989) defines risk communication as "an interactive process of exchange of information and opinion among individuals, groups and institutions. It involves multiple messages about the nature of risk, and other messages, not strictly about risk, that express concerns, opinions or reactions to risk messages or to legal and institutional arrangements for risk management" (1989, p. 21). While the earliest definitions and theories of risk communication addressed the issue of designing a better message, "one which would furnish the lay public with information to convince them to agree with the experts" (Baker, 1990, p. 343), the National Research Council definition emphasizes that risk communication is successful to the extent that it "raises the level of understanding of relevant issues or actions and satisfies those involved that they are adequately informed within the limits of available knowledge" (1989, p. 21).

Benjamin and Belluck (1990) view risk communication in terms of citizen participation and team building. They cite the problem of citizens choosing not to participate in the federally mandated public hearing processes surrounding environmental restoration projects, suggesting that the public often feels ignored by government officials at these forums. Citizens view the government participation programs as pro forma processes, "designed to generate an administrative record that an agency can use as 'proof' that the public was consulted before it makes a preordained decision . . . processes guaranteed to frustrate the public" (1990, p. 50). These authors recommend a formal "risk feedback" process emphasizing the interactive nature of the risk communication process. They suggest that a good starting point for problem resolution is a shared viewpoint of the problem among the various parties and that citizen participation programs foster opportunities for joint problem definition and partnerships in problem solving.

TOWARD A THEORY OF COMMUNITY COLLABORATION IN ENVIRONMENTAL DECISION MAKING

These more proactive views of risk communication suggest a new and empowering communication-based approach to environmental decision making: community collaboration. Community collaboration processes have been suggested by a number of authors in recent years as an alternative approach to solving contentious public policy disputes such as crime, violence, inadequate public education, the provision of social services, rampant growth, environmental degradation and the disintegration of public infrastructure (Bingham, 1986; Carpenter & Kennedy, 1988; Chrislip & Larson, 1994; Crowfoot & Wondolleck, 1990; C. T. Gates, 1991; Gray, 1989; Gray & Wood, 1991; Pasquero, 1991; Potapchuk, 1991). Environmental decision making, including the siting of hazardous waste facilities and decisions related to cleanup plans and technologies, falls squarely within the realm of public policy collaboration. A number of authors have contributed significantly to building a theory of collaboration (Chrislip & Larson, 1994; Gray & Wood, 1991; Wood & Gray, 1991). Some have focused on the process of collaboration (Gray, 1989; Pasquero, 1991; Roberts & Bradley, 1991; Sharfman, Gray, & Yar, 1991; Westley & Vredenburg, 1991), while others have addressed factors which influence the success of collaboration (Chrislip & Larson, 1994; C. T. Gates, 1991; Mattessich & Monsey, 1992; Potapchuk, 1991). Still others have contributed significantly in the area of providing case studies to illustrate the collaboration phenomenon (Chrislip & Larson, 1994; Hall & Weschler, 1991; Logsdon, 1991; McCoy, 1991; Moore, 1988; Norris, 1993; Pasquero, 1991; Roberts & Bradley, 1991; Selsky, 1991; Stamato, 1988).

The general phenomenon of collaboration is defined as a "process of joint decision-making among key stakeholders of a problem domain about the future of that domain" (Gray, 1989, p. 11). Wood and Gray broadened this definition in 1991, arguing that "collaboration occurs when a group of autonomous stakeholders of a problem domain engaged in an interactive process, using shared rules, norms, and structures, to act or decide on issues related to that domain" (Wood & Gray, 1991, p. 146). In short, community collaboration in environmental decision making means involving stakeholders in the decisions which affect them, their health, their economic well-being, and their quality of life. A stakeholder is defined as any individual with a stake in (or concern with) the outcome of a particular decision, whether that decision is related to the siting of a waste facility or the selection of a remediation technology. Stakeholders can include environmental and other public interest group representatives, local elected and appointed officials, people living or owning property in the vicinity of a site subject to environmental decision making, employees and management at the site, representatives of the regulatory community, the business community, technology developers, federal and state agencies, and any others with a stake in the outcome of the decisions. Community collaboration is a communication process which involves a wide range of stakeholders in decision making.

To understand the phenomenon of community collaboration, it is useful to first examine what it is not. Community collaboration is not "decide-announce-defend" or making decisions regarding the development of a remediation plan or the siting of a hazardous waste facility without input from the community. Community collaboration is not a series of one-way messages from "experts" to the public with no opportunity for the public's concerns or values to be heard. Community collaboration is not holding a public hearing to announce predetermined decisions, with no intention of listening or responding to public input. The definition of community collaboration by negation, then, suggests several features. Community collaboration entails a high level of inclusiveness in decision-making processes, so that participation of a wide variety of stakeholder interests is sought and actively encouraged. Chrislip and Larson (1994) suggest that community collaboration is characterized as being a credible and open process, not dominated by the initiating organization or by any single group. To be credible, the community collaboration process must be one of "meaningful work and not . . . a rubber stamp process" (Chrislip & Larson, 1994, p. 82). In an open process, stakeholders feel free to participate to the extent they feel necessary. Stakeholders are not purposefully excluded from the process, and they are representative of a broad array of sectors, for example, government, business, and community groups. Community collaboration provides a process and forum for ongoing, direct, interactive dialogue among a diverse set of stakeholders involved in a remediation program or siting decision. Ideally, stakeholders are involved early in the decision-making process; in fact, they participate in the establishment of the process.

For community collaboration to work, traditional decision makers (e.g., governments and facility proponents) must be willing to share the decision-making power. Pasquero (1991) suggests there are certain "rights" which must be guaranteed through the collaboration process. These include the right to participate, the right to be heard, the right of access to information, the right to be compensated for damages, and the right to say no.

It is critical to the community collaboration approach that stakeholders have the option to say no as a result of the decision-making process, and that the decision to accept risk is a voluntary one. Creighton (1992) cites the example of the Province of Alberta's successful siting of a hazardous waste storage facility several years ago. Geologists and other scientists hired by the government identified a number of geologically suitable (stable) sites near communities throughout the province. Each community was notified by government representatives that it might serve as a suitable location for a hazardous waste storage facility; however, it would be located in that community only by a favorable vote of the entire community, not just a favorable vote of the city council. The provincial government offered to assist the local communities in conducting any studies they felt would be necessary to assure themselves, if they were interested, that the facility would be safely operated and maintained. The result of this voluntary approach to risk acceptance was that stakeholders felt that they were in charge of the decision and that the decision-making process had integrity.

Community collaboration theory is strongly influenced by human communication theory on a variety of levels: interpersonal, small group, organizational, and mass communication. For example, the study of organizational communication and the evolution of Human Relations Theory (Likert, 1971) stress open communication and participative decision making as a means of increasing satisfaction in decision outcomes. Rogers's (1983) Diffusion Theory suggests that communication channels include both mass media and interpersonal contacts and that a number of intermediaries between the media and an audience can influence decision making. Intermediaries can include other participants in the collaborative decision-making process. McQuail's (1984) fifth function of mass communication, mobilization, suggests the ability of the media to promote interests and certain behaviors, including the promotion of interest in remediation and siting issues and active involvement of stakeholders. Hirokawa's Functional Theory offers some initial ideas for a theory of how communication functions in groups to help produce quality decisions (Hirokawa, 1985, 1988; see also Gouran & Hirokawa, 1986; Hirokawa & Scheerhorn, 1986). From the study of interpersonal communication, Uncertainty Reduction Theory (Berger, 1979; Berger & Calabrese, 1975) argues that when individuals meet, they seek to reduce uncertainty about each other, that the more we learn about others, the less uncertain we are of each other, that decreases in uncertainty produce increases in liking among individuals, and that high levels of uncertainty cause increased information-seeking behavior. This theory suggests that community collaboration may foster a reduction in uncertainty surrounding environmental decisions. Many human communication theories and current research projects have significant potential to add to the growing theory of community collaboration in environmental decision making.

The overwhelming conclusion from the community collaboration research and case study analysis is that community collaboration applied to environmental decision making will increase the likelihood of resolving environmental problems and that collaboration offers the best approach and greatest opportunity for overcoming NIMBYism and community opposition to environmental cleanup and siting decisions. It is hypothesized that community collaboration may expedite technology selection and remediation and siting decisions, that it may increase stakeholders' satisfaction in the decision-making process, and that it may improve the stakeholders' perceptions of trust and credibility in the governmental and/or business ventures leading that process. It is further hypothesized that community collaboration and stakeholder involvement in the environmental decision-making process may reduce the likelihood of litigation or other legal or political initiatives intended to stop or inhibit remediation and siting activities and, finally, that it may lead to more enduring decisions.

KIMBALL, NEBRASKA: A CASE STUDY OF SUCCESSFUL COMMUNITY COLLABORATION

Waste Tech Services, Inc., a private firm headquartered in Golden, Colorado, has been one of a very few hazardous waste companies to successfully site an incinerator in the past decade. Gary Severson (1993), director of community involvement for Waste Tech, attributes their success to community collaboration.

Waste Tech was invited to attend a meeting in March 1987 of Kimball's ten-member Economic Development Council to discuss the possibility of siting a hazardous waste incinerator in Kimball. Gary Severson was present at that and most of the subsequent community meetings. During the first meeting, representatives of the firm fully acknowledged that hazardous waste incinerators are a highly controversial and divisive issue, particularly incinerators which accept waste from out of state. In fact, they attempted to dissuade the group from considering the project. They told the community representatives that if they determined they did not want the hazardous waste incinerator in their community, Waste Tech would not remain or try to "sell" them on the idea. Severson encouraged them to study the concept very carefully and offered to provide them with every technical study Waste Tech had available. He offered to allow them access to the company's engineering staff and to provide them with copies of reports, pamphlets, and videos on the hazards associated with incinerators.

His approach was one of being completely open and accessible, and he made the option of siting a hazardous waste facility in the town completely voluntary.

Severson insists that it is critical to begin the communication process through "informal" channels and to sit individually with friends of friends over coffee, to discuss the pros and cons of the incinerator as openly as possible. He met one-on-one with literally hundreds of people, describing the benefits of siting an incinerator in Kimball, but telling them of the downside as well. He always reassured people that it would not be sited in Kimball unless the entire community was satisfied with every aspect of the technology, its operation and maintenance, the transportation to and from the facility, its location, and so on.

Severson soon learned who the key informal decision makers and leaders were, who had legitimacy and credibility in the eyes of others, who were the key stakeholders who could represent significant constituencies. After several months, he was able to work with a smaller number of key people, but was always available to meet with anyone who was interested to provide information and updates on the latest incinerator technology and plan. He listened very carefully to the concerns of the community and always brought those concerns back to the company's engineers in Golden to be resolved.

The Kimball, Nebraska, case is instructive for several reasons. First, the community knew from the outset that the decision to site a hazardous waste incinerator in their community was completely voluntary. They knew going in that they had a choice and that they could turn it down. Second, the process was open and inclusive. Anyone who wanted to learn about the incinerator, the technology, its operation, the transportation patterns, or any other aspect of the proposed facility had complete and open access to studies and reports, as well as to real people who could answer their questions. Interestingly, Severson points out, individual community members were less concerned about the technology and the quantitative risk assessments calculated for the facility than they were about the extent to which they believed they could trust Waste Tech to operate the incinerator safely. The third point is that Severson's approach engendered trust in the process and in the proponents of the facility. He was completely honest with the community about the negative aspects of incinerators, even to the point of providing interested community members with literature on the negative aspects of incineration technology. Fourth, the process was interactive. Severson listened to the community's concerns as much, if not more, than he talked. Not only did he listen, but he incorporated community suggestions into the final design. The community was heard and had input into the decision-making process. Fifth, he was able to identify who the key stakeholders were, and he ensured that they were included in the process on an ongoing basis. Finally, the community was involved in the decision from the outset. They had the opportunity to help define the problem ("Should Kimball serve as a host community to a hazardous waste facility?"), and to be as involved in the decision-making process as they cared to be.

CONCLUSION

The objective of this chapter has been to trace the evolution of the field of environmental risk communication and, more recently, the concept of community collaboration in environmental decision-making. The restoration of environmentally contaminated sites, the safe and effective treatment and disposal of hazardous contaminants, and the preservation of the health of citizens living in the vicinity of these activities represent an enormous public policy challenge. Inadequate communication with the public and a lack of stakeholder involvement in environmental remediation and siting decisions result in public opposition, prolonged cleanup schedules, and increased costs and represent a formidable obstacle to the successful resolution of the nation's environmental problems. Effective risk communication techniques and, in particular, community collaboration and stakeholder involvement techniques—communication empowerment processes informed by human communication theory and research—can help overcome the deadlock which has paralyzed environmental decision making in many parts of the country. This chapter suggests that communication empowerment means offering stakeholders the opportunity to participate in the decisions which affect their health, their quality of life, and their economic well-being through open, inclusive, broad-based, ongoing rational discourse.

PART II

THE POWER OF MEDIA

CHAPTER THREE

Activism in a Moderate World: Media Portrayals and Audience Interpretations of Environmental Activism

David Easter

ENVIRONMENTAL ACTIVISTS, like other activists, have been battling for over a decade against a conservative ideology which finds the whole notion of environmentalism, let alone activism, to be deeply suspect. With the election of President Clinton in 1992, there was a shift from what we could call the hegemony of the right to the hegemony of the center. The election of a Republican Congress in 1994 now pits the presidency and Congress against each other in a partisan conflict, and the hegemony of the center becomes even stronger. The environmental effects of the conservative Contract with America have put considerable political pressure behind varying forms of centrist compromise. While we could initially identify this as shifting political winds, we could also argue that at a deeper level it is inscribed by what Roland Barthes (1972) identified as a key mythology of Western capitalist culture. Put succinctly, at the core of American ideology is what Barthes called "neither/norism," that is to say, the belief that truth does not lie on one side or the other, but rather somewhere in the middle.

Barthes defined myths broadly as the "collective representations" of a culture, from the national flag to big-time wrestling to a major chemical manufacturer's advertorial assertion that "[w]ithout chemicals, life itself would be impossible." This statement is a good example, because the function of myth is to hide its political or ideological nature, to hide the fact that it *is* myth. It is in this sense that Barthes speaks of dominant mythmaking as the process of transforming history into nature in an attempt by the dominant ideology to "lose its name." Chemicals, after all, are not merely products of the conditions, imperatives, and struggles of history; they are the very essence of nature. By this naturalization process myth becomes "depoliticized speech," rendering universal and apolitical that which is in reality socially constructed and inherently political.

Hall's (1982) notion of ideology as the "reality effect" builds upon these semiological insights. Ideology, for Hall, involves the "politics of signification" or "the power to signify events in a particular way." To the extent that this exertion of symbolic power goes unrecognized, the reality effect is achieved, whereby meanings that are ideologically constructed become commonsensical—the natural way of the world. Faced with an image or proposition imbued with the reality effect, people's thought processes are short-circuited to elicit the response, "Who could imagine it otherwise?"

We are drawn to wonder whether the notion of environmentalism has been enveloped by this reality effect. Indeed, allegiance to environmentalism has become virtually commonsensical in our culture. According to a 1992 *Wall Street Journal*/NBC News poll, eight of ten Americans call themselves "environmentalists" (J. Miller, 1993, p. 6). At first blush, this seems like a heartening discovery after years of conservative hegemony. At second blush, however, one has to wonder if the term has any meaning at all anymore. Indeed, who could *not* consider themselves environmentalists these days? Who could imagine it otherwise? We can see how the entire notion has been depoliticized; it has left the political realm of history and entered the universal realm of nature.

We can observe how this has been played out in political and media discourses on the environment. President Clinton, it could be argued, was ushered into office in some part due to his "moderate" stance on just about everything. Instead of being the supreme ideologue, like Reagan, Clinton was elected as the supreme mediator. The much publicized April 1993 "Forest Summit" served as a prime example. The summit was convened to explore the extent to which logging of the ancient forests of the Pacific Northwest should continue and the impact that different policy decisions would have on jobs, profits, and the ecosystem. From the outset the debate was framed in a very particular way: here, ostensibly, two intractable forces were pitted against one another—loggers and environmental activists. Clinton and Gore, so the script went, acted as referees in this politically charged dispute. Then, and only then, could they occupy the transcendental "common ground" where politics gives way to truth or, put another way, where extremism gives way to moderatism.

In a broadcast during the Forest Summit, Judy Woodward of PBS's *MacNeil/Lehrer News Hour* (Hochberg, 1993) echoed the discourses of Clinton, Gore, and media pundits when she described Clinton's purpose as "to bring together two warring parties: loggers, who make a living cutting down trees, and environmentalists, who make it their mission to protect them." An ensuing exchange between Robert MacNeil and Clarence Page of the *Chicago Tribune* neatly set the ideological parameters for this moderatist discourse:

MacNeil: Clarence Page, do you see this as a very risky use of the president's time and charisma?

Page: Yes. . . . This is as risky as gays in the military. There is no obvious compromise. I'm sure the answer is going to be something neither side is going to be pleased with; both sides are going to have to give something up . . .

MacNeil: Isn't that the essence of democracy?

Page: Absolutely right. And these issues have been so polarized for so long, and one of the reasons I give Clinton high marks is that he is willing to seek compromise, to seek common ground. He's taken some hits for that but I think it's a good characteristic.

Enter into the discussion Erwin Knoll, editor of *The Progressive*. Knoll, who as a progressive is an anomaly among media pundits, proceeds to violate the terms of the discourse:

MacNeil: Erwin Knoll, do you applaud the president doing this?

Knoll: There is this notion that this is a clash between environmentalists and loggers. I don't think it is. I think the timber industry for decades has been working against its own long-range interests, by clear-cutting, by exploiting these forests, and now they're reaping the whirlwind and trying to blame it on the spotted owl and the environmentalists. But the fault is theirs for not husbanding their resources in a manner that would have made sense for the long run. So I don't think it's helpful for the president to go out there and act as if they were referees in a fight between the timber industry and environmentalism. That's not the issue.

Knoll was swiftly marginalized in the discussion, and this is understandable given that he transgressed the boundaries of the discourse by refusing to accept the core premise that truth resides somewhere in the middle of two extremes. In doing so, Knoll himself comes off as extremist in a political discourse where truth must lie along the razor-thin divide between "moderate" Democrats and "moderate" Republicans. As explored further below, most media discourse takes place within the boundaries of this moderatist perspective. Furthermore, analysis of audience decodings of the discourse reveals how this moderatist ideology shapes "common-sense" views about environmental issues. In particular, we find evidence, following much recent audience research, that media representations are open to a multiplicity of interpretations and that audience members have considerable interpretive power. At the same time, however, we find that media discourses are powerfully constraining. These findings raise issues about how environmental activists can and should address issues of political strategy and communication empowerment through mass media and other forms of public discourse.

ENCODING/DECODING THEORIES

I conducted an audience study based on an episode of *L.A. Law* (Breech, 1992) that explored the issues addressed at the Forest Summit. The findings have implications for both audience theory and media portrayals—and cultural interpretations—of environmental activism. The study involved the application of Hall's (1980) encoding/decoding model to the *L.A. Law* text. There have been many redraftings of the encoding/decoding model since its inception (see, for example, Fiske, 1987; J. Lewis, 1983, 1991; Morley, 1986). Nonetheless, as Grossberg (1993) has recently observed, the model has become the paradigmatic approach to critical communication studies. The model emerged as a response to two prior media paradigms: effects, and uses and gratifications (Hall, 1982; see also DeFleur & Ball-Rokeach, 1989; J. Lewis, 1991). Early effects research attempted to discern what media does to people, while uses and gratifications research asked what people do with media. Eschewing an approach based on either malignant domination or benign pluralism, the encoding/decoding model sought to grasp the complex interaction between domination and agency in the mass communication process.

As such, the encoding/decoding model reflected a more general perspective called media hegemony theory. Based on the work of Italian Marxist Antonio Gramsci (1971), hegemony theory conceived of cultural forms as key sites of ideological struggle, of struggle over how and what things mean in society. Thus, rather than being simply a matter of manipulation or indoctrination or of pluralistic democracy, culture involves the ongoing contestation among dominant and subordinate groups over how the social order is to be defined and constructed. Thus, like Barthes's notion of myth and Hall's notion of the reality effect, hegemony theory conceives of culture as a battleground over "common sense," over what becomes agreed upon as being the way things are and should be. Common sense thus "constitutes a sense of reality for most people in society, a sense of absolute because experienced reality beyond which it is very difficult for most members of society to move, in most areas of their lives" (R. Williams, 1977, p. 110). Common sense is therefore tenacious and deep-seated, yet for Gramsci it is always only partial, always under contestation.

The encoding/decoding model thus sought to capture this process as it relates to mass communication production and consumption. In this process, certain meanings are preferred, but are not irresistably imposed: "Any society's culture tends, with varying degrees of closure, to impose its classification of the social and cultural and political world. These constitute a dominant cultural order, though it is neither univocal nor uncontested" (Hall, 1980, p. 134). All media texts, then, are structured around a preferred meaning; however, this preferred meaning is not merely received uniformly by individuals. Instead, decoding is contingent on the social position of the viewer. Thus, the Hall model posits three possible readings of a media text: preferred, negotiated, and oppositional. A person whose social position aligns her closely with the dominant ideology may accept totally the preferred meaning of a text; a person whose social position places her in opposition to the dominant ideology may correspondingly oppose the preferred meaning; a person whose social position places her somewhere in between these poles may accept the preferred meaning generally, but modify or oppose certain aspects of it.

Thus, the Hall model moved decisively away from the notion of texts as closed ideological vehicles to texts as bearers of meanings which can only be activated by social subjects, subjects who inflect meanings according to their own social experience. While media texts are "structured in dominance," they are also characterized by "polysemy," open to a multiplicity of interpretations. This question of polysemy has provoked considerable controversy as different theorists have explored the implications of the original model. Most notably, in an important sense the model contradicts itself in its central assertion that all texts are structured around a single preferred meaning that reflects the dominant ideology. Contrary to the semiotic intentions of the model, this implies that all texts contain fixed meanings which exist prior to signification or the process of interpretation (see J. Lewis, 1983). As such, the model only allows for variance in meaning at the level of connotation; meaning is always transparent at the level of denotation. Put another way, the model not only assumes that a preferred meaning exists prior to its reading but also that this preferred meaning is constructed by everyone; variation only occurs at the level of interpretation. In this sense, the model fails to account for all the various dimensions of meaning construction. However, while the Hall model tends to suppress its own implications, a popular theoretical response has involved a swing to the other extreme through a celebratory notion of unlimited polysemy.

Fiske (1987) has taken this notion to the furthest limits by proclaiming that polysemy is a pervasive characteristic of the postmodern "semiotic democracy." Indeed, Fiske argues that the power to construct meanings lies entirely with the audience: "There may be a broadcast version of a television program, but the text that a particular subculture may make of it exists only as part of the cultural process of that audience" (p. 107). Furthermore, the economic imperative to garner audience share compels television's producers to construct relatively "open" texts which "inflect" meanings to accommodate a wide array of social groups and subgroups. Thus, though theoretically acknowledging the existence of preferred meanings in media texts, Fiske virtually denies them any structuring force. To the contrary, the television text sends "invitations to its readers to construct their meanings" (p. 65). It follows, then, that within this negotiated terrain "the balance of power lies with the reader" (p. 66). Ultimately, any attempt by the preferred meaning to "homogenize and hegemonize breaks down on the instability and multiplicity of [television's] meanings and pleasures" (p. 324).

It is beyond the concerns of this chapter to explore the intricacies of the polysemy debate. However, as a means of entering into an analysis of media discourses on environmentalism, I will briefly identify two major problems with the Fiskean perspective. First, as Goodwin (1992) points out, a damaging theoretical slippage occurs "when the moment of meaning production is located in the act of reception" (p. 15). By positing a substantial degree of autonomy to audiences, such a perspective undercuts a key premise of the critical communication paradigm, namely, that "individual subjects have been structured socially in such a way as to make only certain kinds of inner dialogues possible" (p. 15). Given that in postmodern capitalist society the culture industries play a central role in this overall process of social construction, this approach fails to account for "the ways in which media discourses help construct the subject's reaction to media discourses" (p. 15). This relates to a second major problem, which involves the question of the limits to polysemy on the encoding side of the equation. According to Fiske (1987), the sign of television's semiotic democracy is "its delegation of production of meanings and pleasures to its viewers" (p. 236). Yet, as explored through the audience study below, this view makes the erroneous assumption that cultural power is exerted only through monosemic messages.

ENVIRONMENTAL NARRATIVES

We can begin with a narrative analysis of the *L.A. Law* episode. The narrative opens with the partners of the law firm sitting around a conference table discussing the status of current cases. Partner Ann Kelsey announces that she is defending a logging company that is being sued by a worker who lost his arm when his saw hit a metal spike in a tree. The logger is suing two parties: the logging company, for negligence in not detecting the existence of the spike; and the Redwood Warriors, an environmental activist group, which is accused of putting the spike in the tree.

One of Kelsey's partners jokingly asks Kelsey if her Sierra Club membership will be revoked because she's defending a logging company. To this she replies that this time the company is not at fault:

"Tree spikers caused the accident," she says.

"Tree spikers?" another partner asks.

"An activist who drives spikes in trees to keep them from being cut down," responds another attorney.

To which yet another attorney retorts, "Activists? They're terrorists."

"He's also our co-defendant," Kelsey says, eliciting moans from around the table as the scene ends.

Along with establishing the central enigma (Who will be found responsible for the logger's injury?), this scene sets up another set of enigmas: How will Kelsey reconcile the conflict between her allegiance to her client and her allegiance to environmental causes? Are these environmentalists terrorists or actively concerned citizens? How will the co-defendants resolve their ideological conflicts?

The ensuing narrative unfolds largely in the courtroom. Briefly: the logger's attorney charges that the environmental group is guilty for placing the spike in the tree and that the logging company is guilty for failing to adequately protect its workers. The environmental activist's attorney argues that the logging company is solely to blame, due to its "callous disregard" for worker safety amidst its unbridled greed in clear-cutting the forest. Kelsey, in contrast, asserts that the logging company did all it could to protect its workers and should not be held responsible for the terroristic act of the environmental group. However, in the middle of the trial, the judge dismisses the activist from the case due to a lack of evidence, and the jury ultimately finds the logging company president guilty of negligence.

As the narrative moves toward this resolution of the central enigma, Kelsey's internal struggle deepens. After the activist is dismissed, Kelsey suggests to her client that he settle. Refusing, her client responds suspiciously, "They really got to you, didn't they? Those damned Redwood Warriors got you thinking it's my fault." Clearly perplexed, Kelsey denies this assertion.

The episode ends with a telling exchange between Kelsey and the activist's attorney immediately following the jury's decision:

Activist attorney: I don't admire your politics but I like your work.

Kelsey: You don't know anything about my politics.

Activist attorney: I know you keep your politics out of your work and that's a shame.

Kelsey: Are you being radical or just plain rude? You and I and your client are all on the same side of the fence, but you have to reach people with the message. Breaking the law—

Activist attorney: Let me guess. It turns people off and gives us a bad name?

Kelsey: You said it.

Activist attorney: Whereas you're so accommodating you wind up arguing for the enemy.

The episode ends with a closeup of Kelsey, looking distraught.

Another key moment occurs earlier in the episode, a moment which brings us back to our main theme. During a heated argument between the logging company president and the activist, Kelsey says to the activist's attorney, "If we don't help these men find some kind of common ground, there's going to be more violence, more victims like [the logger]."

How do we interpret the meaning of this episode? If we employ the encoding/decoding model, we would first attempt to discern whether there is a preferred meaning encoded within the text. Then we would test this against audience interpretations: Do audience members construct the same preferred meaning? How many accept this meaning and thus construct a preferred reading? How many reject the message, giving an oppositional reading? How many accept certain aspects of the message and reject others, giving a negotiated reading? Alternatively, do audience members construct a variety of preferred readings? In other words, is the text closed and univocal, or open and polysemic? Where do these determinations lie: in the text, in the audience, in the culture, in their interaction?

Without attempting to address all the controversial aspects of these questions, we could attempt to construct a preferred reading of the episode which centers on Kelsey's ideological position, given that she is the story's protagonist. Such a reading would focus on Kelsey's struggles to occupy a middle ground between the "conservative" interests of the logging company president and the "radical" interests of the activist. In this reading, Kelsey emerges as a hero of sorts, who attempts to facilitate a pluralist compromise between two extreme ideological positions—as she is assailed from both sides.

Viewed in this light, the *L.A. Law* episode represents a fictional working through of the tensions and contradictions created in the dispute between corporate and environmental interests. As Carragee (1990, p. 90) points out, "media texts often articulate contradictions within hegemonic ideology" and in doing so underscore the fact that the dominant ideology is not "fixed and seamless," but always adjusting to new historical conditions and attempting to resolve internal contradictions. On this account, we can see the *L.A. Law* episode as a reflection of a centrist attempt to reconcile the need for environmental preservation within a system based on unbridled economic expansion. As such, the episode follows the character of Kelsey as she struggles to maintain an ideological stance which is sensitive to the destruction of the environment, while at the same time defending the needs of business and opposing "unlawful" or "radical" or "extreme" modes of social action. Put in a more Gramscian way, Kelsey could be viewed as the embodiment of the hegemonic ideology's attempt to resolve inner contradictions and thereby maintain a sense of equilibrium.

However, we could also envision other preferred readings. Indeed, it would seem that the text invites a plurality of interpretations, as highlighted by audience readings discussed below. Nonetheless, I will argue, against certain theoretical positions, that this is not because of some inherent instability in this or all texts, nor is it due to some generalized pluralist impulse among program encoders. Rather, we could interpret polysemy here as the manifestation of tensions within the hegemonic ideology being played out dramatically. Kelsey embodies this sense of instability. Attacked from both sides and struggling to maintain—and justify—a stable position, she appears unsettled, confused, distraught, left sighing in frustration in the episode's final shot. Following from this, the text does not close in around a single stable meaning. Rather, as the text hesitates, reflects, interrogates itself, meaning leaks through the seams, opening up the possibility of (at least) three preferred readings:

1. Environmental activists may be right to protest the destruction of the forests, but often their positions and tactics are too extreme. You shouldn't break the law to pursue your cause. Both the logging company and the environmental activists are responsible for the logger's injury. They need to find a common ground, to compromise.

2. The logging company is right. People demand wood; logging companies, like other businesses, are simply meeting public demand and providing jobs for the community. The activists are terrorists and at fault for the logger's injury through unlawful sabotage.

3. Environmentalists are right. Extreme tactics are sometimes necessary to stop the destruction of the forests due to corporate greed. The logging company is responsible for the logger's plight.

As discussed earlier, to suggest the existence of three possible preferred readings poses problems for the original encoding/decoding model, with its conceptual focus on a single preferred meaning. However, also as discussed earlier, the consequent move toward a liberatory notion of polysemy is deeply problematic. Analysis of audience interpretations of the *L.A. Law* episode serves to illuminate the conceptual terrain between these two conceptual poles.

AUDIENCE DECODINGS

I conducted interviews to determine whether the potential readings identified above, or other possible readings, would be actualized in audience decodings. Three subjects were interviewed: Carol, a housewife in her mid-fifties and an upper-class Republican; Susan, a thirty-year-old receptionist, mother, and middle-class Democrat; and Iris, twenty-eight, a social worker who by trade and political orientation is a progressive activist. The research subjects viewed the *L.A. Law* episode separately in their own homes. Immediately following the showing, I asked a series of open-ended questions designed to prompt the viewer to discuss her reactions to the episode. The results were insightful: each viewer constructed a different preferred reading, revealing that at a general level the text was polysemic.

Carol read the episode as favoring the activist's perspective, and she therefore opposed it. She based her interpretation largely on the outcome of the trial. "I would go the other way," she said. "I didn't think [the logging company president] was wrong. I didn't agree with them letting the other guy off, the activist. I thought he should have been blamed. I think you should be allowed to run your business and make your livelihood." This interpretation was clearly informed by her opinion of activists: "I don't like activists in general. I'm not sympathetic. My own beliefs are not that way."

Unlike Carol, Susan decoded the episode as favoring the logging company president. She based her interpretation on two aspects of the text. First, the *L.A. Law* attorney represented the logging company president, which implied that the program supported his perspective. Second, her interpretation was based on how she believed the text constructed the activist: "They had the radical environmentalist and his radical lawyer, with long hair, and [the activist] was just mumbling during the court hearing. So they made him look like a nut and he was really to blame." Thus, according to Susan's decoding, the text paints the logging company president as the "underdog" who is ultimately victimized by the activist, who wrongly "gets off scot-free." Using the encoding/decoding terminology, Susan negotiated with what she believed to be the preferred meaning of the episode. She did not sympathize with the logging company president, yet she did not identify with the activist's position either. She said: "They want you to think that the environmentalist is at fault, which he might have been, you know—his tactics might have been wrong." Thus, while she believed the program favored the logging company president, her own view comports with Kelsey's: she felt that both parties were to blame and a common ground should be sought.

What is interesting about the readings of Carol and Susan is their move to close down the meaning of the potentially polysemic text. Both of them decode the text as having a single preferred meaning, and neither of them in their responses pointed to any ambiguities in the episode. Iris, in contrast, decoded the episode as having a dual meaning. For her, the preferred meaning was embodied by Kelsey, who struggled to reconcile the excesses of both greedy corporations and extremist activists. However, in keeping with her social position as a progressive, Iris opposed this meaning as an unwarranted compromise, stating bluntly: "The company was definitely to blame, because they don't really do things to protect workers and they don't really give a shit about what happens to the forest."

We can draw two major conclusions from the audience decodings. First, we find a clear determining link between the decoders' social positions/political orientations and their readings of the text. Second, we find that the text is polysemic, open to a multiplicity of readings. This counters the notion that people agree on a preferred meaning, but that they respond to it differently. Here, a single preferred reading does not emerge; rather, we find three preferred readings of the episode.

If we were to leave it here, we find support for the Fiskean notion that television is a "semiotic democracy" in which viewers have a great deal of power to construct their own meanings from programs that invite this pluralism. However, while the *L.A. Law* text may be polysemic at the general level, a closer exploration reveals that at a key subtextual level meaning closes down tightly. While the three decoders constructed the episode differently, their readings converged noticeably on a key dimension—its portrayal of environmental activism. Susan, when asked why she believed the episode favored the logging company president, said: "Just the parts where they're portraying the activist and his lawyer as just kooks, instead of [the environment] as being a real issue."

Iris, who as an activist has a direct concern about public perceptions of activism, was unsettled by what she saw as the episode's negative portrayal of her vocation. She said that the episode portrayed the activist as "some crazy guy who goes around chaining himself to trees, doing stuff that is especially violent to other people. That's how they try to portray activists, so I think that most Americans who watch the show would think that he's kind of crazy and violent, that his tactics are just as bad as what the logging company was doing." When asked what specifically in the episode led her to reach this conclusion, she referred to the use of the word "terrorist": "Well, they try to make him look like a leftist who doesn't really care about how to go about stopping the deforesta-tion, kind of like a terrorist. I assume that's what they were trying to do because of the way they threw the word 'terrorist' around, that people are going to be turned off by that, afraid by all that."

Interestingly, but not surprisingly, while Iris objected to what she perceived as a biased characterization of the activist in the episode, Carol viewed such a portrayal as an accurate depiction of activists in the real world. When asked what she thought of the activist, she responded: "Arrogant and aloof, and like, 'I did it, and just prove that I did wrong, and I have a right to save.' . . . That's what gets me about activists is that they think they have the right to break the laws or anything else just to prove something because they think it's their right." When asked to characterize the activist's attorney, she stated: "I think he was one of these yuppie types that go for the causes. Which I guess you have to have someone to do that. But I'm not normally for activists, I don't like their tactics."

There are three things worth noting in this statement. First, the phrase "go for the causes" is a loaded one in our culture. Its semantic force is pejorative, and in this context could be paraphrased as meaning that the activist lawyer does not really pursue causes because he deeply believes in them, but rather because he is given arrogantly to pursuing causes for the sake of pursuing causes. Second, the mythic discourse of what Barthes (1972, p. 150) called "inoculation" is at play in her second statement, which again is pejorative: we need to put up with aberrations like activists because we are a free society. Activists are only to be taken seriously in that they reveal democracy in action. Finally, we find a universalizing characterization of activists in the phrase "I'm not normally for activists," which comports with what Barthes (p. 151) described as the mythic discourse of "identification." Paraphrased, this would mean that all activists are the same and that all activists are misguided and should be opposed *in toto.* Activists become the others, but not others with unique attributes and contributions, but rather aberrations from the normal or, as Barthes put it, "analogues who have gone astray."

IMPLICATIONS

Audience Research

Overall, one major conclusion emerges: while the episode is generally polysemic, there is a powerful discourse operating within the narrative that closes down the meaning of the text. Put another way, while this discourse about activism does not emerge at the general level to achieve the status of a preferred reading, it does work to constrain the polysemic potential of the text in the service of a dominant ideological perspective. In fact, if we analyze the discourse about activism as a subtext, we find that the Hall model is applicable at this level. All three decoders constructed the same preferred meaning: activists are others, bizarre, dangerous, contrary to the American way, aberrant citizens, and so on. Carol accepted the preferred meaning. Iris opposed it. Susan negotiated with it, opposing its total marginalization of activists while accepting its critique of activists' tactics.

This finding led me to ask a deeper question about the extent to which the determination of meaning lies primarily within or outside the text. Put another way, is the text closed down by its own structure, or is it simply an instance of a general closure within our culture, in which it is an automatic reaction to associate "activism" with negative connotations? Going back to the text, I found that both the activist and the logging company president could be interpreted negatively. In my reading, the logging company president was portrayed as overbearing, rude, boisterous, and uncompromising. Yet, in the audience study, the negative attributes of the activist resonated much more powerfully among the decoders. It becomes clear that this interpretation was partially grafted onto the text from outside. Iris, for example, complained several times about how the program "threw the word 'terrorist' around," when in fact this word was used only once in the entire episode.

To see if a decoding pattern would emerge, I showed the episode to thirty college students. Their written interpretations fell in line with the original findings. Half the students interpreted the episode as favoring Kelsey's moderatist perspective. A quarter of the students saw the program as favoring the logging company president, and a quarter saw it as favoring the environmental activist. By sheer numbers, we could say that the moderatist perspective might be the preferred meaning, but the evidence was far from conclusive. It was conclusive, however, when it came to the discourse about activism. I asked students to characterize the logging company president and the environmental activist. While the students' personal views on the issue varied, their views of how these characters were portrayed in the episode did not. The strongest word used to describe the logging company president was "greedy," a term that was used several times in the text. Much stronger words were reserved for the activist, however: "bum," "slimeball," "arrogant," "unrepentant," "moron," "sneaky," and "very liberal." This reveals clearly that we have an instance in which a powerful cultural discourse is resonating powerfully within a specific cultural text.

We can draw one major conclusion from this finding in relation to audience theory. The study suggests that audience researchers must be wary of the tendency to focus solely on polysemy while missing other ways in which meaning may be limited. As J. Lewis (1991) observes, "we have become seduced into thinking that popular culture must be univocal to be powerful or hegemonic," when in fact "an ambiguous TV program can be just as manipulative as an unambiguous one, it simply moves in multifarious ways" (p. 205). We need models to explore these multifarious ways in which ideology works, rather than reverting to a simplistic model of media effects, be it a pessimistic approach that sees domination in everything or an optimistic approach that sees resistance in everything. The original encoding/decoding model, whatever its shortcomings, sought to carefully negotiate this dialectical terrain, as should continuing audience research endeavors.

Environmental Activism

The findings of the audience study appear deeply problematic when applied to attitudes toward environmental activism in our society. The discourse about activism, regardless of where one stands on the question, is a powerful one. As noted at the beginning of this paper, this is not surprising to activists in the field. Yet, given how the media constructed the debate at the Forest Summit, for example, we are led to ask not merely how activists are marginalized, but rather how "different" activists—such as labor and environmental—are divided among themselves. The L.A. Law episode offers a telling example. On the witness stand, the injured worker assesses blame for his accident as follows: "That nut [the environmental activist] put a spike in the tree and Etter [the logging company president] didn't do jack." The worker places the blame equally between the two, or does he? Clearly, the worker blames the activist for endangering his workplace. As for the logging company president, he is at fault, primarily, for failing to prevent the tree spiking, not for any willful action that could endanger workers' jobs, such as massive deforestation through clear-cutting. The implication here is that if the logging company president had been more vigilant in protecting workers from environmental activists, the workers would pledge their allegiance to the company in its war against ecoterrorists.

In both real and media-induced ways, the battle lines were similarly divided at the Forest Summit, which serves to underscore a crucial strategic imperative: Without a more coherent alliance between the labor and environmental movements, activism at both levels loses the ideological (and, ultimately, political) battle to corporate interests. These interests, buttressed by moderatist-oriented media coverage, have thus far gained significant ideological advantage by attempting to define the antagonism as one between environmentalists and workers—precisely the scenario that is most disadvantageous to both. The media clips leading into the pundit roundtable on the *MacNeil/Lehrer* segment discussed earlier, consistent with other media coverage at the time, were dominated by images of angry loggers venting spleen against angry ecoactivists in an ideological scenario which served corporate interests by portraying the conflict as one between environmental protection and jobs. This effectively paints over the real sources of the problems facing both parties in the alleged dispute.

While grass-roots environmental activists have attempted to counter the consequences of corporate and media representations of the environmental debate, the same cannot necessarily be said of mainstream environmental groups. For many environmental and labor activists, these groups have capitulated to the moderatist line under the rationale that it is better to accept scraps than nothing at all. Indeed, as Dowie (1994) observed, "[t]o a growing number of environmentalists outside the Beltway, chummy breakfasts with Al [Gore] symbolize the compromised gradualism that has put the movement on the road to becoming an endangered species" (p. 518). Dowie's proposed strategy is that grass-roots activists do some inside-the-Beltway lobbying of their own, but not at the White House and Congress, "but [at] the Sierra Club, the Environmental Defense Fund and the National Wildlife Federation" (p. 518). Put another way, perhaps the environmental movement would do well to avoid moderatism in a moderate world.

CHAPTER FOUR

Constituting Nature Anew Through Judgment: The Possibilities of Media

Kevin DeLuca

THE INCREASING PREVALENCE of talk about the environment in many different areas, including politics, international relations, economics, academia, and popular culture, seems to have done little to alter the trajectory of modern civilization toward environmental ruin. A primary reason for this is that mainstream environmental discourses have been institutionalized within the dominant articulation or paradigm out of which the environmental problems arose. This dominant articulation in modern industrial civilization is commonly known as "progress" and runs as follows: Humanity, by dominating nature through the use of instrumental reason (formal reason and technique) and technology (the relation of techniques and social forms), will achieve security. The deconstruction of progress requires an analysis of technology, since technology is the material means through which the domination of nature is achieved. Most human experiences in the lifeworld are technologically mediated so that the co-constitution of self and world through perspectives in judgment is mediated by technology (including media).

As the technological world lurches from one environmental crisis to another, there is a wide continuum of responses, ranging from turning to technology for solutions to the problems (ignoring unforeseen and often harmful side effects) to arguing for abandoning technology altogether and returning to a more "primitive" state (as if there ever was once a human society innocent of technology). All the responses recognize technology as central to the situation, share an implicit conception of technology "according to which it is a means and a human activity," and adopt "the instrumental and anthropological definition of technology" (Heidegger, 1977, p. 5). Such a definition is correct only in a very limited way, and it misses the essential transforming nature of technology, which changes human perception and the environment. This limited perspective on technology is particularly prevalent and damaging among environmental groups—Earth First! and certain factions of the Greens leap to mind as groups that have such an especially negative instrumental view of technology that they call for abolishing it. This is not particularly surprising since environmentalists charge themselves with protecting nature, an area often visualized as being free of the taint of technology, and since technology is often the means for destroying nature. This view is damaging, however, when it leads environmentalists to misunderstand the fundamental importance of technology to the environmental movement. There are two ways in which technology is central to the environmental movement.

It is almost commonplace to note how the first pictures of Earth from space in 1966 made evident the frailty of the planet and sparked a global ecological consciousness. One of humanity's highest technological achievements, space flight, made possible a perspective essential to environmental thinking over the past three decades. On a less grand scale many key environmental issues—saving the whales, protecting African wildlife, preserving rainforests, and so on—are driven by the concerns of people who are made aware of and led to act upon these issues through the media. In other words, on many issues most people's only contact with the environment to be saved is through communication technology. Thus, the environmental movement is a technological movement insofar as it takes place in a context made possible by communication technology. Further, media enable the global awareness that is central to the environmental movement since many local people do not particularly want their home environment to be "saved."[1]

Second, environmental groups, including radical groups such as Earth First!, depend on communication technology, both their own and that of media corporations, in their struggles to save and protect nature and in their efforts to change public consciousness concerning environmental issues. Quite simply, environmental groups rely on media tactics, especially the construction of image events staged for mass media dissemination, as their primary rhetorical activity as they struggle to effect social change.

Since the centrality of technology to both environmental awareness and action warrants an in-depth exploration of technology, the following section looks at the essential characteristics and effects of technology by examining the work of Don Ihde and Marshall McLuhan.[2] The chapter then identifies how practical relations with technology are transformed into a "technological worldview." Next, by comparing the thought of McLuhan to that of Bateson, the chapter investigates the relation of technology and conscious purpose to the larger ecosystem and examines how adverse effects (error) can be mitigated. Finally, the possibilities of technology in promoting systemic wisdom and judgment are explained, with specific reference to examples of media tactics of environmental groups.

A PHENOMENOLOGICAL EXPLORATION OF TECHNOLOGY

The work of Ihde and McLuhan focuses on the relation of humanity and technology but with different yet complementary emphases. In contrast to McLuhan, who is concerned with the effects of technology in interaction with the larger cultural world—the totality of effects, Ihde focuses on the essential characteristics of specific human/technology interactions. While McLuhan is more concerned with how technology transforms the social world, Ihde is more concerned with how technology transforms individual perceptions.

For Ihde, technology or technics (he uses these terms interchangeably in various works) connotes a "sense of human action engaged with, through, among concrete artifacts or material entities" (1983, p. 1). This is in contrast to technique, which is "an isolated, defined end which allows the construction of means" (Angus, 1984, p. vi) and which does not require a "material object" (Ihde, 1983, p. 1). In *Technics and Praxis* (1979), *Existential Technics* (1983), and *Technology and the Lifeworld* (1990), Ihde phenomenologically explores human/technology relations in order to ascertain the essential characteristics of technology. He cites two categories of human/technology relations: focal and background. There are three types of focal relations: embodiment, hermeneutic, and alterity. In embodiment relations, a human experiences through a technology, for example, seeing through a telescope or feeling through a dentist's probe. Such an experience involves an extension or amplification of one human sense, a reduction of the other senses, and also a reduction of the sense amplified. A probe allows one to feel more minutely the surface of the tooth but prevents one from feeling the warmth and wetness of the tooth. The experience of distance through the technology is transformed into an experience of irreal near-distance. The object perceived through a technology appears as a sensorily reduced object. In embodiment relations, the technology that is used to experience something changes the experience. The moon as seen through a telescope is changed by the telescope so that it is not just the moon but the moon-through-a-telescope. While transforming the experience, the technology is semitransparent because the technology is the means rather than the object of focus.

For Ihde, hermeneutic relations involve experiences of or with technology. They are the focus of perception and are acted on as a text. As Ihde explains, "In a hermeneutic relation, the world is first transformed into a text, which in turn is read" (1990, p. 92). An aspect of the world is known only as translated through the technology. If I read in the newspaper that it is seventy-eight degrees and sunny in Los Angeles, I know that reality only through the paper. By watching television, in particular PBS documentaries, I learn of and become concerned about the Amazon rainforests. Hermeneutic relations allow me to have a vast knowledge of a world of which I have no personal or lived experience. As Ihde puts it, "Through hermeneutic relations we can, as it were, *read* ourselves into any possible situation without being there" (1990, p. 92).

Ihde introduces the notion of alterity relations in his latest work, *Technology and the Lifeworld*. Ihde borrows the term "alterity" from Emmanuel Levinas in order to distinguish human/technology relations in which the human relates *to* the technology as a quasi-other. In contrast to embodiment or hermeneutic relations, which retain a reference to the world, in alterity relations there is no necessary reference to the world. The technology is the object of perception, not the mediator. Examples range from cherished objects ("a long-cared-for automobile" [Ihde, 1990, p. 98]), to sacred technological objects, to technological competitors (video games or computer chess): "[W]hat the quasi-otherness of alterity relations does show is that humans may relate positively or presententially *to* technologies. In that respect and to that degree, technologies emerge as focal entities that may receive the multiple attentions humans give the different forms of the other" (Ihde, 1990, p. 107).

In background relations, technology transforms my experience of the world by replacing nature in my immediate experience of the world and reforming the context of my world. I walk on pavement—my feet need never touch the earth. In the city at night, the glow of electric lights replaces the starry heavens and the dark of the night. The materials that form my shelter have been so transformed that I no longer recognize them as coming from trees, rocks, and sand—from nature. As Ihde argues, "[T]he background role is a field one, not usually occupying focal attention but nevertheless conditioning the context in which the inhabitant lives" (1990, p. 111). Ihde does not write much about background relations, but they can transform one's perception of the world as much as using a telescope does: "With the expansion of our technology, we have in effect, translated our concepts into artifacts, radically restructuring not only our conception of nature but the texture of our ordinary experience as well. . . . [O]ur world of artifacts may be no more than the thinnest of layers covering the rhythm of living nature, but it is that layer we confront in our daily experience" (Kohak, 1984, pp. 12–13). In contrast to embodiment and hermeneutic relations, in background relations technology is not part of the process of perception but rather is the context of perception. Nonengaged technology, automated technology, and the products or artifacts of technology are the background of a technological society. Background relations do not affect the process of perception; they affect perception by changing what is perceived.

This distinction between embodiment/hermeneutic relations and background relations is important when exploring the relation between nature and humans and the mediation of that relation by technology. Nature is the primordial ground of being which is mediated through the senses and culture (which vary historically). In embodiment and hermeneutic relations, technology in interaction with the senses creates a perception of nature. Different technologies help create different perceptions. For example, experiencing the Serengeti

Plains of Africa through television is different from being there or reading about it. A dominant medium or combination of media may create a perceptual or noetic background so that an oral culture, dominated by speech and the ear—acoustic space—will have a more involved, intimate relation with an "animate" nature than will a print culture, dominated by the visual sense, which will objectify and fragment a "mechanistic" nature. Embodiment and hermeneutic relations with technology will result in different perceptions of nature, but primordial nature is only perceptually and conceptually changed. In other words, a different technology leads to a different thematization and therefore a shift of perceptual or noetic background, but as technology and its artifacts increase in quantity, noematic background relations increase in importance. Technology and artifacts as background start to replace primordial nature as background. What can be perceived changes. The context of perception, of lived experience, changes. The context or background always serves as a limit, but a fluid limit, as attested to by the many conceptions of nature throughout history. However, by having "translated our concepts into artifacts, radically restructuring not only our conception of nature but the texture of our ordinary experience as well" (Kohak, 1984, p. 12), we have created a context or background that reinforces a part or figure and therefore creates a more rigid limit. The figure or part has created its own ground or whole. The abstract, conceptual construct has created its own concrete reality. Noetic background relations have given rise to a technological noematic background: "Though the theoretical construct of a mechanically ordered matter in motion may bear little resemblance to the living nature of the field and the forest and so may never have appeared convincing before, it is a faithful reflection of a world of artifacts and as such compelling to a humanity whose experience of nature is restricted to contact with artifacts" (Kohak, 1984, p. 13). The primordial ground, the world as horizon of horizons, still exists, but nature as background for thematization of concepts has been replaced by artifacts as background.

McLUHAN AND THE EFFECTS OF TECHNOLOGY: RATIO OF THE SENSES

Marshall McLuhan is concerned with how humans and media interact, how that interaction reconfigures patterns of perception, and how a medium in interaction with perception and other media translates the cultural environment. (For McLuhan, the words "media" and "technology" are interchangeable.) McLuhan concentrates on the effects of technology. For him, the medium is the message because each new medium enters an environment and translates and alters it. Though the effects of the technology vary depending on the particular environment, the "effects of a technology do not occur at the level of opinions or concepts, but alter sense ratios or patterns of perception steadily and without any resistance" (McLuhan, 1964, p. 33). For McLuhan, like Ihde, every technology extends a human capacity and reduces others (because there is an equilibrium in the sensorium). The wheel extends the feet or human locomotion, but the greater speed entails less involvement with the environment through which one passes. McLuhan defines technology as a way of translating one kind of knowledge into another mode: " [T]echnologies are ways of translating one kind of knowledge into another mode. . . . All media are active metaphors in their power to translate experience into new forms. The spoken word was the first technology by which man was able to let go of his environment in order to grasp it in a new way" (1964, pp. 63, 64).[3]

Technology is always a response to a problem, an irritant—stress is the stimulus for invention. Every new technology is explicit. It is a response to a figure from the background of culture. However, as it is pushed to the limits of its potential it reaches a break boundary, reverses, becomes part of the ground, and has effects opposite of those for which it was intended. For instance, the road, designed to make travel between two cities easier, pushed "beyond its break boundary turns cities into highways" (McLuhan, 1964, p. 49), as with Los Angeles. Fertilizers and pesticides, invented to help us produce more bountiful and less damaged crops, pushed beyond a break boundary become part of the ground and now result in poisoned food and water. There are two important points to note about this structure of extension and reversal. The first is that each medium is entering an already existing culture which affects and limits the effects of the medium: "There is, for example, no way of refusing to comply with the new sense ratios or sense 'closure' evoked by the TV image. But the effect of the entry of the TV image will vary from culture to culture in accordance with the existing sense ratios in each culture" (McLuhan, 1964, p. 54). The second point is that this structure applies to individual technologies and to a medium or a combination of media that defines a cultural epoch.

If McLuhan's structure of the transforming effects of technology—extension of one capacity, reduction and reordering of the other senses, reversal of the intended and initial effect of the technology, and translation of knowledge and the environment from one mode to another—is correct, it can help people understand the present environmental situation and perhaps enable them to use that awareness for wise action instead of stopgap reaction. For McLuhan, integral awareness of the effects of a new technology on the environment and patterns of perception is essential to parrying the violence of the new effects. The example of the phonetic alphabet clarifies how awareness may help:

> Oral cultures act and react at the same time. Phonetic culture endows men with the means of repressing their feelings and emotions when engaged in action. To act without reacting, without involvement, is the peculiar advantage of Western literate man. . . . Only alphabetic cultures have ever

mastered connected lineal sequence as pervasive forms of psychic and social organization. The breaking up of every kind of experience into uniform units in order to produce faster action and change of form (applied knowledge) has been the secret of Western power over man and nature alike. (McLuhan, 1964, p. 88)

Print intensified the effects of the phonetic alphabet, which included the dominance of visual space, figures without ground, stasis, abstraction, objectification, fragmentation, individualization, and introspection.

This century has seen or felt the reversal of the technology of the phonetic alphabet. McLuhan argues that "[t]oday the great principle of classical physics and economics and political science, namely that of the divisibility of each process, has reversed itself by sheer extension into the unified field theory" (1964, p. 48). Electricity is instantaneous, erasing lineal cause. Television and computers are part of the reversal, the reemergence of the oral, of acoustic space, of the play of figure and ground, of tribalism, of lived experience. As McLuhan concludes, the "immediate prospect for literate, fragmented Western man encountering the electric implosion within his own culture is his steady and rapid transformation into a complex and depth-structured person emotionally aware of his total interdependence with the rest of human society" (1964, p. 59). McLuhan might well have said that man will also become aware of his interdependence with nature. This is provided that humans do not become numbed, docile servants of their technology.

If McLuhan is right, it helps explain the rise of grass-roots, emotional, direct-action groups such as Greenpeace[4] and Earth First!, as opposed to traditional, centralized, paper-pushing, bureaucratic lobbying groups such as the Sierra Club or Friends of the Earth. Perhaps due to the rise of electric technology, the new groups perceive the world in a more integrated, involved way. They recognize the need to avoid looking at nature as enemy or standing reserve. Even though the world seems to be threatened by technology and its products (and humans), electric technology can be involved in helping humanity avoid destruction by promoting the oral, the acoustic space, an organic synthesis of all the senses, and the reunification of action, thought, and community. In other words, the bias of electric technology is reversing the bias of writing and print. However, a return to an electric version of the oral and acoustic space does not guarantee an abandonment of the concept of nature as standing reserve or resource storehouse. It will still be a world of artifacts that forms the texture of our ordinary experience, preventing a lived experience of primordial nature, the ground of our being. Such a lived experience of nature seems necessary for Western humanity to become aware of its "total interdependence" with nature, to become aware that the unit of survival is not the individual organism but the organism plus environment (Bateson, 1972, p. 483).

FROM PRACTICAL RELATIONS TO TECHNOLOGICAL WORLDVIEW

McLuhan's way of looking at technology helps us step back in order to get an idea of how we ended up with a technological worldview. If technology arose in response to human survival needs in the face of an overwhelmingly powerful natural world, the domination of nature (as developed in scientific technology) was a heating up or intensification of this original impetus. We have now gone beyond a break boundary: there is now a technological worldview that threatens the survival of humanity because it has replaced nature with a technological milieu. This generalization accounts for changes brought by technology but not for specificity or particularity. It doesn't explain why out of all the cultures throughout history which have had practical relations with technology, modern Western culture has developed a technological worldview. The totality of this domination is well noted by Heidegger (1977): "Metaphysics grounds an age, in that through a specific interpretation of what is and through a specific comprehension of truth it gives to that age the basis upon which it is essentially formed. This basis holds complete dominion over all the phenomena that distinguish the age" (p. 115).

How did a human/technological metaphysics come to dominate this culture in this age? Heidegger (1977) answers that the essence of the modern age arises from the fact that by freeing itself from the bonds of the Middle Ages, Western humanity could become subject: "Man becomes that being upon which all that is, is grounded as regards the manner of its Being and its truth. Man becomes the relational center of that which is as such" (p. 128). The world is "conceived and grasped as picture. What is, in its entirety, is now taken in such a way that it first is in being and only is in being to the extent that it is set up by man, who represents and sets forth" (pp. 129–130). Nature, if it is "to enter at all into representation as events of nature," must conform to "the plan or projection of that which must henceforth, for the knowing of nature that is sought after, be nature: the self-contained system of motion of units of mass related spatiotemporally" (p. 119). Not only is nature restricted to a certain form, humanity is limited. "There begins that way of being human which means the realm of human capability as a domain given over to measuring and executing, for the purpose of gaining mastery over that which is as a whole" (p. 132). Heidegger's *Geschichte* adds some historical specificity to the account of the transformation of practical relations to a technological worldview. However, he doesn't answer the question, Why Western culture? What were the bonds of the Middle Ages and how did humans free themselves? How was Western humanity able to become the subject? Western humanity's relation to technology suggests some answers.

The primary bond of the Middle Ages was the spoken word. As Ong puts it, "Primary orality fosters personality structures that in certain ways are more communal and externalized, and less introspective than those common among literates" (1982, p. 69). The phonetic alphabet in combination with print made possible visual space, abstraction, objectification, fragmentation, point of view, and individualization. It made possible human as subject, figure as ground, looking at and objectifying an exterior world: "By separating the knower from the known, writing makes possible increasingly articulate introspectivity, opening the psyche as never before not only to the external objective world quite distinct from itself but also to the interior self against whom the objective world is set" (Ong, 1982, p. 105). Only Western culture had the technology of the phonetic alphabet and print, which made possible the transformation of practical relations with technology into a technological worldview, a metaphysics with humanity/technology at its center. It made possible the rise of the conscious purpose of survival to the metaphysics of survival, the attempt by the part to determine the whole.

SYSTEMIC WISDOM

McLuhan, Gregory Bateson, and others think humanity is at a turning point in its history. As humanity reaches the limits of dominating nature, whether humanity will survive its "victory" over nature has become a widespread concern, brought into popular consciousness through global warming, ozone depletion, acid rain, general pollution and waste disposal problems, and overpopulation. This is not just a situation of specific, isolated problems, a mere enumeration, but rather a pattern that points to a systemic crisis. A changing of the pattern or configuration of our culture is essential. The question becomes, How does one, enmeshed in the culture, recognize and act to change a pattern? Furthermore, what constitutes the pattern and what can change it? Technology does not determine a culture; however, the bias of a technology forms the background or environment out of which certain possibilities, problems, solutions, and ways of perceiving become more likely. McLuhan's structure explaining the effects of technology is a way of understanding the background we are in.

McLuhan concentrates his analysis of technology on embodiment and hermeneutic relations and their effects. The world, the ground, for McLuhan is "the cultural environment defined by a continuous translation between a plurality of media" (Angus, 1989). McLuhan focuses his analysis on technology in interaction with human perception, on intentionality, or, as Bateson would call it, conscious purpose. McLuhan is concerned with patterns of perception in a technosphere. He doesn't deal with how the wider ground of nature and the horizon of the world are fluid limits to the possible thematizations and effects of technology—in other words, with how the nontransformed environment limits the transformed environment.

However, McLuhan's theory of technology and its effects implicitly provides a way of understanding the larger relation of perception or conscious purpose to ground. A fertile way to think of McLuhan's epistemology is to compare it to that of Bateson. McLuhan's concept of the unit of importance is not the individual in a physical body. Instead, it is the individual and the environment, as implied by his conception of media (technology) as extensions of humans—the wheel is an extension of the foot; clothes, of the skin; the spoken word, of the ear; the printed word, of the eye; electricity, of the central nervous system and consciousness; and so on. This corresponds to Bateson's essential unit: organism plus environment or mind. In so conceiving of the self, McLuhan both extends the idea of self out into the world and decenters and historicizes the self. The self is not a foundational unit but a cultural construction—an oral culture has a different basic concept of self than a literate culture. Furthermore, McLuhan removes technology from the status of an Other, something foreign to us and independent of us; he asserts that technology is us: "These media, being extensions of ourselves, also depend upon us for their interplay and their evolution" (1964, p. 57).

McLuhan focuses on the interaction of perception and technology and the resultant thematizations, the part of the whole system Bateson would call conscious purpose. Conscious purpose is the part that transforms the whole. It is awareness chained to purpose. Both Bateson and McLuhan are concerned to show that whenever a system or environment is determined by conscious purpose, the rate of change increases and disaster becomes more likely. Bateson writes that people and cultures are "self-corrective against disturbance, and if the obvious is not of a kind that they can easily assimilate without internal disturbance their self-corrective mechanisms work to sidetrack it, to hide it, even to the extent of shutting the eyes if necessary, or shutting off various parts of the process of perception" (1972, p. 429). McLuhan further explains that "[t]he very success we enjoy in specializing and separating functions in order to have speed-up, however, is at the same time the cause of inattention and unawareness of the situation. It has ever been thus in the Western world at least. Self-consciousness of the causes and limits of one's own culture seems to threaten the ego structure and is, therefore, avoided" (McLuhan, 1964, p. 93).

This explanation is why McLuhan is not a technological determinist. Technology is only a part of humans and a larger system (culture and nature), and McLuhan is aware that humans are part of this larger system. Those who accuse him of technological determinism probably subscribe to the arrogance of a humanistic determinism. McLuhan explains that technology is often part of conscious purpose, which, if unchecked by systemic wisdom, determines the whole, the environment, since "the specialist is one who never makes small mistakes while moving toward the grand fallacy" (1964, p. 118). McLuhan is constantly pleading for understanding, general awareness, or wisdom, as is Bateson: "Wisdom I take to be the knowledge of the larger interactive system—that system which, if disturbed, is likely to generate exponential curves of change" (1972, p. 433). For McLuhan, "media study considers not only the 'content' but the medium and the cultural matrix within which the particular medium operates" (1964, p. 26). Heidegger also turns to reflexivity, wisdom, or reflection as the antidote for conscious purpose or procedure: "Man will know, i.e., carefully safeguard into its truth, that which is incalculable, only in creative questioning and shaping out of the power of genuine reflection. . . . Reflection is the courage to make the truth of our own presuppositions and the realm of our own goals into the things that most deserve to be called in question" (1977, pp. 136, 116).

The danger is in having conscious purpose (instrumental reason) guide our actions—the part determining the whole, the figure constituting the ground. As Bateson notes, it "is in our power, with our technology, to create insanity in the larger system of which we are parts" (1972, p. 466). The antidote to insanity is wisdom or reflection: "When the technology of a time is powerfully thrusting in one direction, wisdom may well call for a countervailing thrust" (McLuhan, 1964, p. 75). The balance may be provided by a medium with a different bias. The need, then, is to promote wisdom. Both McLuhan and Bateson see art and creativity as central to wisdom and to controlling conscious purpose:

> The artist is the man in any field, scientific or humanistic, who grasps the implications of his actions and of new knowledge in his own time. He is the man of integral awareness. . . . [I]n experimental art, men are given the exact specifications of coming violence to their own psyches from their own counter-irritants or technology. . . . While the arts as radar feedback provide a dynamic and changing corporate image, their purpose may not be to enable us to change but rather to maintain an even course toward permanent goals, even amidst the most disrupting innovations. We have already discovered the futility of changing our goals as often as we change our technologies. (McLuhan, 1964, p. xi)

Art as perceptual judo may enable humanity to fend off the violence of new technology while heading toward goals decided through wisdom or judgment, not conscious purpose or instrumental reason.

Bateson (1972) also talks of the need for humility, since "man is part of larger systems and the part can never control the whole" (p. 437). Bateson also calls for the creativity of art, for "in the making [of art, man] must necessarily relax that arrogance in favor of a creative experience in which his conscious mind plays only a small part" (p. 438).

JUDGMENT: PLURALITY OF PERSPECTIVES

McLuhan and Bateson's appeal to art seems limited, even nebulous, for two reasons. One is the separation of art and everyday life in our culture; an appeal to art would therefore seem to have little impact on daily life. The second is Bateson's incomplete theorizing of systemic wisdom, which is left as a mysterious, unconscious process. A turn here to Ian Angus's more completely theorized concept of judgment will allow us to make clear the possibilities of promoting judgment in daily life and the role of technology in helping to make judgment possible.

Judgment involves a rehearsal of perspectives that enlarges the immediate perception of instrumental reason (formalized conscious purpose) into awareness of a larger whole—system, culture, background, nature. The rehearsal of perspectives in judgment leads to the "co-constitution of self and world in judgment" (Angus, 1984, p. 156), which is a continuous activity. (This conceptualization of self as an activity that is intrinsically connected to a larger environment meshes with McLuhan's and Bateson's concepts of self.) Making, when extended to include not only art but the making of daily life—making a fire for warmth as opposed to turning up a thermostat, making dinner as opposed to eating at McDonald's—engages judgment by revealing techniques to be manifestations of the practical context. Heating with wood as opposed to central heating, and growing food in a garden as opposed to shopping at a supermarket, involve participation in making, which makes visible the labor involved in the construction of the world, makes evident techniques as manifestations of practical context, and helps deconstruct "the world conceived and grasped as picture [and nature] as a spatiotemporal magnitude of motion" (Heidegger, 1977, pp. 129, 120).

Making deconstructs the representation of the world as picture, as object, as finished product. There is "a difference between a participatory technology which lets the human meaning of a subject's act stand out and the automated technology which conceals it, creating the illusion of autonomous functioning" (Kohak, 1984, p. 25). Making in or even using several media or technologies also promotes judgment because the different biases of media provide different translations or perspectives of the world. Individuals and cultures "have tended to flourish under conditions in which civilization reflects the influence of more than one medium" (Innis, 1950, p. 7). McLuhan writes:

> It may be that a great part of the secret of the brain's powers is the enormous opportunity provided for interaction between the effects of stimulating each part of the receiving fields. It is this provision of interacting-places or mixing-places that allows us to react to the world as a whole to much greater degree than other animals can do. But our technologies are by no means uniformly favorable to this organic function of interplay and interdependence. (1962, p. 7)

Since the dominance of one medium may lead to a dangerously narrow focus, a loss of interplay, there is a need for a plurality of media.

In every perception in interaction with a technology (embodiment and hermeneutic relations), there is a theme, background, and horizon or limit. The limit to sight is the invisible. A telescope makes more visible, but the horizon is still the invisible. The limit to sound, to speech, is silence. When one translates from one perception-technology to another, something is lost and something else is gained since translation involves a change of background and horizon. The translation of a book into a movie is a common example. Judgment or systemic wisdom is gained because the changing of horizons gives one access to what was once a horizon or limit to perception and exposes conscious purposes and different perspectives. A major danger with technology is the use of technology in embodiment and hermeneutic relations which discourage or prevent a plurality of purposes, translations, and perspectives. For example, one can experience a lake from a factory as a dumping place for toxic waste, but if one then tries to experience the same lake from a boat as a place to fish and swim, one realizes the danger and short-sightedness of the conscious purpose of lake as toxic dump. That perception determines the whole, for it transforms the background (lake) and prevents the experiencing of the lake in any other way. Changing technologies or media leads to awareness of horizons, conscious purposes, and perspectives and therefore fosters judgment. Wittgenstein (1988) said that "[w]hereof one cannot speak, thereof one must be silent" (p. 189). If talking about saving a forest is not raising awareness, chaining oneself to a tree or sabotaging logging equipment might raise awareness by providing another perspective. More concretely, reading a pamphlet with the statistic that eighty thousand acres of rain forest are chopped down every day may not provoke a reaction because print promotes detachment and a horizon of print is involved action. However, to hear someone tell a story about the clear-cutting of a rainforest is likely to elicit an emotional reaction because speech promotes involvement and a horizon of speech is detachment. Neither medium is better than the other. Indeed, they complement each other. The combination of a pamphlet and spoken story (and slide show) would engender the wisest response, as various translations give one access to the limit or horizon of each medium, exposing conscious purposes, providing different perspectives, and making judgment possible.

In short, technology helps make judgment possible in two ways. In embodiment and hermeneutic relations, technology in interaction with perception provides a plurality of translations which in turn make possible a plurality of perspectives and judgment. In background relations, as well as embodiment and hermeneutic relations, technology can help make possible a plurality of purposes and in turn a plurality of perspectives and judgment. It is important to remember McLuhan's warning that not all technologies are "uniformly favorable to this organic function of interplay" and pluralities. This is especially so for automated technology and technology in background relations. The universalization of automated technology and background technology threatens to close off possible perspectives and judgment. For example, suburban tract housing is designed with basically one conscious purpose, profit (and perhaps shelter), and as technological background can thwart other purposes—house as home, as art, as place to play, as part of a community, as part of the ecology of a particular place. Technology as background formed by one or only a few conscious purposes offers less flexibility and fewer possibilities than a techno-logical background formed by a plurality of conscious purposes or a natural background (which is not formed by conscious purpose). A tree offers more possibilities than a two-by-four.

When thinking about a technology as participatory or automated or as involved in embodiment and hermeneutic relations or background relations, it is necessary to recall our earlier definition of technology as the relation of techniques and social forms. For example, in the United States television is embedded in social forms that make it participatory for a few and automated for the many. In a different matrix of social forms, television could be partici-patory for the many.

There has been a trend in social forms toward automated technology and specialization (one conscious purpose), which makes sense in a culture domi-nated by instrumental reason. Specialization of individuals, companies, com-munities, cities, states, regions, and nations, along with automated technology, has had dire effects at all levels, from the local to the global, not the least of which has been the narrowing of perspectives and the impover-ishment of judgment.

As we face a global environmental crisis which is so pervasive that all aspects of our ways of living are implicated, technology is often rightly seen, whether linked to instrumental reason or on its own, as a primary villain in the tragedy of global environmental degradation. However, that is not technology's only possible role in the modern world. Just as instrumental reason transcended and bounded by judgment is redeemed, technology in the service of judgment may play a crucial role in resolving our epistemological-environmental crisis. As the analyses of Ihde and McLuhan show, technology in particular interactions and in the totality of the effects of those interactions transforms us, our perceptions of the world, and thus our world. Technology is us, and we are part of a larger system. Technology as part of instrumental reason or conscious purpose has played a major role in the articulation of the myth of progress, which is a celebration of instrumental reason set free from telos. Goals are always in response to problems, and the answers tend to produce more problems. For example, fossil fuels are creating tremendous amounts of pollution and are running out. Some people have seen a solution in nuclear energy, but that leads to a new problem: nuclear accidents and nuclear waste. However, humans cannot exist without technology, which is to say that technology is necessary but not a necessary evil. Technology can also help enable humanity to rise above instrumental reason and act with judgment. Technology, through translations and through a plurality of perspectives, allows us to see the world in many ways. We end up with a richer and deeper understanding of the ground of our being.

The positive possibilities of technology within the context of judgment are evident in the interactions of environmental groups with media.

ENVIRONMENTAL GROUPS, MEDIA TACTICS, AND NEW PERSPECTIVES

- Members of Earth First! unfurled a three-hundred-foot-long black plastic ribbon down the front of the Glen Canyon Dam in order to simulate a crack in the dam. On another occasion, Earth First!ers dressed in bear costumes and blocked traffic in Yellowstone National Park to protest development on grizzly bear habitat. (Short, 1991, p. 172)

- Love Canal residents drove to Albany, New York, to present Governor Carey with two coffins symbolizing the plight of the children and adults living on the toxic waste site (Gibbs, 1982, p. 96). In a forum with Governor Carey, when it was their turn to ask questions, the Love Canal activists/mothers "flooded the stage with their three-year-olds and four-year-olds. Then they turned to the governor and asked if he intended to protect these children from the deadly chemicals. Surrounded by toddlers, the governor capitulated on the spot." (Greider, 1992, p. 167)

- Members of Kentuckians for the Commonwealth set "up a 'lemonade stand' in the state capitol, with samples of contaminated water from various eastern Kentucky communities." (Van Gelder, 1992, p. 62)

- Greenpeace activists have steered rubber rafts between whaling ships and whales, chained themselves to harpoons, plugged waste discharge pipes, simultaneously hung banners from smokestacks in eight European countries in order to create a composite photograph that would spell out "STOP" twice, dressed as penguins to protest development of Antarctica, delivered a dead seal to Downing Street, and used drift nets to spell out "Ban Drift Nets Now" on the Mall in Washington, D.C. (Brown & May, 1991)

What are we to make of these and a host of other such image events—tree hugging, tree sitting, chaining themselves to the gates of landfills, using bodies to block machinery, even acts of ecotage? Are they the desperate stunts of the powerless? Are they tactics designed to get attention for the real rhetoric (speeches, pamphlets, books) of such groups? If, following Bowers, Ochs, and Jensen (1993) and others, we lend some legitimacy to these image events as nonverbal means of persuasion, what does that say of the "social movement" in which these groups are principal players? The aforementioned image events staged for mass media dissemination comprise the central rhetorical activity of these environmental groups as they attempt to produce social change. As Lois

Gibbs, a leader at Love Canal and founder of Citizens Clearinghouse for Hazardous Wastes, writes, "We had to keep the media's interest. That was the only way we got anything done" (1982, p. 96).

Image events have become the primary form of rhetorical activity for radical environmental groups, such as Greenpeace, Earth First!, and grass-roots environmental justice groups, as they strive to create social movement with regard to ideographs such as "progress" and "nature." These image events can exist and have meaning only through the use of communication technologies. Greenpeace, for example, was born in a direct action that failed to achieve its goal but succeeded as an image event. Since then (1971), they have used image events to deal with a host of environmental problems (whaling, sealing, nuclear weapons and waste, toxic wastes, incinerators) and in the process have become an internationally famous organization supported by over two million members and a $50 million budget. Image events have enabled Earth First! to get its issue (wilderness preservation) on the public environmental agenda and its philosophy (intrinsic worth of other species and deep ecology) heard by the public—at least to some extent. The more than seven thousand environmental justice groups use image events as a key tactic in their effort to plug the toilet of the industrial system (Greider, 1992, p. 169). Greider despairingly calls these tactics "the politics of rude and crude" and claims that they reveal "the disconnectedness that prevents them [citizens] from entering into any kind of enduring, responsible relationship with those in power" (Greider, 1992, p. 163). Greider misreads the possibilities of image events because he understands them through the frame of traditional deliberative rhetoric that aims at reform within the system; he takes into account neither how television requires a different form of rhetoric nor how producing a social movement requires that one confront the system.

While rhetorical theorists from Aristotle through Bacon to Perelman have recognized the importance and power of "bringing-before-the-eyes," "making pictures," and "creating presence," today, "in the age of television, dramatic, digestive, visual moments are replacing memorable words" (Jamieson, 1988, p. x). Kathleen Jamieson even argues that "[s]peech in such settings would dilute the power of the nonverbal message being telegraphed to audiences, regardless of their native language, throughout the world" (1988, p. 115). Thus, far from being the desperate stunts of the disillusioned, image events are the central mode of public discourse both for conventional electoral politics and alternative grass-roots politics in an age dominated by commercial television. While the civil rights movement of the 1950s and 1960s was catalyzed by powerful pictures *and* eloquent words, radical environmental groups rely almost solely on image events to create social movement. Indeed, it is telling that there are no famous environmental speakers and no memorable environmental speeches, except perhaps for Chief Seattle's letter to the president, which was fabricated by a white man in the 1970s.

My support of environmental groups' adaptation of image events as neces-sary tactics is not meant to suggest that television is a level playing field. Obviously, elected officials, especially the president and members of Congress, as well as business leaders and corporations, enjoy an enormous advantage over environmental groups in terms of access to media, particularly television, and control of their image (due in no small measure to the fact that the media are themselves giant corporations with a vested interest in the status quo). The implications of these disadvantages need to be explored. Still, in order to participate in the most important arena of public discourse environmental groups must use the tactic of image events. The distinction here is one of strategy versus tactic (de Certeau, 1988, pp. 36–37). While those in positions of institutional power are able to use image events in strategic ways, for radical environmental groups the use of image events is a tactic, "a maneuver 'within the enemy's field of vision' . . . and within enemy territory," a recognition that they "must play on and with a terrain imposed on [them] and organized by the law of a foreign power" (de Certeau, 1988, pp. 36–37). The image events of environmental groups are tactics that operate in the territory of the system but outside the sense-making rules or grid of intelligibility of the system, a necessary condition if they are to create social movement.

To dismiss image events as rude and crude is to cling to "presuppositions of civility and rationality underlying the old rhetoric" (Scott & Smith, 1969, p. 7), a rhetoric that supports those in positions of authority and thus allows civility and decorum to serve as masks for the preservation of injustice and condemns the dispossessed to nonbeing (Scott & Smith, 1969, p. 8). Indeed, Aristotle's *On Rhetoric: A Theory of Civic Discourse* (1991) can be read as a primer on how to maintain hegemony. Such an understanding of rhetoric assumes an "agreement on basic values and a belief in the perfectability of the system" (Cathcart, 1980, p. 268) and is antithetical to the very purpose of groups that are trying to produce social movement by creating "doubts about the legitimacy and moral-ity of the establishment" (Cathcart, 1980, p. 271). Lois Gibbs of Citizens Clearinghouse for Hazardous Wastes explains that "[t]he movement is outside the system" (Greider, 1992, p. 168), and thus it must rely on "confrontational rhetoric [that] challenges the system's values and its perfectability" (Cathcart, 1980, p. 268; see also Simons, 1972, on coercive persuasion).

Image events are necessarily rude (barbarous, unrefined, uncouth) and crude (in a raw or natural state; lacking grace or taste); since they are attempts at resisting the conditions imposed by ideographs, they are meant not to make sense in the existing conditions. Since dams are concrete manifestations of progress (witness how many dams the World Bank funds/forces in "underde-veloped" countries), simulating the cracking of the Glen Canyon Dam does not register as making sense on the grid of intelligibility as defined by "progress." Risking human lives to save whales and seals is unjustifiable when nature is a storehouse of resources for human use; thus, such image events destabilize the ideograph "nature." Delivering dead seals to politicians and offering them lemonade made with polluted water do not translate into politics informed by instrumental "reason." Tactical image events are resistant practices, "gestures that defy translation, throw sense off track, and, thus, short-circuit the system through which sense is made" (Biesecker, 1992, p. 357), and they make possible the rearticulation of the synchronic structure of ideographic clusters (industrialization).

M. McGee (1980) asserts that the task of the rhetorical theorist is to prove the existence of social movement through a "well-argued inference that changes in human consciousness are of such a nature that 'social movement' has occurred, or that the rhetorical activity of a group of human beings would produce 'social movement' if it were effective" (p. 244). The latter has been the task of this section with regard to the rhetorical activity of image events performed by radical environmental groups. Image events, made possible by media, introduce new perspectives into the mass-mediated sphere of public discourse, thus contributing to a plurality of perspectives that makes judgment possible. More than that, though, I want to suggest, following Biesecker, that for a critical rhetorician "the task is to trace new lines of making sense by taking hold of the sign whose reference has been destabilized by and through those practices of resistance, lines that cut diagonally across and, thus disrupt, the social weave" (1992, p. 361). In other words, the critical rhetorician's role in helping to make judgment possible consists of making sense of practices too often dismissed as nonsensical by dominant perspectives.

A minor theme of this section, then, has been to trace new lines of making sense with regard to the signs "rhetoric" and "politics," two signs that are destabilized when the image events of environmental groups are taken seriously instead of ignored or dismissed as the antics of the unruly. The lines of rhetoric need to be redrawn (as previously suggested) in order to make sense of an arena of public discourse dominated by commercial television, wherein "television news is predicated on synecdoche" (Jamieson, 1988, p. 112) and the "moving synoptic movement has replaced the eloquent speech" (Jamieson, 1988, p. 117). The acts of environmental groups, from image events to ecotage (acts of which function primarily as image events), exceed the bounds of a politics limited to the electoral or the peaceful and open the possibility of conceptualizing politics so that blocking a bulldozer, plugging a pipe, or smashing a machine is not an illegal act of obstructionism, vandalism, or terrorism but a political act that calls into question the morality and legality of acts by corporations that displace people and ravage the environment.

Image events defy the conditions for sense making imposed by the ideographs "progress," "nature," and "technology" (and the linkage of these ideographs in the articulation of industrialism), thus opening space for tracing new lines of making sense—social movement. Specifically, Greenpeace, Earth First!, and environmental justice groups use image events to contest the linking of economic progress with nature as a storehouse of resources. Greenpeace, by spray painting the fur of baby seals and sailing between whaling ships and whales, argues against reducing animals to economic resources and instead proposes that animals have intrinsic worth and inalienable rights.

Earth First!, by deconstructing dams, hugging trees, and blocking or sabotaging machinery, contests the definition of the land as a resource and instead suggests that "there is no ontological divide between human and nonhuman" (Oelschlaeger, 1991, p. 301), that biodiversity has value in itself, and, following Aldo Leopold's land ethic, that "a thing is right when it tends to preserve the integrity, stability, and beauty of the biotic community. It is wrong when it tends otherwise" (Leopold, 1968, pp. 224–225).

With their image events, environmental justice groups are fighting an articulation of industrialism which understands progress (economic) as linked to the domination of nature, for the domination of nature involves not only the domination of external nature but the domination of other humans and the domination of one's own inner nature (Horkheimer, 1947; Horkheimer & Adorno, 1972; Leiss, 1972). As Larry Wilson, a community leader from Yellow Creek, Kentucky, explains, "The system was invented by the people who are poisoning us. The rules say they get to argue over how much cyanide they can put in our coffee, how much poison they can put out before they have to take responsibility for it. That's not a system we can ever win in" (Greider, 1992, p. 166). In this system certain groups of people (e.g., minorities and the working class) get abused as a natural resource (labor power) and polluted as nature. For example, the Clean Air Act allows 2.7 billion pounds of toxic chemicals to be spewed into the atmosphere every year (Easterbrook, 1989, p. 28). Environmental justice groups want to move the meanings of "progress" and "nature" so that governments are more concerned with people and the environments they are embedded in and less eager to greet corporations with open pockets and closed eyes, as does Kentucky with symbolic road signs that announce "Kentucky is OPEN FOR BUSINESS" (Van Gelder, 1992, p. 64). Lois Gibbs (1993) observes: "Over the past ten years the Movement For Environmental Justice has redefined the word environment. No longer does the media, the general public or our opponents see the environmental movement as one that is focused on open spaces, trees and endangered species alone. They have finally got it! The Environmental Justice Movement is about people and the places they live, work and play" (p. 2).

In a world where powerful corporations are eager to paint environmental justice groups as NIMBYs ("not in my backyard") and to ostracize Earth First!ers as Luddites (certainly a word that needs to be redefined), the role of the critical rhetorician is to help reconfigure the grid of intelligibility so that environmental justice groups make sense as NAMBYs ("not in anyone's backyard") and Earth First! actions count as political acts designed to change the conditions of possibility through moving the ideographs that set the conditions.

When the image events of environmental groups are read as attempts to move key ideographs, challenges to and constructions of progress and nature become key sites of struggle, oppression, and hope for people attempting to invent societies less riddled by the domination of nature in all its aspects.

NOTES

1. This is, admittedly, a simplified explanation of the complex phenomenon of local resistance to environmental efforts. This resistance can be driven by poverty, greed, coercion, distrust of ecological "imperialism," or a philosophy of people in nature that resists the ideology of nature that requires nature to be separated and isolated from humans. Also, of course, local groups found many environmental efforts.

2. The choices of Ihde and McLuhan are meant to be exemplary of two important traditions in the philosophy of technology. Phenomenology has made important contributions to the study of technology, particularly in the work of Heidegger. Ihde is working out of this tradition. In communication circles, media theorists such as Harold Innis, McLuhan, James Carey, and Joshua Meyrowitz have provided a fertile alternative to effects research. McLuhan is certainly the most famous and controversial of this group and perhaps the most important.

3. I do not correct or add to the sexist language used by some of those quoted in this chapter for the reason that such sexist language is not merely a matter of terminology but is often of theoretical and historical significance. In my own work I try to avoid sexist terminology and sexist thinking, though probably not with complete success.

4. McLuhan's philosophy of technology was of tactical importance to some of the original members of Greenpeace. See Robert Hunter, *Warriors of the Rainbow* (1979) and *The Storming of the Mind* (1971).

CHAPTER FIVE

Talking to Each Other about the Environment: Using Video Production to Instruct Adolescents about Recycling

Rod Carveth and Roger Desmond

THIS CHAPTER DESCRIBES an attempt to increase recycling knowledge and behavior by inviting junior high school students to become writers, directors, and actors in brief television programs about recycling. We sought to facilitate home recycling by inviting preadolescents to become gatekeepers for home recycling. We sought, in short, to provide Earthtalk about recycling by a population that has been relatively ignored in the environmental communication literature: adolescents, the heirs of the planet and its concomitant problems. There are several advantages to a strategy that addresses this population:

1. They are easy to reach. School programs now address various aspects of environmental threats. Where curricula do not exist, they will be mandated in the near future.

2. Many students of this target age are already proenvironment; they perceive that they will inherit a planet with overfull landfills, vast amounts of toxic waste, polluted groundwater, and so on. It is likely that they do not embrace the fatalism or cynicism of their parents or other members of the adult population. They have grown up amid a number of communication campaigns aimed at substance abuse, AIDS prevention, literacy, and so on, and are familiar with risk reduction messages.

3. They are more likely to be accepting of recycling as a necessity than adults are. Existing research indicates that traditional American values (e.g., support for private property rights, support for economic

growth, and faith in material abundance) are antithetical to a strong environmental stance (Van Liere & Dunlap, 1981). In contrast, people with a strong liberal ideology have been found to support specific environmental regulations (Samdahl & Robertson, 1989). By extension, people who have not reached maturity are more likely to embrace an openness to positive messages about their environment.

4. By empowering this population, we can use this group as a means of conveying recycling information to other groups, such as their parents and siblings.

We used an approach that has never previously been employed in this domain: junior high school students created public service announcement programs aimed at their own population. We knew that video production is a highly attractive component of education for this age group, and in our experience, we find this population to be resistant to traditional lecture approaches. The essence of our approach was to help our students to review the vast literature on risk communication and to synthesize their learning into television scripts that would presumably persuade and inform their peers.

THE NATURE OF RISK COMMUNICATION

As in any new field of study, conceptual clarity in risk communication is still evolving. The most often cited definition of risk communication is "any purposeful exchange of information about health or environmental risks between interested parties" (Covello, von Winterfeldt, & Slovic, 1986b, p. 172). Other definitions include psychological, social, and political dimensions in the definition of the field of risk communication. As Kasperson and Stallen (1990) point out, conceptual discussions about the nature of risk communication are prematurely prescriptive in nature in that each researcher tends to focus on a message formula that has been successful in a given campaign. In many ways, the evolution of risk communication mirrors that of academic communication study over the past fifty years: an initial emphasis on message elements and a subsequent inclusion of audience as the significant concept in the communication process. In the study we are about to report, a decision was made to allow audiences to formulate messages that they deemed effective as persuaders.

Further examples of parallel development of risk communication include discussion and investigations of the concept of source credibility. For a long time investigators have been concerned about why individuals are much more worried about the dangers of nuclear fallout than they are about more realistic dangers such as sidestream smoke and lead poisoning. As one expert in the field states the case, "[I]t appears that people are spending most of their time avoiding risk from radiation so that they can go skydiving" (Cohn, 1989, p.

61). One probable reason for this perception is the enhanced credibility of federal regulators such as the Environmental Protection Agency (EPA), with its headline-grabbing victories over the last decade in combating corporate polluters.

By contrast, the mass media have low credibility among the public because of their slowness in making the public aware of environmental issues. For example, groundwater contamination was a serious problem for twenty years before the media paid attention to its dangers. Traditionally in communication study, credibility has been reduced to three dimensions: trustworthiness, competence, and dynamism. Risk communication adds a fourth factor: consistency. That is, there is accumulating evidence to suggest that some publics evaluate the credibility of risk communicators on the basis of past experience as receivers and the success of previous communication efforts of the sources. Furthermore, risk communication has found attractiveness of the information source to be another important component in the credibility formula. But unlike the conclusions of the persuasion literature, homophily (similarity) does not appear to be a component of attractiveness; in other words, people desire experts that they can trust who are clearly more knowledgeable than they are (Renn & Levine, cited in Lichtenberg & MacLean, 1990, p. 159). For a while, it seemed apparent that mass media were the best way to disseminate risk communication messages; however, more recent thinking casts doubt on the efficacy of the news media to provide information necessary for individual risk decision making. For example, results of a twenty-year investigation of German news media indicate that on a wide variety of environmental issues, such as air, water, and forest pollution, news coverage has become increasingly negative, while objective indicators of these issues have shown either improvement or no decline in environmental quality over that period (Keplinger & Mathes, cited in Lichtenberg & MacLean, 1990, p. 159). The study provides some evidence for a common (but typically erroneous) perception by the public that media do not reflect reality, but instead create it. Other reasons that the media are not the best disseminators of environmental risk include their emphasis on sensationalism and their inability to present scientific information lucidly, as well as the recent tendency of corporations to fight back aggressively with self-generated video press releases and use of alternative media to counter what they perceive to be misinformation. The ultimate result is confusion and suspicion on the part of news viewers and readers.

Recent evidence suggests that community sources of information, schools and youth organizations such as 4-H Clubs and Scouts, are more effective than the news media in providing communication about environmental risk (Reinfeld, 1992). An emphasis on conservation and the economic benefits of recycling has proved to be more effective than a concentration on risk alone in motivating students to recycle. Some media that have been successful in schools are colorful posters, comic books, costume characters, and puppets. Successful efforts in schools appear to reflect a long-standing finding in risk communication: data alone will not be believed nor heeded (Cohn, 1989). What is needed to make such efforts successful is to include information about the personal salience of the issue, the observable benefits of recycling, and the notion that student behaviors can make a difference. Youth especially are turned off by sheer numbers and by risks that are not personally relevant. For example, in attempting to combat drug abuse, the Partnership for a Drug-Free America recently decided to reorient their messages from fear appeals (e.g., "This is your brain. This is your brain on drugs.") to more positive appeals stressing the benefits of being drug free. The reason for this shift is that while the campaign has been successful in reinforcing the beliefs of nonusers and scaring off occasional users, such appeals have little effect on regular drug users because such appeals are neither believable nor personally relevant (i.e., young drug users don't believe they can be killed by drugs).

RESEARCH ON RECYCLING

The subdiscipline of risk communication has the potential to facilitate recycling in at least two ways: through persuasion and through education about the nature of environmental risks. In the past decade, efforts to influence recycling behavior through attitude change have met with little success (Golding, Krimsky & Plough, 1992; Heath & Nathan, 1991). As Oskamp et al. (1991) found, environmental attitudes were not associated with curbside recycling behavior in adult populations. It appears that "pure persuasion" attempts in the absence of environmental education are doomed to failure if the goal is to increase compliance with municipal recycling laws. Educational programs have been much more successful in that simple conservation knowledge has been found to predict recycling behavior (Arbuthnot, 1974; Oskamp et al., 1991). Similarly, Lansana (1992) found that awareness of the positive benefits that could accrue from recycling were more important in predicting recycling behavior than were the traditionally dominant demographic variables of income, education, and age. Research on the success of recycling programs in 264 communities (Folz, 1991; Folz & Hazlett, 1991) reveals that participation in both mandatory and voluntary recycling programs is greater in communities that include a recycling component in the local school curriculum and encourage children to share this information with others at home.

Children and adolescents are inundated with communication about AIDS, pregnancy, substance abuse, gun control, and child abuse prevention strategies. These messages are presented on television, in school, on milk and candy cartons, in comic books, and virtually everywhere else where a young audience can be found. While little research exists on the upper limits of information overload, it is possible that the net effect of message multiplication is dilution of their impact; children are being "talked at" more frequently and from more directions than in any previous generation. In addition, critics observe (see Poore, 1993) that environmental education suffers from two problems: (1) it promotes a politically charged environmentalist agenda and (2) it does not instruct students what to do, but tells them to tell others what not to do. The project outlined in this chapter represents an attempt to change the direction of risk messages from adults talking to adolescents to adolescents communicating with their peers.

FOCUS AND OBJECTIVES OF THE PRESENT STUDY

The focus of the investigation was on the potential of self-produced video programs for the communication of environmental risks associated with waste disposal practices in Connecticut. The target population was junior high school students (ages eleven to thirteen). Students researched and wrote brief television scripts regarding recycling, damage to the ecosystem resulting from the absence of recycling or from inappropriate recycling techniques, procedures involved in waste separation, human health risks surrounding inappropriate disposal techniques, and other waste issues. Four five-person production teams researched and produced four taped programs that were five to eight minutes long. All four productions were completed by July 1991.

The focus for the study was on waste management in the state of Connecticut. Connecticut is one of only a few states to pass a statewide mandatory citizen recycling law.[1] Currently, over 50 percent of the state's landfills are at or near capacity, and the remaining landfills are relatively small. Consequently, the state of Connecticut passed Public Law 87-544, which mandated that towns implement recycling programs by no later than July 1, 1990.[2] The goal of the law is to recycle 25 percent of the solid waste stream. In addition to the recycling mandate, the Connecticut Department of Environmental Protection proposed a solid waste management plan that included educating residents and businesses about the benefits of waste reduction.

The objectives of our project were as follows:

1. To increase awareness in the target population of the public health risks associated with improper waste disposal techniques

2. To initiate intentions by the target population to use approved waste disposal techniques

3. To provide junior high schools with a curriculum for teaching environmental risk through video production techniques

In the process of developing these project objectives, small teams of students were assigned the task of researching and developing videotapes concerning one or more of the following issues:

1. recycling, as mandated by state law

2. landfills and ground or water contamination

3. recycling as an aesthetic issue, leading to a more beautiful state environment

4. how recycling could save costs for businesses and consumers

METHOD

Development of Pre- and Post-Tests

The authors researched key issues in waste management, using academic libraries as well as the state library in Hartford. Thirty-one multiple-response knowledge items were initially developed. The goal was to create items that tapped the essential issues in the whys of recycling and items which underscored the magnitude of the problem. An engineer from a local environmental consulting firm who served on the project advisory board inspected each item for accuracy and eliminated two items that proved to be debatable among experts.

In order to assess the readability and discrimination power of our test, we had 31 junior high school students complete the tests. As a result of their test patterns and feedback, 5 items were eliminated, for a total of 26 knowledge items. Fourteen attitude items were developed from open-ended interview questions with groups of seventh graders.

The questionnaire contained two measures which served as dependent variables in this study:

1. *Recycling Knowledge Scale*—subjects were asked to answer 26 multiple-choice questions concerning recycling techniques, laws, and impact. The scale was composed of the total number of correct answers to the multiple-choice questions.

2. *Recycling Attitudes Scale*—subjects were asked to indicate their agreement with 14 items designed to assess the degree to which they thought recycling would benefit society. Subjects recorded their agreement with each statement across five response options ranging from 1 = "strongly disagree" to 5 = "strongly agree" (8 of the items were worded negatively toward recycling and were thus reverse scored). Scores for the scale for recycling attitudes were constructed by summing the items together. Reliability for the scale was assessed by Cronbach's alpha. The reliability coefficient was deemed acceptable (Cronbach's alpha = .795, $n = 168$).

Procedure

Students completed self-administered pre-test questionnaires in their classroom settings. Two weeks after the administration of the pre-test, students were asked to view the videos from all production teams. The presentation of the four videos took approximately twenty minutes. Two weeks following the presentation of the videos, students were administered the post-test, which included the items from the pre-test as well as questions assessing the general quality, information value, and production values of the videos.

Sample

One hundred sixty-eight seventh graders (70 male, 98 female) from four junior high schools in the greater Hartford area completed pre- and post-tests. None of the students participating in the data analysis were involved in the actual production of the videos themselves. Three groups were compared. Group One was composed of students from two schools located in suburban, middle-income districts. Students were also primarily white. One production team from each school participated. The n for Group One was 111.

Group Two was made up of students from an inner-city junior high school, with a primarily black population. Two production teams from the school completed one video each. The n for Group Two was 40.

Group Three was made up of students from a school district that draws its population from both urban and suburban residents, due to its location between two towns. These students served as a control group as they had neither produced nor viewed the recycling videos. Thirty-five students completed the pre-tests. Post-tests were administered twenty-eight days later. A number of the students were uncooperative with the research procedures: 18 post-tests were unusable due to lack of completion. The final n for this group was 17.

RESULTS

Knowledge Gain

Initially, the 26 knowledge items were compiled into a knowledge index with a total gain score from pre- to post-test. A one-way analysis of variance was conducted, using three groups as independent variables and knowledge scores as the dependent variable, in order to check for overall differences. The overall F ratio was not significant ($F_{2,\ 165} = .575$, $n.s.$). Inspection of the group means revealed the differences shown in Table 1. T tests for before/after mean differences revealed that the gain for Group One was significant ($t_{165} = 3.74$, $p < .001$), indicating a significant knowledge gain by the suburban school group after viewing the videos. T tests for Group Two and Group Three showed no gain.

Table 1
Pre- versus Post-Test Knowledge Scores for the Three Groups

	Group One	Group Two	Group Three
Pre-Test Knowledge Score	13.18	10.00	7.76
Post-Test Knowledge Score	14.30*	10.52	9.00

* post-test knowledge score is significantly different from pre-test ($p < .05$) knowledge score according to
t test.

Chi-square analyses to assess pre/post-test differences were performed on the individual items of the recycling knowledge scale. Results revealed that significant differences were found for 17 items. The items are listed in Table 2 along with the correct answers and their respective chi-square results.

Attitudes

T tests were conducted to assess pre/post-test differences for the individual items of the recycling attitudes scale as well as for the summed scales as an index. No significant differences were found for any of the individual attitude items. However, for 8 of the 14 attitude items in the pre-test, 75 percent or more of the subjects responded "strongly agree" or "agree." In fact, the mean response to the 14 items was slightly over 4, indicating that most subjects showed agreement with each item in a positive (i.e., prorecycling) fashion. When the 14 items were grouped as an index, there were no significant increases in attitudes toward recycling, but at pre-test, the mean of all school groups was over 52.0 (the maximum score being 70); students were favorably disposed to recycling before any treatment.

Subjects were also asked to indicate their agreement with 4 items designed to assess their reactions to the videos. The items and their respective means and standard deviations are listed below.

I like these programs. ($M = 3.59$; $s.d. = 1.27$)

These programs are for kids my own age. ($M = 3.18$; $s.d. = 1.36$)

These programs are like other shows on television. ($M = 2.56$; $s.d. = 1.42$)

The programs are funny. ($M = 3.36$; $s.d. = 1.26$)

Students generally liked the programs and found them funny. Overall, students were somewhat neutral as to the age-appropriateness of the videos. Students also indicated slight disagreement as to the similarity of these videos to other shows on television. That may be due to students' video sophistication; they are exposed to a variety of slick television shows with higher production values than the experimental videos contained.

Table 2
Differences on Individual Recycling Items

Item	X^2	Significance Level
1. The average person throws out how much trash per day? *Answer:* 3 to 5 pounds.	25.99	p < .001
3. In Connecticut, most of the trash is: *Answer:* Buried in the ground.	22.04	p < .0001
5. A place where trash is buried is called: *Answer:* A landfill.	29.53	p < .001
7. Starting in January 1991, people in Connecticut will be required by law to: *Answer:* Separate recyclable materials (such as paper, glass, and metal).	14.63	p < .001
8. The main reason why the law mentioned in Question 7 was passed is: *Answer:* The landfills in Connecticut are almost full.	11.97	p < .005
9. Which of the following are *durable* waste products? *Answer:* Used batteries and tires.	18.07	p < .001
10. Which of the following are *nondurable* waste products? *Answer:* Paper cups.	13.25	p < .05
11. When we recycle paper, how much do we save out of every dollar spent on paper for the home or office? *Answer:* $.40.	11.58	p < .001
12. Besides converting waste into new products, we can also fix some things to be reused. Which of the following items are easily reusable? *Answer:* Soda and beer bottles.	20.24	p < .001
13. What is the best way to handle grass clippings and leaves from yards? *Answer:* Allow them to decay in compost heaps.	35.17	p < .001
14. Instead of burying food packages, some people say we should burn them. What is a disadvantage of burning food packages? *Answer:* It releases dangerous hydrocarbons into the air.	27.33	p < .001
15. What percentage of our solid waste is currently dumped in landfills? *Answer:* 80%	21.73	p < .001
17. PCBs are: *Answer:* Used as insulators in some appliances.	9.01	p < .002
19. Very simple and inexpensive recycling programs which are currently in use have: *Answer:* Decreased the amount of garbage by 25%.	17.54	p < .001
20. Incinerators transform our garbage into: *Answer:* Mounds of ash.	60.44	p < .001
22. Garbage incinerators produce heavy metals, such as lead, arsenic, and cadmium, which: *Answer:* May cause problems to our nervous systems and/or cancer.	23.65	p < .001
25. Recycling and composting: *Answer:* Can greatly decrease the amount of garbage to be burned.	14.09	p < .001

* - d.f. = 1

Students were also asked to rate their liking for each video separately. The ratings for the individual videos are as follows:

I liked the "Talking Trash" video. ($M = 2.34$; $s.d. = 1.36$)

I liked the "Recycle Rap" video. ($M = 2.98$; $s.d. = 1.41$)

I liked the "Environmental Jeopardy" video. ($M = 1.65$; $s.d. = 1.15$)

I liked the "Adventures of Recycle Man" video. ($M = 4.13$; $s.d. = 1.30$)

Students appeared to like the action adventure video the best and the game show the least. The talk show and rap video received lukewarm reviews.

Finally, students were asked what their favorite video was. Over 60 percent indicated that "Adventures of Recycle Man" was their favorite. The finding may have occurred because the students liked that format the best.

DISCUSSION

The results of this study revealed that student-produced videos on recycling helped contribute to knowledge about recycling. The magnitude of this difference was moderate, but quite apparent for individual item analysis. In terms of what commonalities appear across items that were missed, the most common factor is detail. Students did not gain in their knowledge of highly specific "factoids," such as the actual costs of recycling and savings from recycling or the percentage of noncompliance for national landfills. Two items (item 23 and item 24) actually show a decrease in knowledge of the term "source separation." What students did learn were knowledge items reflecting recycling procedures, health risks resulting from failure to recycle, awareness of cost benefits that generally accrue from recycling, and some scientific information concerning chemical contamination of landfills and groundwater.

Suburban versus Inner-City Students

The trend in knowledge gains by suburban students is quite clear: they learned much more from exposure to student-produced videos than did their city counterparts. While this trend is somewhat puzzling, it is also clear that suburban students started with a greater awareness of the benefits of recycling and thus subsequently added more to their knowledge base than did the inner-city students. Another important reason for this difference is that upon interviewing the city children, the authors learned that as of March 1992, the city of Hartford was not picking up recyclables from individual residences, only from apartment buildings.

The videos appeared to have no effect on creating more positive attitudes toward recycling. However, it should be noted that students already had positive attitudes toward recycling. Students had generally positive attitudes toward the videos, preferring the narrative (dramatic form) the best. While the present analysis suggests that the narrative form is best for conveying information about recycling, future research should investigate the efficacy of this format disseminating information about recycling.

Overall, the results provide some evidence to suggest that having students produce videos about the environment (in this case, recycling) and then disseminating those videos to other students may increase environmental awareness.

Objectives

In terms of our original objectives, objectives 1 and 2 centered on increasing awareness of the need for recycling and increasing intentions to use recycling techniques in the target population. In light of our knowledge gain data, the project is most successful in a suburban population where recycling programs are already in progress. Our data reveal that attitude change was minimal due to preexisting positive attitudes toward recycling, so we cannot claim success in meeting objective 2. We believe, however, that the producers and consumers of the video programs, armed with increased knowledge of the need to recycle, will continue to discuss the topic with peers and to increase their recycling behaviors. Teachers in three of our four target schools reported that there was increased talk about recycling in the weeks following our programs. Objective 3 was directed at providing a model curriculum for school systems. Three school systems now have access to our programs, and others have made inquiries.

We also sought to increase awareness of the "deadline" for a local landfill crisis. The anwers to test items 7, 8, and 15 show modest increases in knowledge of the issues surrounding the need for immediate implementation of recycling. In addition, there is a current need in science education to be more attractive to girls. Our data analysis revealed no gender differences in learning from the program; there was evidence that girls were slightly higher in knowledge than boys before treatments and initially were more favorably disposed to recycling. Two of our four production teams involved females as producers, and our observation was that they were extremely attracted to the production of environmental videos.

In follow-up conversations with our junior high producers, it became evident that it was that group that gained the most in knowledge, but since they were involved in much of the research that became the pre-test, we did not administer tests to the producers. We observed, however, that it was the production teams that were excited and motivated by the issues surrounding recycling; the immersion in the topic moved several of the scriptwriters to monitor recycling activities in their own families and to comment on lapses in compliance by their schools. Given the popularity of video production among this population and the increasing availability of cameras and editing equipment in homes and schools, the next step in this line of research should be to invite the entire target population to become producers. Combining scriptwriters and studio staff would create an effective means of inductive learning about this topic and would be a powerful means of empowering students to communicate about their environment.

Benefits

We see the benefits of this project as follows:

- The project provided students with knowledge about the risks associated with pollution, awareness of methods to alleviate such risks (such as recycling), and methods by which to communicate information about environmental risks and risk reduction methods.

- The project provided area junior high schools with a curriculum for teaching risks to the environment from improper waste disposal techniques as well as environmental benefits gained through the mandated recycling procedures.

- The project provided students with training and practice in video scriptwriting and production.

- The project introduced basic elements of natural science curricula in a nontraditional and innovative manner.

- The project coordinated student efforts from different schools within Connecticut.

RECOMMENDATIONS

In future projects such as this, we recommend that video-based programs be developed in schools that have some type of environmental curriculum in place. The contrast in results between our inner-city and suburban schools suggests that curriculum support is necessary to provide a forum for discussion of student research. Our suburban district incorporates several hours of environmental discussion into science classes per year, and we believe this partially accounts for knowledge gain in the project. Our inner-city school, although excellent in science education, features environmental science only for gifted classes. Future projects would benefit from a cooperative start-up in the fall and careful coordination with the science teachers to provide support for the video and research. We did not have the benefits of an early start-up and coordination because of a lack of quick cooperation from our local school district administrators.

In terms of actual video development, we took pains to make sure that video ideas and script development were from students and not adults. We served as research consultants and resource persons for productions, but we did not intervene. We strongly recommend such nonintervention for future projects of this nature to ensure student interest. Based on our analysis of test items, any evaluation materials and actual video content should be careful to employ language that students understand. We tried to pre-test language, but post hoc data analysis illustrates that students missed items and dialogue that was too technical. In follow-up interviews, students frequently commented on the acting ability of their peers, with suggestions such as "use more professional actors." While such a suggestion may seem impractical, we perceive some merit in separating writers/researchers from talent. School staff could help identify students with dramatic ability to act in videos, with writers/researchers serving as directors. This could help to ensure better production values.

While this project was rewarding for the authors, on a large-scale basis it would only be cost-effective if classroom teachers were capable of instructing students in video production. Clearly, this is on the horizon. An additional benefit is that teachers can use the technology for a wide array of lessons beyond recycling. Conversations with area teachers indicate a growing thirst for hands-on production training as part of their in-service requirements.

Finally, we are certain that the procedures we employed will be beneficial with respect to other areas of concern to educators; our technique can be adapted to such problems as AIDS, substance abuse, and numerous other risk areas. The enthusiasm that our young producers displayed for research and video production is a previously untapped resource for risk communication.

NOTES

1. Most states leave it to local municipalities to develop their own recycling laws.

2. As with many other states, Connecticut's law could be seen as a reactive measure. In 1976, Congress passed the Resource Conservation and Recovery Act (RCRA). The RCRA encouraged individual states to develop comprehensive solid waste management plans by providing technical and financial assistance to the states for these plans. Unfortunately, the funding for this assistance lasted only a few years, leaving it to the states to continue or develop their own solid waste management programs on their own. Many states initiated programs when solid waste management became a serious problem (Carless, 1992).

PART III
RESOURCES OF LANGUAGE

CHAPTER SIX

Forever Wild or Forever in Battle: Metaphors of Empowerment in the Continuing Controversy over the Adirondacks

Susan Senecah

IT MUST BE understood from the outset that the history informing the current controversy surrounding the Adirondack Park in upstate New York is extremely complex and rich, spanning more than two hundred years. It is a tightly woven and interlocking, some might say hopelessly knotted, web created by the beliefs and actions of the backwoods guides, farmers, loggers, lumber barons, entrepreneurs, adventurers, Gilded Age elites, wealthy politicians, preservationists, and other individuals and families who determined the area's history and continue to impact it today. Their collective and historical experiences and memories, now framed as metaphors, continue as powerful drivers of the contemporary debate. As they are used, both consciously and unconsciously, these metaphors serve to empower some groups, to obstruct others, and to rhetorically encourage the deadlock.

The diversity of public/private ownership of the Adirondack Park, its complex history, and the politically charged balance it requires between development and preservation suggest that the controversy is more complex than issues around, for example, protecting a national park. As Bill McKibben (1992) aptly observes, "Anyone with enough fence can make a Yellowstone [National Park], and then walk away and leave it alone" (p. 42). The Adirondacks are different. Certainly, if some of these conflicting issues can be resolved in the Adirondack Park, then it might serve as a global model for similar situations (Davis, 1993) in which economic communities must survive and even thrive intermingled with protected wilderness.[1] Ultimately, the Adirondack Park challenge is about reconciling public values on private land and about reconciling yesterday with the future.

This study focuses on the rhetorical discourse produced by the various competing voices that were heard following the 1990 release of the Commission on the Adirondacks in the Twenty-First Century's report, *The Adirondack Park in the Twenty-First Century*. Specifically, this analysis focuses on the use of metaphors in the discourse produced by the most active and influential groups in this intense public argument between preservation and development and between local and state control.[2] It attempts to identify metaphorical themes in the present discourse, to explain their meanings within their historical and cultural pasts and the present, to suggest the consequences of continuing to frame the conflict by using the same metaphors, and to explore the potential for breaking the stalemate.

THE ROLE OF METAPHORS IN CONSTRUCTING AND REFLECTING REALITY

Rhetorical critics have long been intrigued by the "language-oriented approach to sociological rhetorical criticism" (Brock, Scott, & Chesebro, 1990, p. 283) that is broadly called sociolinguistics. Gronbeck (1978) defines the sociolinguistic process as resting on the presumption that human beings are "symbol-using (symbol making, symbol misusing) animals" and that "symbols—and the society which invents, promulgates, and sanctions them—are determinative of an individual's perception or apprehension of the world, attitudes, values, and behaviors" (pp. 157–158). A sociolinguistic approach to rhetorical criticism[3] is usually context- and time-specific, focuses on language as its point of departure and primary object of study, and examines the energizing force of language on societal structures; that is, the embodiment of action, not simply the reflection, presentation, or pointing toward action (Brock et al., 1990). Often, methodology includes qualitative textual analyses in an effort to establish language patterns that will increase the understanding of the rhetorical acts and will open up new insights not otherwise available about the nature of a people's reality or the framework of what is claimed as real (Gergen, 1978; Royce, 1964).

Metaphors can be thought of as linguistic ways of imaging reality. They are couched in feeling as well as in rationality and thus yield an affective as well as a cognitive understanding (Olds, 1992) of this mindscape. Although they are the language of common speech, metaphors are more than decoration or elaboration; they are indigenous to meaning (Brock et al., 1990), intervening as models lifted from one aspect of experience and applied to another. New meanings are thus created from the context of the old yet are still interwoven with the old meanings. According to Burke (D. C. Williams, 1989), new meanings are born from the old, but remain forever "attached to, enveloped in . . . the old, each feeding symbiotically from the other" (p. 206).

Unlike metaphors in literary works, rhetorical metaphors often are marked by rather pedestrian qualities. Rather than being carefully chosen for the poetic richness of the image suggested, the rhetorical metaphors that are thrown together in common speech often seem disjointed and even silly. Nevertheless, in many situations, the speakers and listeners construct a shared meaning. As Hart (1990) suggests, often the "cacophony of images produces an integrated, emotional whole" (p. 213).

We cannot communicate without using metaphors. Lakoff (1990) observes that "[m]etaphorical thought, in itself, is neither good nor bad; it is simply commonplace and inescapable. Abstractions and enormously complex situations are routinely understood via metaphor in automatic and unreflective ways" (p. 1). Therefore, metaphors in persuasive discourse have received a good deal of scholarly attention. As a master form of depiction that equates one thing with another (Osborn, 1967), metaphors result from as well as provoke thought (Hart, 1990). A study of metaphors can therefore offer insight into a rhetor's and an audience's motivations and worldviews in a number of ways.

First, metaphors selectively highlight ideas. Osborn (1967) argues that humans cannot communicate without using metaphors; important ideas within a culture will find their way into the language in the form of metaphors. Second, metaphors are often generative, suggesting new relationships between ideas. In this way, they can be powerful tools in persuasive discourse. Jamieson (1980) asserts that metaphors simultaneously create inventional possibilities and impose inventional restraints. That is, a chosen metaphor lends itself to being extended in some ways that are culturally appropriate and to being restricted in some ways that are culturally inappropriate. For example, one might say that one's heart bleeds for the situation of another, but extended metaphors to include the digestive or elimination systems would not be appropriate.

Third, metaphors can also mask ideas and values in that some metaphors become so routinely used and embedded in a culture that this "blind acceptance" (Lakoff & Johnson, 1980, p. 237) may obscure and even justify other values. For example, calling components of nature "natural resources" not only directs a view of trees as detached raw products, but also can blind one to recognizing or valuing the critical biodiversity required for the health of an old-growth forest. Lakoff (1990) asserts that "the use of a metaphor with a set of definitions becomes pernicious when it hides realities in a harmful way" (p. 1).

Finally, metaphors have entailments. That is, if one thing is equated with another, a series of accompanying worldview elements may be set into motion. For example, if a group has "won a battle," then there must be an enemy. Using the previous illustration, "natural resources" would also imply other utilitarian values such as the following: (1) nature should be used and to do otherwise would be to waste it, (2) nature can be inventoried and used, detached from any consequences for other natural elements, and (3) nature can be taken apart, understood, and controlled. Water becomes cubic feet to be "harnessed," and animals become "furbearers" and "game" to be "harvested."

Examining texts for coherent patterns of metaphor use, then, is profitable. Whether archetypal (Osborn, 1967), such as light/dark and up/down, or specific within historic and cultural contexts, metaphors allow the critic to gain further insight into rhetor, audience, and, in the case of this study, the roots of ideological conflict. Cataloging the language use is not enough, however. Hart (1990) suggests that "the good critic concentrates on the intellectual operations signaled by the use of these stylistic tokens" (p. 224). What is at issue, therefore, is not the truth or falsity of a metaphor but the perceptions and inferences that follow from it and the actions that are sanctioned by it. How we understand truth depends on how we understand situations. Metaphors help us understand situations.

Words or objects alone do not change reality. Changes in conceptual systems, however, do change what is real for us and affect how we perceive the world and act upon those perceptions. Because much of our social reality is understood in metaphorical terms, a critic would do well to look closely at a discourse's metaphors. For the current metaphors of the Adirondack controversy to yield insight, however, one must first explore their historical and cultural roots.

SETTING FOR ENVIRONMENTAL CONFLICT

The Adirondack Park

In the northernmost part of New York State lies a most unusual area of beauty and controversy known today as the Adirondack Park, a day's drive away from 70 million people. Its history is well documented.[4] Its lands were given to the state of New York after the Revolutionary War, offered as payment to veterans of the same war, turned down by most as being too hostile and primitive a wilderness, and subsequently leased and sold to timber interests, railroads, and wealthy elites who desired a haven in nature away from the bustle of New York City, 150 miles to the south.

By 1892, greedy lumber barons and locomotive-sparked forest fires had denuded most of the easily accessible mountains, leaving streams silted and causing flooding as far south as Albany as well as threatening the water supply to the other cities in the southern parts of the state. The 1890s may have been gilded and self-serving, but many of the gilded who had political power also shared an interest in forests that was almost cultlike in its intensity; these threats to the northern forests were compelling enough reasons for them to take drastic action. In 1885, the state legislature declared in statute that the remaining publicly held lands were to be held as what they called the Forest Preserve.

In 1892, New York State further declared that an entire area composed of both public and private lands would be designated as the Adirondack Park. To delineate the new park's boundaries, a line was drawn on a map using blue ink. This line became known as the Blue Line, a boundary "that has long inspired both contempt and admiration" (McMartin, 1994, p. 16). In 1894, the state declared that the Forest Preserve, the state's scattered holdings within this park, would be held as "forever wild," resulting in a spectacularly beautiful preserve of lakes, woods, and mountains never to be logged or developed. In the ensuing century, several state purchases increased the Forest Preserve so that by 1994, 42 percent of the total park was "forever wild." That is, from the original 681,374 acres, the state's holdings have expanded to their present 2.5 million acres, with 1 million acres of this "forever wild" Forest Preserve further designated as "wilderness," where motorized vehicle use is prohibited and undisturbed natural succession is allowed. It would take a constitutional amendment to change any of this structure.

The Blue Line delineating the boundaries of the Adirondack Park also has been expanded several times to encompass its current 6 million acres, the largest public park in the United States outside of Alaska. It covers one-fifth of the state, is equal in size to the neighboring state of Vermont, and is nearly three times larger than Yellowstone National Park. It includes the headwaters of five major drainage basins, 2,800 lakes and ponds, and more than 1,500 miles of rivers fed by an estimated 30,000 miles of brooks and streams. It contains such a complete variety of ecosystems that in 1989 the United Nations designated it a global biosphere in and of itself: the Adirondack Champlain Biosphere.

Yet it is not a park in the usual meaning of a vast, unbroken public domain for public recreation. Before the park was ever designated as such, the area was well known to many. Large portions of the area were, and still are, owned by forest and mining corporations, wealthy families, and private organizations, the latter with exclusive memberships often consisting of the wealthiest elite of the corporate and political worlds. These parcels account for 28 percent of the park.

Parts of the park also had long been known to native peoples (although only small numbers actually inhabited these areas)[5] and, beginning in the 1700s, by hardy, self-sufficient Adirondackers, an independent, proud, and often colorful population of guides, hunters, trappers, lumberjacks, crafters, farmers, and families. The heirs to the original Adirondackers' legacy and culture continue to make their living and raise their families in the park. The park, therefore, is not only a seasonal home to 210,000 visitors, an annual destination spot for an estimated 9 million tourists, and a potential paradise for real estate developers. The Adirondack park is also home to 130,000 permanent residents scattered throughout the park in 110 hamlets and communities, some of which often top the state's list for unemployment and poverty rates. By the park's centennial in 1992, these residents and their communities composed 30 percent of the park.

In sum, the Adirondack Park encompasses twelve counties and 6 million acres, of which 42 percent is public and 58 percent private. In size, diversity, and ownership, it is unique in the United States, which is why ideological clashes, sometimes fierce, have historically marked the debate over control of its future.

Growing Pressures

Yet, until 1973, the Adirondack Park in northern New York existed more as a map designation than as a physical entity. Then, because of increasing real estate development and recreational pressures—a consequence of the construction of the Northway, a multilaned highway from New York City straight north through the park to Montreal—state government created the Adirondack Park Agency (APA) and charged it with administering both a master plan for the care and custody of the state lands and a land use and development plan for the regulation of the private lands. Taken together, these plans were to set the guidelines for protecting both the parklike atmosphere and the economic well-being of the people of the park.

Since its inception in 1973, the APA has frequently clashed with Adirondack residents and local governments over agency policies and practices. This, in fact, is a gross understatement because the resentment and anger on the part of many communities over park representation on the board of commissioners, and the power and the perceived arrogance of the APA, have erupted in various home-rule, grass-roots efforts to intimidate, sabotage, and even eliminate the APA.

Some of the precursors to the parties in the present controversy began at this point. For example, the League for Adirondack Citizens' Rights was formed almost instantly and quickly grew to 24,000 members. Its goal was to push for abolishing the APA. A forerunner of the Wise Use/property rights groups that nationally emerged in the later 1980s,[6] the league argued against anyone, especially the APA, telling Adirondackers what to do with their private land. Its tactics were aggressive, including dumping manure on the steps of the APA's offices, an action that was thwarted after gasoline had been spread but before the match had been struck.[7] The league operated for many years, but was inactive by 1990 for a variety of reasons.

Another group, the Adirondack Council, also traces its origins to this same time period. Representing the interests of its members and member organizations—the Wilderness Society, the Natural Resources Defense Council, and the Association for the Protection of the Adirondacks—the council was and still is concerned with preserving the open spaces of the Adirondacks and supporting the APA and its regulatory power over what the council considers inappropriate development.

Until the late 1980s, these two visible groups badgered each other in a sort of rhetorical tug of war over the legitimacy and authority of the APA, but the APA continued to operate. It was understaffed for the job it was required to do and, according to early staff members, also perhaps a little too caught up in the sense of the APA's historic mission. Together, these two factors contributed to slow processing of permits and to occasional lapses in good judgment about what should be regulated and how. These became obligatory stories in any anti-APA conversation until one might believe that they described the majority of APA experiences. At any rate, the early APA staff members could not be accused of lacking motivation and dedication. On the other hand, many Adirondackers, while agreeing that some regulation was needed, were especially resentful that local governing boards were left out of the process. At the same time, the state of New York continued to appropriate various sums for land acquisitions to add to the Forest Preserve in the Adirondacks.

During 1988, this routine changed. New York State attempted to buy only a portion of a large land parcel in the Adirondack Park that had been put up for sale by a forest products company. By the time the state reacted to pressure from an outraged public and environmental groups for expedition of the matter, the property had been sold to another interest, who then negotiated with the state for a combination of outright purchase and easement rights at a much higher price per acre than the original selling price.[8] A better way had to be found.

In January 1989, in response to what was perceived as unbridled land speculation, unwarranted development in the region, and the inadequacies of the APA to regulate certain areas such as shorelines, Governor Mario Cuomo, in his State of the State Address, announced the establishment of the Commission on the Adirondacks in the Twenty-First Century. Peter Berle, president of the National Audubon Society and former commissioner of the New York State Department of Environmental Conservation under Governor Hugh Carey, was appointed chair. The fourteen-member panel was charged with making recommendations on how to manage the park lands, both public and private, so as to maintain a strong economic base compatible with the park's open-space characteristics into the twenty-first century.

The Report: *The Adirondack Park in the Twenty-First Century*

The eagerly anticipated commission report was finally released on May 9, 1990, a month late. It was ninety-six pages long and proposed 245 recommendations. According to the report, titled *The Adirondack Park in the Twenty-First Century*, the park was in danger. From within the park, development threatened its forested mountains, its shorelines, and its roadsides. From outside the park's Blue Line boundary, larger threats loomed from a booming population looking for recreational property to buy, from changing economies in the timber and tourism industries, and from acid rain and deposition of airborne toxic substances.

The commission also contended that the fate of the park, to a large degree, rested with a small number of owners, primarily the forest products companies and private, wealthy families who owned large, undeveloped parcels, because rising land values and increasing costs were making it difficult for these landowners and farmers to withstand development pressures. The commission claimed that increasing personal wealth had sparked an explosion of second-home and condominium development. The report further contended that the pace of land sales and the breakup of large parcels would determine the final form of the park before the century was over and that the full buildup in the park under current APA regulations could bring the park's population to well over one million people. Stricter regulation was needed.

Of the 245 recommendations, a few received more public attention and debate than all the others combined. This triggered a new round of heightened tension, anger, and distrust. Briefly, these recommendations called for:

- a one-year moratorium on building or development

- the state acquisition of an additional 654,850 acres for the Forest Preserve

- a one-dwelling-per-2,000 acres threshold for rural lands (representing 87 percent of the private holdings in the park)

- a one-year moratorium on changes in land use and development within 660 feet of any shoreline in all land use areas except hamlets

- a two hundred-foot setback from the edge of shorelines, roads, or recreation corridors for new construction

- earth colors and vegetative screening for existing buildings in certain situations

- the extension of the Blue Line to include certain additional lands and islands

Even before its release, Governor Cuomo's commissioned report had sparked heated debate both in support of and in opposition to its anticipated recommendations. Several news reports asserted that the seeds of distrust were planted when the commission was first created in 1989 and critics charged that it was too closely aligned with preservationist groups. The flames of hostility were further fanned when the commission held only two of its thirteen public hearings within the park. When the report's release was delayed a month past deadline, grass-roots groups began springing up in suspicion and in anticipation of what the report would say. The one dissenting member of the commission, Robert Flacke, issued a "minority report" scoffing at many of the report's claims. Although he later apologized for issuing his rebuttal three weeks before the report was issued, his action only added to the growing anger and second-guessing.

When the report was released in May 1990, the recommendations were greeted by howls of protest that were soon followed by demonstrations and even death threats to commission members. The commission's executive director, George Davis, and other members were surprised by the venomous hatred inspired by the report.

Within just over a year after the report's release, over a dozen groups of various ideological persuasions had emerged to join the existing groups, all claiming to know the best course to take in managing the park. So loud were some of the opposing voices that the debate was kept at a rolling boil for about eighteen months after the report's release; as it continues to simmer, the debate still prevents progress toward a resolution of the stalemate.

So powerful was the influence exerted by some of the voices that Governor Mario Cuomo immediately distanced himself from the commission's report and refused to act on any of its recommendations. By 1994, he still had not. Further, his Twenty-First Century Environmental Bond Act, a proposed financial mechanism for the state to continue the acquisition of park land and assist communities with infrastructure projects, failed at the ballot box in November 1990 by less than 1 percent of the vote. The Adirondack Solidarity Alliance, a newly formed opposition group, took credit for killing the Environmental Bond Act. In addition, although several pieces of legislation have been introduced in the subsequent five years to modify and/or mollify the commission's recommendations, none have passed. The process for planning for the long-term management of the park froze in the summer of 1990.

A primary reason for this is that nearly the entire park is in the district of one state senator, Republican Senator Ronald Stafford, often referred to as "AdiRONdack" Stafford. He has been adamant about not supporting any more regulation in the Adirondacks than currently exists. He can afford to be adamant, as he has been the second most powerful person in the Republican-controlled senate for some time, and past and present senate majority leaders have deferred to him on Adirondack issues; this means that Stafford holds the absolute power of life or death over any bill having to do with the Adirondacks. This is possible because in New York State politics, a few powerful majority members of the senate can determine whether a bill that has support for passage will even make it to the senate floor for a vote. Since January 1993, Stafford has also headed the Senate Finance Committee, so that he, to a degree, holds the purse strings on every senate bill needing appropriation. Senators are extremely reluctant to even consider crossing him.

In 1991, just one year after the commission's report, the vitriol seemed to lessen. However, that same year, Senator Stafford again introduced his annual legislation to abolish the APA altogether and distribute its duties among other state agencies. Although the legislation failed as usual in the Democratic-controlled assembly, the action had the effect of tearing off the thin scab on the old, deep wounds felt by many in the continuing battle. Meanwhile, the APA continued to be strapped with reduced funding, inadequate staffing levels, and an almost doubled workload, leading to the even slower processing of permits and adding to the frustration of those Adirondackers who viewed the existing regulations as too restrictive in the first place.

CONFLICT AND SYMBOLISM

Because so many groups were active in the time following the release of the commission's report, only a few representative groups can even be mentioned. Their rhetorical dramas will sound familiar to any scholar or activist who has heard the competing voices on just about any wilderness issue. The litany of battle metaphors is standard, with clearly delineated good and evil.

Groups Supporting the Report

The Adirondack Council (18,000 members in New York, 400,000 total through its three remaining national member organizations) is commonly described as the leading preservationist watchdog of the Adirondack Park. One of its member organizations is the oldest Adirondack preservationist group, the Association for the Protection of the Adirondacks (1,500), founded in 1902 by some of the more prominent and wealthy seasonal visitors to the park. The other two are the Natural Resources Defense Council and the Wilderness Society.

The Sierra Club (45,000 in New York State, over 500,000 nationwide) and the National Audubon Society (500,000 nationwide) are the two national environmental groups that have been active in the Adirondack Park campaign. The Residents Committee to Protect the Adirondacks (800) emerged as a local group in 1990 to give a voice to the Adirondackers who agreed that the park needed many of the protections recommended in the commission's report and that the traditional way of life and economic well-being of the park residents should be safeguarded.

Groups in Opposition to the Report

Some grass-roots opposition to the APA has been expressed within the park since 1973, when the APA was legislatively created to regulate both private and public lands within the park. However, in 1989, at the same time that the Commission on the Adirondacks in the Twenty-First Century began its task, the oppositional message of the Wise Use/property rights movement was starting to rise to national notice and influence. Even before the commission's report had been released in 1990, the Wise Use ideology spoke to some Adirondackers' fears of land grabs by a scheming, nonrepresentative government. Wise Use leaders refer to the park as a "scenic gulag" and to environmentalists as "watermelons"—green on the outside but red on the inside. Within a year of the report's release, an astonishing number of property rights groups sprang up in the Adirondacks, all representing various degrees of vitriol and adherence to conspiracy theories and using various tactics from verbal intimidation to threats, vandalism, and violence.

The Citizens Council of the Adirondacks (4,300 members) emerged as the earliest and most extreme of the groups opposed to the commission's report. The group was founded in late 1989 by Donald Gerdts, who believed that a conspiracy existed between the commission and what he termed radical preservationists. Gerdts's penchant for profanity was expressed in speeches, flyers, and faxes to environmentalists. He was originally dismissed as a lunatic, even by many Adirondackers, but his views gained credibility as his inflammatory rhetoric, media skills, and his ability to get things organized gave voice to many Adirondackers' pent-up anger and frustration over what they perceived as state restrictions on their private property rights in the Adirondack Park. Pictures of colonial Minutemen, the Liberty Bell, and Paul Revere on his midnight ride marked the group's press releases and letterhead. In a very short time, Gerdts became almost a household word.

The Adirondack Solidarity Alliance (3,300) subscribes to a sort of constitutional fundamentalism that charges that the state defrauds Adirondackers of their rights to life, liberty, and the pursuit of happiness, including their right to own and enjoy property. In June 1990, to protest the state's closing of a narrow road that originally ran through what is now a nonmotorized wilderness area, they hauled the huge boulders that the state agency had placed across the road to the town square at nearby Schroon Lake. On the boulders were spray-painted the words "Stones of Shame." After several days, they hauled the boulders to Albany and deposited them in front of the state capitol. For several months, the alliance also investigated and advocated the possibility of the Adirondacks seceding to neighboring Vermont and the indictment of Governor Mario Cuomo as a criminal.

The alliance has two symbols. One is a galloping red horse, taken from the colonial practice of letting a red horse run through the town's streets to give warning of attack and time to arm. Whenever the alliance displays the red horse in a protest, it is accompanied by a banner reading "Adirondack Rebellion." The other symbol is a long-taloned, splayed, red eagle rimmed with stars. On its breast is a heart on which is printed "USA," and on its head is a star imprinted with the initials of the group.

METAPHORICAL ANALYSIS

Framing the Analysis

Why a Wise Use/property rights message found a few loud voices in the Adirondacks is not surprising. Wherever public values are extended to private property or wherever the cumulative public consequences of private actions are considered, some owners can be expected to fear that their land will be taken under eminent domain or that they will be unfairly pressed to sacrifice for the benefit of others, whom they often view as rich elitists. This drama of the little guy and the common folk as victims of conspiracy and tyranny, and the call to battle with no compromise, mark much of the discourse produced by supporters of the Wise Use ideology. These feelings often are expressed in the language of national, nostalgic pioneer myths and the Revolutionary War ideals of freedom, the pursuit of happiness, and protection from confiscation of private property without just compensation. These touchstones mark much of the discourse produced by the opponents of Adirondack regulation as well. Indeed, the active ties between the Wise Use movement and some of those involved in the Adirondack opposition are solid and readily acknowledged.

The puzzle is not about why Wise Use ideas find support and expression among some Adirondackers. The puzzle is about why, in the time following the commission's report, so many Adirondackers allowed this relatively small group to have more volume, more recognition, and, by extension, more legitimacy than any other voice in the Adirondack debate. That legitimacy is measured by the power the group has to paralyze any attempts to move the conflict beyond stalemate toward resolution.

A good part of the answer has to do with Adirondacker history. The property rights message taps feelings of fear, distrust, or insecurity about present and future situations. It taps much more in many Adirondackers because these present feelings confirm scenarios that are grounded in collective Adirondacker cultural and historic memories. These conspiracy scenarios, as far-fetched as they may seem, ring true or at least familiar to many Adirondackers. Because their forebears experienced them and they now live with this legacy, the scenarios have an immediacy and authenticity anchored in the memories and stories and biases of Adirondack culture.

The emotional buttons so easily pushed by many of the Adirondack opposition groups are found most prominently in the metaphors of a "park" and the Blue Line boundary. These are reminders of an authentic drama played out in the past and projected into the present fear of a political conspiracy to take Adirondacker land to create a playland for rich elitists. These metaphors serve as constant reminders of how invisible and hence powerless many Adirondackers perceive they became and still are. As such, the metaphors of powerlessness are ironically empowering. By evoking them loudly in a public forum, Adirondackers force the audience to acknowledge their existence and the potential of their anger.

The Blue Line

The Adirondack Park is a powerful metaphor, not for what it depicts, but for what it does not acknowledge and therefore renders invisible. Something designated as a park usually is expected to be an unbroken piece of land often kept in its natural state as public property for aesthetics and recreation. A park is not usually expected to have permanent human residents who own land within it and make their living on it. Similarly, the original intention of New York State when it created the park was for it to eventually become all public domain (Terrie, 1992).

In 1892, when the Adirondack Park was legalized as "all lands now owned or hereafter acquired by the state," the powerful Blue Line was drawn on the map to mark this wild area, and in a stroke, the proof of the park's existence became tangible. The psychological effects of this transformation cannot be overemphasized: in that one action, the new park's human inhabitants were immediately rendered voiceless and invisible to those outside the park. Even to those early wealthy park visitors, the Adirondackers seemed out of place or, at least, useful only to the extent that the locals could serve the visitors' needs in their great camps that they built in the park.

This perception continues today. The upstate region of New York was and still is generally viewed as a mostly empty, wild area, even by some state legislators.[9] This is the residual consequence of the 1892 park act, which never acknowledged the private lands within the park. Neither did it address how private land was to be treated or how it would be acquired. Even now, although it is quite apparent that all of the land within the Blue Line will never be acquired as public land, the original intent remains the state's ultimate goal in the minds of many Adirondackers.

The Blue Line, therefore, acts as more than a simple park boundary. It is a powerful metaphor that is used far more by the park residents than by any other group in the Adirondack debate. Groups opposed to the report frame the Blue Line as a tangible, identifiable marker, an actual place. Whenever it is written, it is capitalized. The color blue is used at opposition meetings and rallies; there are blue balloons and blue painted signs and blue ribbons pinned outside legislators' offices and on clothing during protests and lobbying activities. The names of some opposition groups contain it, for example, the Blue Line Council and the Blue Line Confederation, with its *Blue Line News*. Whereas to some the Blue Line marks a protected, wondrous natural place of pristine beauty, to others the Blue Line became, and still is perceived as, a divider and a marker rendering the Adirondackers within it invisible or trapped in, as one group calls it, "a scenic gulag."

Since its debut on a map in the park's very earliest days, the Blue Line has also appeared on every official state map, continually providing a visual marker delineating a specific area and thereby fostering the interpretation that this land is different from the land on the other side of it. When the Blue Line was originally drawn on the map and the Adirondack Park was created, the image of a park and all its attendant attributes came into sharp focus in the media's eye and the public's mind. Just as dramatically, Adirondackers and their communities faded out of focus until they were invisible. The only thing that most people saw or wanted to see was the park. In this light, the common metaphorical reference to the commission's report as a "blueprint" takes on stronger inferences.

Since first being drawn, the park's boundaries have been extended several times from its original area of fewer than 3 million acres to its present 6 million acres. Every time these boundaries were extended, more people were enclosed by and seemingly sucked into oblivion by the advancing Blue Line. Not only was the newly enclosed land immediately regulated more strictly, but its inhabitants were rendered instantly invisible and powerless. The report recommended expanding the Blue Line once again. No wonder there was outrage.

Tapping into the collective memories of the Adirondacker experience, the groups opposed to the report also argued that the state still harbored the goal of acquiring all of the land within the Blue Line to create an elitist, environmentalist playground. Whether this happened through eminent domain or purchasing conservation easements, the goal was the same: to make the Adirondackers disappear, quite literally by pushing them off their land or figuratively by rendering them invisible.

It was this struggle against being invisible that also drove the Adirondack opposition groups' explosion against the report's recommendation that houses and roofs be painted in earth tones so that the structures would blend in and not be noticed. It should be noted that this proposed regulation has been in effect in other places for some time, for example, along federally designated rivers under the 1968 National Wild and Scenic Rivers Act. The reasoning is that if experiencing a landscape is what draws tourists to an area, then minimizing the impact of structures on that landscape is of benefit to the economic base. To protesting Adirondackers, however, having houses that blend in only reinforces the invisibility they already feel.

Invisible in the Great Camps

According to the literature of groups opposed to the report, if preservationists cannot push Adirondackers outside of the Blue Line, herd them into hamlets, or by extension make them invisible in their houses, then these wealthy elitists who want a private playground will disenfranchise them. According to this drama, the report gives Adirondackers two choices: Move out or become a servant to the rich. The two options are linked to another powerful cluster of metaphors used by opposition groups, extreme and moderate, that hearken to authentic experiences embedded in Adirondack history and culture.

In the park's history, along with the perpetual tension between private and public lands, was an equal or greater tension between classes of rich and poor. When New York declared its intention to preserve its forests and acquire all the land delineated by the Blue Line in the creation of the park, it signaled a powerful message to the wealthy that here was an opportunity to buy land cheaply for private reserves and then perhaps sell it back to the state later at a handsome profit. Clubs such as the Adirondack League, the Ampersand Preserve, and the Whitney Park cheaply bought up huge parcels of land in the late 1800s for their own private playgrounds and potential future profit.

These private great camps were exclusive and extensive. By 1904, fifty-five of them occupied nearly three-quarters of a million acres of the Adirondack Park, a full third of all the private land in the park (Terrie, 1992). This figure did not account for the smaller parcels held by wealthy individuals and the vast private holdings by timber and mining interests.

The creation of the park boundaries with the stroke of the Blue Line and the meteoric rise of the private preserves had a dramatic effect on Adirondackers caught in the events. Adirondackers were used to thinking of the area as one big forest where the boundaries that existed usually did not signal exclusivity and prohibition of entrance or use. Adirondackers and visitors could fish, hunt, cut wood, and go wherever they wanted. It was never an issue if a stream passed through several ownership boundaries or if stalked game took the hunter onto someone else's land. This changed dramatically when the wealthy created their preserves and built their great camps where they "would not be forced to rub shoulders and share their game with the hoi polloi" (Terrie, 1992, p. 50).

Two factors created the most animosity with Adirondackers in the past, and today they still find powerful metaphorical expression in the opposing groups' literature. First, these wealthy preserve owners were serious about wanting the land to themselves. They fenced in their preserves, each one covering tens of thousands of acres, posted the land with "no trespassing" signs, and hired armed guards to patrol the perimeter. Between the camps of the wealthy and the state's "forever wild" Forest Preserve, the region became a patchwork maze of forbidden land.

This legacy is echoed in the opposing groups' metaphors, with the roles of wealthy elitists and super-rich now played by environmentalists and state officials. Even the ostensibly more moderate groups assert that the commission's report is a slap in the face to Adirondackers, a wish list of preservationists who want to make the Adirondacks the exclusive domain of the super-rich, inaccessible to all but expert hikers and campers. It is all part of a plan to chop up the land to provide a playground for the wealthy and to deprive the Adirondackers of their livelihoods and culture.

Second, the wealthy members of these exclusive clubs and private great camps were a collection of the most famous, politically connected, and powerful people of that era, not just of New York City but of the entire country. The list reads like a who's who of the Gilded Age, a sort of "land baron cartel" (D'Elia, 1979, p. 19), including J. P. Morgan, Alfred J. Vanderbilt, a couple of Roosevelts, railroad magnate William Seward Webb, and many others. They were part of an era marked by two distinct classes, very rich and very poor. It was thought that the wealthy were entitled to the finer things in life. The underclasses, while aspiring to be rich themselves one day, were relegated in the meantime to the role of serving the wealthy. And serve they did. They washed and ironed the multiple costumes that the family and guests needed for formal dinners, relaxing, bowling, gambling, or boating. They provided all of the labor-intensive tasks required to maintain a paradise playground for the wealthy.

However, when an Adirondack worker went home for the day or after the summer season, he or she passed by posted and often guarded land to return to modest dwellings at best. The contrast was stark and the message was clear: Adirondackers were not included or wanted unless they could be useful in doing the bidding of the rich. For example, in the multiple-building Sagamore great camp, originally owned by the Vanderbilts, a collection of buildings for the staff was built behind and over a rise from the main camp on the lakeshore. The servants lived in this ironically placed "upper" camp, for they were never to be seen unless properly dressed for service, and most of the Vanderbilt guests never saw this other camp or even knew of its existence. It was invisible.

The resentment grew deep and continues to be a very powerful force. Hence, the opposition groups' warnings of servitude and slavery in the Adirondacks—that the wealthy elite still want the Adirondackers to haul their water and carry their logs—ring clear to many. The more extreme property rights groups predict that Adirondackers will be forced to live in concentration camps working as slave laborers for the APA. Swastikas were painted on the Adirondack Council's office.

Therefore, when the groups supporting the report insist that increased wilderness will bring more tourists and that meeting their needs could be a cornerstone of the Adirondack economy, the proposition echoes against past Adirondacker experiences. The commission and some supporting groups have good intentions when they support the notion that the bulk of economic and housing development should take place in the hamlets and towns to preserve as much open space as possible as a tourist draw. To property rights groups, however, the image of Adirondackers having their land taken and then being herded into the hamlets triggers resentment and anger at a familiar patronizing pressure, one that tells them to stay put in certain places to serve outsiders who will have access to the land.

Reinforcement of Metaphorical Themes

The central questions, of course, concern how to get beyond this polarization. What competing ideological points need to be at least acknowledged and legitimated to move this issue beyond impasse? How can these competing voices all be given ownership in and responsibility for a management plan that safely leads the park into the twenty-first century?

Unfortunately, several of the groups that were supportive of the report reinforced the opposition's metaphorical themes, especially the theme of invisibility. Whether this was done deliberately or unintentionally, the ultimate effect has been to buttress the opposition groups' arguments and trigger the obstinate entrenchment of positions. The report's supporters have, ironically, empowered the opposition. Therefore, to move this conflict closer to resolution, important factors need to be recognized and mediated.

First, it is incumbent on the environmental groups to recognize that the present tensions are based in large part on valid historical and cultural claims of Adirondackers. In multiple interviews with lobbyists and spokespeople for the most active environmental groups, it was clear that those who know and love the "forever wild" parts of the Adirondacks also are very concerned with viable, appropriate economic development that will provide income and a tax base to support good schools, health care facilities, and other infrastructure needs of the Adirondack communities. Several environmentalists insisted that the stories about pushing people out of the park were once true to various degrees, but maintained that this was past history and should not even be an issue. Nevertheless, it is, and they should treat it seriously. The experiences and events may indeed have occurred in the past, but the memories and attitudes regarding them are very much a part of the present. By not recognizing the current struggle as another chapter in a long, complex, and interwoven historical and cultural narrative, these groups, and some more than others, illustrate both why Adirondackers feel they must struggle for recognition and respect and why when Adirondackers can achieve this to any degree, they feel empowered.

Groups supporting the report claim that their motivation is not to prevent people from living in the park or to make them invisible, but to find the balance between preserving unique natural spaces and providing economic security. Finding a balance is a popular metaphor used extensively by both sides. It implies that a balance does not now exist, that some aspects are unduly receiving more attention than others. Yet this imbalance is never identified. Further, these groups must recognize that their campaign to preserve open space in the Adirondack Park continues to empower the opposition groups to perpetuate the conflict. That is, the environmental groups frame their appeals around those very aspects of preserving open space that reinforce the siege mentality of the opposition groups and reinforce the invisibility of the Adirondackers.

For example, many publications and direct mail appeals by the Adirondack Council and most of those from the National Audubon Society's national and northeastern regional offices acknowledge no communities, no towns, no schools, no people in the Adirondacks. Although this is perhaps not intentional, Audubon's local, regional, and national literature unfortunately reinforces the invisibility of Adirondackers simply by not acknowledging their existence or casts them as wanton destroyers within the drama. Much of the literature of the Sierra Club does the same. Specifically, the area within the Blue Line is metaphorically cast as a biological treasure chest, a jewel, a green oasis in an urbanized Northeast, a timeless splendor, a spiritual retreat, the most magnificent natural resource in New York, and one that should be a national treasure. Its vast vistas and pristine habitats and unique species are said to be priceless.

But the park, these groups claim, is in peril and crisis. This jewel is being assailed by unbridled, unwarranted, irresponsible, and massive development threats. The park is in the throes of a development boom. Greedy, land-grabbing developers are snapping up wilderness tracts for condominiums. Vistas are being marred, shorelines maimed, and water contaminated. The wilderness risks being tamed; therefore, protected public and vulnerable private lands must be managed responsibly using the weapons of regulations. To do otherwise would be to spend the inheritance of future generations.

In this preservationist attack drama, the opposing groups are only masked as down-home Adirondackers. In reality, they are greedy real estate developers and timber interests yearning to make a killing in the unbridled building boom. Convincing photos accompany these appeals and invariably depict shorelines, mountainsides, wilderness areas, and roadside vistas marred by garish or crowded second-home developments. These common themes are backed with convincing statistics, maps, and before and after pictures of development. The point is not that these claims are contrived, because they are not. The point is that they are not complete and do a disservice not only to Adirondackers but also to those who support preservation.

CONCLUSION

According to the opposition groups, many Adirondackers harbor a perception that they have been pushed out of the process of planning for the future of their lands. As this study discussed, they were pushed out of focus and visibility by suddenly being included in a park marked by a blue line. Then they were pushed out of the lands and streams that became posted great camps and preserves. Then their dignity was denied by the disdainful attitudes of the wealthy playing in their private great camps. Then in 1973 they perceived that their local control was compromised by the external, politically created Adirondack Park Agency. Many felt that it was imposed on them because the state believed that the local governments could not manage their own communities responsibly. Then the commission on the Adirondacks in the Twenty-First Century issued its report, *The Adirondack Park in the Twenty-First Century*, in May 1990. Adirondackers felt that they once again had been pushed out of the decision-making process.

Regardless of how many of the report's 245 recommendations were beneficial and supportable, a few of them were extraordinarily powerful in reviving past and present animosities. The opposing groups were loud and media savvy, and they used many standard property rights arguments and metaphors, but in this case these arguments tapped into much deeper, more personal, and more entrenched beliefs based on the historical and cultural Adirondacker experience. Therein lay these groups' success at galvanizing enough attention and support, or at least tolerance, as to appear to be representing the majority of the

Adirondack population. The interaction between opposing groups continues to be a mutually destructive relationship.

The opposition groups were surrogates for a population of Adirondackers who had been trying to get noticed and legitimized for a long time, and the issues they raised have influenced powerful New York state senator Ronald Stafford, whose district is mostly in the Adirondack Park and who continues to have informal veto power over Adirondack issues.

Dick Purdue (1990), supervisor of Indian Lake, noted that "[t]he issue is power, not environment." According to Purdue, the Adirondackers experienced little meaningful goodwill in the process by which the report was produced. Further, they were depicted as wanton enemies of the park environment. Finally, the Adirondackers perceive the environmentalists as being not so much interested in defending the land as they are in defending their own exclusive power in the park.

Groups like the Adirondack Solidarity Alliance and the Citizens Council provided visibility and exhilaration to many Adirondackers; they empowered them. Even if individuals never joined any of the groups, they could cheer them on and identify with their aggressive, abrasive attacks on state politicians and proponents of open space. At the very least, they could relish the squirming in Albany. In addition, the threats and profanity acted as a sort of consummatory rhetoric (Scott & Smith, 1969), productive not in getting them infrastructure and economic development assistance, but in getting them noticed—finally.

Although contrasting metaphors of upstate/downstate, inside/outside, and rich/poor were common in the discourse following the report's release, others were far more powerful in reinforcing how Adirondackers became and still are perceived as invisible, incapable, and expendable. Were groups opposed to the report, especially those led by nonnative Adirondackers, aware of the historical and cultural experiences of the Adirondackers to an extent which allowed them to deliberately pick and choose their narratives and metaphors for best advantage? Probably not to the degree that it might appear, but they certainly knew when they hit sensitive triggers and chronically raw wounds.

On the other hand, one certainly can assign some blame to the environmentalist groups and the commission members. Had they considered the history and culture of the Adirondackers, they could have engaged the commission's task in a way that would have empowered local Adirondack communities to own part of the process and to choose certain pathways. Ideally, commission members would have recognized their own potential biases at work on many fronts, from commission representation to assessing local and state needs and desires to exploring and framing the recommendations for their implementation. Unintentionally, supporters of some or all of the report's recommendations reinforced these historic biases. Their sincere love of the wilderness and their strong commitment to protect it blinded them to the reactions that some of the recommendations were sure to ignite.

In hindsight, then, it is easy to blame the environmentalist groups and representatives on the commission. Such blame, however, is unfair because most of the report's 245 recommendations had to do with economic development and local community infrastructure needs such as landfill closures, roads, and sewage treatment needs. Indeed, the 130,000 residents of the park were fully acknowledged in the report's recommendations. In addition, all of the groups in support of the report expressed concern that Adirondack communities be vibrant and economically healthy. Why were these concerns not heard by Adirondackers?

This analysis sought to explain why these recommendations were overshadowed and silenced by just a very few voices. It is unfair to speculate whether the commissioners and the environmental groups should have been attuned to the historical and cultural perceptions that needed to be addressed. For some of them, their organizational mandate has always been to promote wilderness preservation, and that is the focus of their literature; hence, few to no people ever appear or are referenced in any of their campaign literature. This does not mean that they are plotting the demise of the communities, yet within the Adirondack context, this is the message perceived by many. Also, some groups failed to appreciate the important roles that the historical and cultural experiences play in how contemporary events are framed or interpreted, especially in regard to the metaphorical power of the Blue Line and tourism as indicators of invisibility.

The lesson from this analysis is that whatever rhetorical strategies are pursued in advancing any preservationist goals in the park, they should be augmented with others that reaffirm the dignity and capabilities of Adirondackers. Will it be easy or simple? Of course not. Since the report's release, the sides have become more polarized, and any attempts to bridge them in either direction are viewed with skepticism. For example, the preservationist Adirondack Council has wisely attempted to make its interest in park residents more visible, but their latest efforts are generally viewed by opposing groups as fronts and smokescreens. Meanwhile, the APA has presumed the authority to mandate earthen colors for some new construction in the park, "the better not to see you with, dear," notes a newsletter of the Blue Line Council (1994, p. 1).

However, the Residents Council for the Protection of the Adirondacks, a newer, in-park group that supports most of the report's recommendations including the wilderness/open space protection measures, is making small but significant headway. Rather than negatively empowering themselves by defensively boycotting and stonewalling any initiatives, its members are positively empowering themselves by stepping into the process to provide a mediating voice in the conflict, in spite of being viewed as sellouts by most other Adirondacker groups.

UPDATE

Since the commission's report in 1990, several bills have been introduced in the New York state legislature to deal with the future of the Adirondack

Park and to strengthen the Adirondack Park Agency. They have all failed in the senate. In January 1992, Governor Cuomo introduced legislation calling for a new covenant, one that proved that land preservation and economic development could be compatible.[10] In that the metaphor of "covenant" suggests a sacred and therefore trustworthy quality, it is useful. At any rate, it failed. In fact, any rumor of any Adirondack bill triggered the familiar competing metaphors. Some of the releases directed people to begin stocking up on guns and ammunition.

After three years, public pressure for action was high since reactions to the 1990 report had stalled any progress toward financing land acquisitions and local infrastructure needs (e.g., landfill closings) across the entire state. In 1993, several versions of an Environmental Protection Act (called the Trust Fund) were circulated and debated, although the fear was that once again Senator Ronald Stafford would stonewall any legislative efforts, and that was what almost happened. In the final forty-five minutes of the twenty-six-hour marathon leading to the end of the 1993 session, Senator Stafford pushed for local veto power on any state purchases of open space, virtually eliminating any future land acquisition in the Adirondack Park. The legislative mood soured and the clock was ticking. As the *New York Times* (Dao, 1993) noted, "When Senator Ronald Stafford says not in my district, a whole state goes without" (p. B1). Pandemonium broke out among the environmental lobbyists and their assembly supporters. The entire proposal stood on the verge of collapse. However, as often happens in public policy formation, strange political twists outside the scope of this paper drove the issue to resolution.

A speedy negotiating session later called an "Adirondack thaw" and a "last legislative gasp" (Wehrwein, 1993), conducted literally on the fly between the two chambers in the final dawning hours, resulted in a state/local control compromise that would allow the future purchase of eighty-five open spaces scattered across the state and selected in a 1990 Open Space Plan to be exempt from the local veto. Fifteen of those parcels, including the crown jewels, were in the Adirondacks.

Passing legislation, however, is one thing; implementing it is another. Swept out of office as part of the November 1994 national Republican landslide, Mario Cuomo lost his bid for a fourth term as governor, and in 1995 the political reins passed to George Pataki, the first Republican to head New York in twenty years. Senator "AdiRONdack" Stafford was reelected and held onto his seat on the Senate Finance Committee. Because the upstate vote helped elect Pataki, many in the Adirondacks were originally cheered by his antiregulatory, less-government-is-better stance. They immediately began lobbying for the Adirondack Park Agency to be gutted and many of the commissioners replaced. However, when no local government officials from inside the Blue Line were among the more than two hundred people on the new governor's transition team shaping new policy, their enthusiasm waned and cries of "Adirondack Apartheid!"

punctuated editorials and opposition groups' literature. The Adirondack Solidarity Alliance, now an active member group in the national property rights coalition Alliance for America, also launched a foundation to prepare a lawsuit challenging the constitutionality of the APA in federal court, buoyed by the introduction of federal "takings" legislation by upstate Republican Congressman John McHugh.

Still unresolved at the time of this writing, Pataki's severe state budget proposal, enormously controversial on many levels, proposed to divert funds dedicated by the hard-won Environmental Protection Act to the general fund, putting environmental protection and infrastructure needs at odds with welfare and Medicaid cuts, state worker layoffs, and higher state university tuition. The governor has inherited the ideological legacy of the 1990 report, *The Adirondack Park in the Twenty-First Century,* and by the time his current four-year term is complete, the twenty-first century will be at the doorstep. Unless the new administration is wise enough to learn the lessons of the past that are driving the present Adirondack Park controversy, it will be endlessly searching to define and create that elusive panacea of balance.

Burke's (1957) rhetorical philosophy evolves from the view that "language is a strategic response to a situation from which motives can be derived" (p. 3). Some reporters who wrote about the aftermath of the report's release correctly framed the issue as one of control. But the larger, more far-reaching issues were and continue to be about the origins of this competition over control in the private/public lands of the Adirondack Park and Adirondacker responses to opportunities to be empowered. The metaphors reveal these issues and offer insight into how the arguments could be framed differently to lessen the sense of battle and the absolutes that have defined these issues for so long.

It is important that the Adirondack issues be resolved, because many places in the world, where there are a mix of people, plants, and animals living around each other, are in the same pull between public values and private land. Writer Bill McKibben (1992) asserts that

> if the Adirondacks have a future, then much of the rest of the world has a future: We need the Adirondacks in part because it could point a middle way. And if we can't solve our problems here, in the relatively wealthy northeastern United States, it is too much to expect that the Brazilians and the Rwandans and the Burmese are going to solve theirs. . . . Once these mountains supplied huge quantities of timber, vast amounts of iron ore—now they could supply the ideas necessary around the environmentally disintegrating world. (p. 42)

A profitable place to start is to examine the metaphors.

NOTES

1. Indeed, the Adirondack model, even with all its persisting problems and stalemate, is being closely studied to help fashion a private/public land arrangement in the Lake Baikal region of Russia. A delegation led by commission chair G. Gordon Davis is part of the Russian/American team to plan for the ecologically sustainable development of the vast forests nurturing the world's largest and deepest lake.

2. Much of the literature examined here was produced by several of the most visible and vocal groups: the Adirondack Council, the Adirondack Conservation Council, the Adirondack Cultural Foundation, the Adirondack Defense Fund, the Adirondack Mountain Club, the Adirondack Solidarity Alliance, the Association for the Protection of the Adirondacks, the Blue Line Confederation, the Blue Line Council, the Citizens Council of the Adirondacks, the Environmental Planning Lobby, the Fairness Coalition, the League for Adirondack Citizens' Rights, the National Audubon Society, the Residents Council for the Protection of the Adirondacks, and the Sierra Club, Atlantic chapter. In addition, more than one thousand newspaper articles were analyzed from the following newspapers across New York State from 1990 into 1994: the *Albany Times Union*, the *Binghamton Press Sun Bulletin*, the *Buffalo News*, the *Catskill Daily Mail*, the *Deposit Courier*, the *Glens Falls Post Star*, the *Gloversville Leader Herald*, the *Jamestown Post Journal*, the *Kingston Daily Freeman*, the *Legislative Gazette*, the *Middletown Times Herald Record*, the *New York Post*, the *New York Times*, *Newsday* (Nassau), *Newsday* (New York), the *PJ Tri State Gazette*, the *Plattsburgh Press Republican*, the *Poughkeepsie Journal*, the *Rochester Democrat and Chronicle*, the *Rockland Journal News*, the *Schenectady Daily Gazette*, the *Staten Island Advance*, the *Syracuse Herald Journal*, the *Syracuse Post Standard*, the *Troy Record*, the *Utica Observer Dispatch*, the *Watertown Daily Times*, and the *Yonkers Herald Statesman*.

3. For a comprehensive yet brief overview of the evolutionary link between rhetorical criticism and sociolinguistics, see Brock, Scott, and Chesebro (1990, pp. 282–287).

4. Although the Adirondack Park may not be well known to the general U.S. population, a wealth of historical sources, including an abundance of primary sources, exists because of New York State's importance in the early history of the United States. The Association for the Protection of the Adirondacks established and maintains the Adirondack Library housed at Union College, Schenectady, New York. Another rich archive of primary as well as secondary material is housed at the residence of long-time and passionate Adirondack advocate Paul Schaeffer in Niskayuna, New York. In his house, hand built of Adirondack stone, is the Adirondack Room, where many of the most important preservationist meetings of the past fifty years have been held. For excellent, comprehensive books about Adirondack history, see Terrie (1985) and Graham (1978).

5. James Fenimore Cooper's best-known novels, such as *The Deerslayer* and *The Last of the Mohicans*, were set in the Lake George and Lake Champlain areas of the Adirondack Park.

6. The Wise Use movement, also termed the antienvironmental movement, is a coalition of ranchers, corporate interests, private property owners, and public interest organizations formed to combat environmental regulations. Advocating "multiple use" of public lands and greater sovereign control of private property, the movement has become involved in a variety of local and state environmental controversies. See Gottlieb (1989) and Arnold and Gottlieb (1993).

7. For a firsthand account of the origin and activities of the League for Adirondack Citizens' Rights, see *Adirondack Rebellion* by Anthony D'Elia (1979), one of its founders and most dedicated and active members.

8. New York State attempted to buy ninety-six hundred acres of land put up for sale by Diamond International (a forest products company). Diamond International was offering the property for $193 per acre, but the state could offer only $145, because the land acquisition

process prevented the state from offering an amount above the appraised fair market value for the land. Additionally, the state wanted only a portion of the property, and Diamond International wanted to sell the property to one buyer. Consequently, Lassiter Properties, Inc., of Georgia, a land speculator, purchased the property for $177 per acre. The state eventually was able to purchase a portion of the property (fifty-five thousand acres) from Lassiter, but only after environmental groups and an outraged public pressured Governor Mario Cuomo to appeal directly for the expedition of the purchase. New York State paid $10.8 million, or $194 per acre, for the land. The sale consisted of a combination of outright purchase and acquisition of easement rights of the property.

9. Two recent examples witnessed by the author in her capacity as environmental policy analyst for a New York state senator reflect this common discounting of the 130,000 people living in 110 communities in the Adirondack Park. First, at a 1993 New York statewide organization's executive board meeting attended by the leadership of corporations, unions, and state agencies, the subject was raised of possibly including on the board a member from the upstate Adirondack region. The chair noted, "Well, I've heard that there are people living up there, so maybe we should go up and find one." Second, in several letters written to a New York state senator, the constituents complained that they were appalled to learn that not even half of the land in the park was owned by the state. They urged the senator to do all he could to make sure the rest of the land would be promptly acquired.

10. "Working landscape" is a currently popular metaphor used to describe this balance. The working landscape metaphor is fraught with danger, however. The connotation desired is of a landscape, an open space, that is legitimate because it is productive and economically pulling its own weight. The reasoning is that if open space can be viewed as contributing to a community's economic benefit, then it is worthwhile and desirable. The danger lies in its tapping into the powerful work ethic in American culture. If landscapes are worthwhile because they work (earn), then landscapes that cannot work, such as mountainsides and inaccessible, backwoods wilderness, are not worthwhile; at the very least, their value is difficult to measure. This metaphor plays into the utilitarian ideology that not to use nature for profit is to waste it. Here the landscape itself is doing or not doing the work—an inference that is much more dangerous.

CHAPTER SEVEN

The Rhetorical Function of "Earth in the Balance"

Warren Sandmann

WHY ARE WE in the midst of what even the most conservative of scientists and politicians admit is a potential ecological catastrophe? Is it because of the rate at which we produce both toxic and "ordinary" waste? Is it because of our continued dependence on fossil fuels and their effect on the atmosphere? Is it because we are wearing out the best of our farmlands and overgrazing and destroying marginal land? Is it because we are destroying rainforests on an assembly-line basis? Is it because we are overpopulating the earth at an alarming rate?

The simple answer, of course, is yes to all of the above. But a more complex answer, and a more complex question await us. Given the evidence of our own senses, the compilation of data, and scientific research, why are we still engaging in what appears to be destructive behavior? Al Gore, vice president of the United States, believes he has at least the start of an answer to this more complex question. Gore believes that we engage in this seemingly self-destructive behavior because we have created a symbolic relationship with the planet that places humanity in any number of roles except one: spiritually connected to the planet. As Gore (1992) states it, "The more deeply I search the roots of the global environmental crisis, the more I am convinced that it is an outer manifestation of an inner crisis that is, for lack of a better word, spiritual" (p. 12).

Gore has more thoroughly developed this basic thesis in a 1992 book entitled *Earth in the Balance: Ecology and the Human Spirit.*[1] With Gore's involvement in the 1992 presidential race, some of the material in this book became part of the public debate. What was primarily discussed, however, was the section detailing the possible costs of curing this crisis. Given the venues for discussion, such as the vice presidential candidates' debate, this is only normal. What has received less attention, during the election and since, is Gore's detailed treatment of the symbolically created relationship between humanity and the planet.

In this chapter I intend to explore more fully the arguments and examples Gore offers to bolster his claim that the ecological crisis is rooted in a symbolic dysfunctional relationship between humanity and the planet. Gore offers us a picture of this relationship between humanity and the planet as one that has been mediated through our culture, our history, our philosophy, our economic theories, and our theology. Gore is reminding us of humanity's ability to symbolically create social and material realities. Our symbolic relationships do not just create symbolic reality; they have material implications as well. In better understanding Gore's message and rhetorical technique, those people interested in and involved in improving our environment will also better understand the necessity of symbolic power in the battle over the environment. That battle is not simply one fought for land, air, and water; it is also (and more importantly) a battle over the symbols that we use in the struggle. Gore's message, and the message of this essay, is simple: The manner in which we use these symbols (as well as the manner in which these symbols use us) has a major and possibly decisive impact on our planet.[2]

To understand better this relationship among symbol use, humanity, and the ecological conditions of our planet, we need first to understand better the relationship among symbol, social reality, and material practices. A brief overview of some of the work of Burke, Hall, McGee, and others will set the groundwork for a critical analysis of Gore's major arguments, as well as allowing us to consider some of the implications of Gore's argument as they relate to the manner in which communication can and does empower environmental action.

SYMBOLS AND/OR REALITY: A BRIEF OVERVIEW

And however important to us is the tiny sliver of reality each of us has experienced firsthand, the whole overall "picture" is but a construct of our symbol systems. To meditate on this fact until one sees its full implications is much like peering over the edge of things into an ultimate abyss. And doubtless that's one reason why, though man is typically the symbol-using animal, he clings to a kind of naive verbalism that refuses to realize the full extent of the role played by symbolicity in his notions of reality. (Burke, 1966, p. 5)

In this excerpt, Kenneth Burke offers us one perspective of the relationship among symbols, humanity, and reality. In order to survive in the world in which we live, we have no choice but to create it in terms of our symbol use and then live in that world as a real world. That "created" world is more than just a symbolic construct, however, in that it has real material effects on human behavior.

The Burkeian concept of the terministic screen offers the clearest example of the effect that language and symbols have on human behavior. Burke's terministic screen should be thought of as just that: as a screen, or filter, that lets in certain items and restricts others. Alternately, it can be seen as a perspectival point of view. From one position, we are granted a "view" of part of reality. From another perspective, we are granted another "view" of reality. Given that we view reality through a filter or from one perspective (or possibly a series of perspectives), we must act on the basis of this limited view of reality. As Burke puts it, "Even if any given terminology is a reflection of reality, by its very nature as a terminology it must be a selection of reality; and to this extent it must function also as a deflection of reality" (p. 45). Our perspective, our terminal screen, is our world. These perspectives, these screens, are symbolic creations in themselves—collections of terminologies.

Adding to Burke's realm of the symbolic, M. C. McGee (1980) theorizes how symbols influence and even control human behavior. McGee has tried to revitalize the concept of ideology, to dissolve the contradiction between those who speak of ideology as a trick perpetuated in order to maintain an otherwise unacceptable political and social arrangement (materialists) and those who speak of ideology as simply a "voluntary agreement to believe in and to participate in a 'myth' " (symbolists) (p. 2). To dissolve this contradiction, McGee argues that it is necessary to understand that both myth and ideology function as symbolic power, as collections of symbols that have a material effect on human behavior and on the manner in which humanity constructs its reality, both individually and, more important, collectively. In McGee's terms:

> If we are to describe the trick-of-the-mind which deludes us into believing that we "think" with/through/for a "society" to which we "belong," we need a theoretical model which accounts for both "ideology" and "myth," a model which neither denies human capacity to control "power" through the manipulation of symbols nor begs Marx's essential questions regarding the influence of "power" on creating and maintaining political consciousness. . . . [S]uch a model must begin with the concept of "ideology" and proceed to link the notion directly with the interests of symbolism. (p. 4)

All human behavior, McGee argues, is based on our participation in a "mass consciousness," and such a consciousness is always "false." This does not mean that we are simply "automatons" with no capacity for independent action, nor that we are simply living out various alternative political/social dramas constructed by an elite. What this means is that the concept of "truth" is "always an illusion." Truth is always a product of rhetoric, of persuasion, and as such it is always an expression of power through the use of symbols (pp. 4–5). How does this symbolism influence individual and mass behavior? McGee offers the concept of the ideograph, collections of "political language" which manifest ideology in their "capacity to dictate decision and control public belief and behavior" (p. 5). McGee argues that the ideograph controls both the elite and the populace equally when he states that "[w]hen we consider the impact of ideology on freedom, and of power on consciousness, we must be clear that ideology is transcendent, as much an influence on the belief and behavior of the ruler as on the ruled" (p. 5). Ideology as manifested in the ideograph is, in essence, a symbolic enthymeme (Bitzer, 1959). Given our existence and partici- pation in a mass consciousness, the use of a term such as "liberty" to warrant behavior such as war makes the ideograph "liberty" an enthymeme calling up an appropriate response on the part of the members of the mass conscious- ness/audience. What is important in understanding the concept of the ideo- graph is that it is more than a term or collection of terms that is used to create a "poetic myth." Ideographs call forth specific behaviors from individuals and groups and manifest themselves in material actions. Ideographs, in other words, offer justifications for behavior and help us to answer the question, Why did they do that? Ideographs are the symbols that we use (and that use us) to create our world. That created world is the only world we have, since our only way of making sense of the world is through symbols.

Both Burke and McGee focus on the role of language in influencing human behavior. Implicit in both of their theories is an understanding that existing societal structures and political organizations and theories (representative gov- ernments, capitalistic and socialistic economies, and the institutions that arise from these economies) also influence human behavior. To McGee and Burke, these structures are also symbolic constructs and induce material effects. Stuart Hall (1985) explores the interrelationship between discourse practices and socie- tal institutions by presenting us with a rereading of Louis Althusser in an attempt to better illustrate the construction of the social structure and its role in influenc- ing human behavior by symbolically constructing the human subject.

Hall argues that Althusser has offered some very important theoretical changes in understanding the practice by which social structures and social beings are determined by more than one structure (e.g., economics) and through which social structures and social beings can live with the multiple determinations of a variety of social structures. Hall asserts that Althusser is rediscovering what Marx originally stated: that while a social formation is a "structure in dominance" with certain tendencies and configurations, it is also a "complex structure in which it is impossible to reduce one level of practice to another in some easy way" (p. 91). Basically, Hall is arguing that Marx originally theorized and argued for the complexity of different material-determining factors in constructing social meaning and social structure, especially in the manner of symbol use and symbolic behavior. In other words, individuals respond to symbols in different manners at different times and under different conditions. Their socialization to symbols is not solely determined by a preexisting structure (p. 92).

Where Althusser's major advance in returning Marxism to its theoretical roots comes, Hall argues, is in his insistence on articulation as the practice of creating social and political structures that are neither dependent and determined by preexisting structures nor the completely autonomous practices of "free" individuals. Preexisting structures, such as the state or capitalism, have constraining and influencing power, but they are not necessarily determinative. That is the role of ideology, the practice of the "arbitrary" fixing of connections among structures, practices, and new structures. In terms of language theory, it is the establishment of a connection between the sign and the signified that creates social meaning. It goes beyond the Derridean practice of continually deferring the signified while acknowledging that there is no necessary connection between the signified and the sign. What Hall is calling for is the active practice of creating linkages, of articulating social practice and social identification through the political struggle of assigning meaning to symbols. Practice is the process of creating structure. Again in terms of language theory, it is the process of creating the link between the sign and the signified, of assigning meaning to a symbol, knowing that there is already a structure that has assigned meaning to this symbol, working within this structure yet not being wholly determined by this structure.

Hall and Althusser offer the possibility of changing our ideologically and symbolically constructed human behavior. We are still inhabitants of a symbolically created world, and these symbols still influence our behavior, but we also have the ability both to create new symbols and to create new behaviors for the old symbols. Burke and McGee's emphasis on language as the mechanism of articulation provides us with the start of an answer in the understanding of how cultures re-create social situations.

In better understanding this relationship among symbols, societal structures, and human beings, we are now better able to understand the arguments being presented in Gore's book. By utilizing this knowledge of the relationship among language, culture, and material practice, communication theory can help to bring about an invigorated environmental action. What those who study the relationship between symbol and society present to us who live and operate in a symbolic society are the tools necessary to create the conditions for change. Our reality is not just the product of our symbol use. It is also a product of the synthesis between material structures and practices and symbol use that reinforces and questions these structures and practices. To create change, we have to acknowledge the role that both symbol use and material practice play, and we have to adopt strategies that have an impact upon both elements. The basic tools that we as communication professionals can offer to all those who wish to create change are the tools of symbol use.

EARTH AND HUMANITY: WHAT IS THE RELATIONSHIP?

Gore presents both material and symbolic causes and results of the ecological crisis, but the tone of the overall document is rhetorical in nature. The material results of our ecological shortsightedness, according to Gore, are firmly rooted in our symbolic relationship with the earth, with each other, and with the socioeconomic structures of contemporary society. In essence, even with the material consequences of this crisis, "ecology" is presented here as a rhetorical construct, a symbolically and discursively constructed element of social and material reality. It is not "simply" a discursive construct, nor is it "simply" a material fact. The manner in which we relate to the environment is not direct. It is mediated by a number of factors, including our philosophical stance toward the place of humanity in the world, our social and economic structures that give meaning to elements of the earth such as humans, and our spiritual sense of who we are and what place we should have in the world.

An example of the manner in which humanity sees itself as disconnected from the rest of the earth can be seen in Gore's examination of the symbolic construction of "waste." In discussing the problem of increasing personal, industrial, and governmental waste, Gore argues that in our contemporary society, we have a perception of waste as useless. What is even worse is that this perception is combined with a belief that natural resources not used for commercial purposes are also "waste." Gore highlights the symbolic nature of this perception by noting our language in referring to the use of natural resources. He states that "[e]ven the words we use to describe our behavior reveal the pattern of self-deception. Take, for example, the word consumption, which implies an almost mechanical efficiency, suggesting that all traces of whatever we consume magically vanish after we use it" (p. 147). The use of the term "consumption" implies that we use a product until it's gone. But this term blinds us to the fact that when we "consume" anything we still produce waste. What's even worse in this symbolic relationship is we produce two kinds of waste: the "waste" of what we don't consume and the "waste" that is left over after we consume.

There are other "deceptions," both material and symbolic, involved in our relationship with natural resources and consumption of them. For example, Gore argues that the use of incineration in the treatment and disposal of waste is an example of deception in that we take solid waste and simply transform it into air pollution and toxic ash. There is no treatment; there is only transformation and short-term gain: the ash must still be dealt with and the air for future generations will be tainted by the process (p. 156). The treatment and disposal of waste, and our perception of the "consumption" of natural resources, are emblematic of this dysfunctional symbolic relationship with the earth. As Gore puts it, "[O]ur civilization is presently built on a matrix of interlocking economic and social activities that emphasize the constant consumption of new 'things' " (p. 160).

While the "culture of consumption" that Gore here identifies is a combination of material and symbolic behaviors, the rules that guide it are largely symbolic. It is a social structure empowered and maintained by symbolic means.[3]

Gore argues that the root cause of ongoing economic crises is a failure to understand the new relationship between humanity and nature. The old assumptions were that nothing that people could do would have a permanent effect on the world and that there was a simple and localized cause-effect relationship between human action and the environment. The new reality, however, is that humanity is now a natural force that affects the planet much as the moon affects the tides, and that all of our actions are a part of a system of interactions. There is not just a simple cause-effect relationship with a local element of the environment. The problem, however, is that our thinking is still guided and governed by the old assumption, the old master metaphor that divides us from the planet, the old image of us as smaller than the planet.

The role of metaphor is important here. To most casual users and even students of language and symbol use, a metaphor is a simple figuration, "[A] figure of speech in which a term that ordinarily designates an object or idea is used to designate a dissimilar object or idea in order to suggest comparison or analogy" (*American Heritage Electronic Dictionary*, 1990). Considered this way, a metaphor is simply a means to extend and develop an argument. Because of the role that language and other symbol use play in constructing our social reality, however, a metaphor is much more. Perry (1983) makes a similar argument. He states that we need to consider metaphor less as an addition to an argument and more as the argument itself. Metaphors, Perry argues, function to constitute people and ideas in a social reality. The metaphor creates our "truth," the same "truth" that McGee has argued is always an illusion and always "real" at the same time.

In utilizing this understanding of metaphor, Gore's development of a metaphorical relationship in which humans are smaller than or insignificant to the planet takes on new importance. What happens when we examine this metaphor? First, humans in this metaphor are seen as inhabitants of an at best indifferent world, a world that is largely (if not entirely) beyond their control and impact. Given this construction, humans are justified in any behavior that benefits humankind, regardless of its impact upon the planet. The planet does not care for humans; the planet will take care of itself. Humans are separate from the planet and therefore lack any connection to the planet. This is a relationship that in essence portrays all of humanity as temporary guests of a very beneficent host. It is as if we all were simply staying at the Planetary Hilton, eating food prepared by people we never see, having our lodgings cleaned and maintained by more people we never see, swimming in the pool that is serviced by yet more people we never see, and then simply paying a solely economic bill when it's time to move on to the Planetary Hyatt. There is no real cost other than the transfer of some form of economic counter.

Perhaps a better understanding of this metaphorical relationship will come from using yet another metaphorical relationship: the world as a well-stocked supermarket and humans as simply customers. We take whatever we want from aisle after aisle of well-stocked shelves. Those shelves are magically (or so it seems) restocked each night so that every day brings us more and better goods. We don't know where these goods come from. We never see them being produced. We simply take what we want, and once again, all it costs us is one simple economic counter. The real "cost" of what we take never appears in this metaphorical supermarket/world, because we never have to pay anything other than an economic counter. This dependence on a purely "economic" cost is a major element of what Gore sees as our dysfunctional relationship with the planet.

Isn't this just another metaphor, however? Another way to explain a perception? It is this, but it is also a fairly accurate depiction of the actual material practices that most people (especially in "advanced" Western and capitalistic countries) engage in. When we buy our products at the supermarket, we are doing just that: buying products. There is no direct interaction with the producers of the product. There is little if any knowledge of how these products came to be on the shelf. The store is stocked overnight. Trucks come from all parts of the country, with shipments from all over the globe. We have little if any knowledge as to the basic components of these products. We react to these items as products, as elements that are essentially different from ourselves, even though we are made of many of the same basic components. All we have to give for these products is a piece of paper, metal, or plastic: an economic counter for an element of the earth. This is the instantiation of the metaphor, the intersection where the metaphorical/symbolic relationship between humanity and the planet meets the material practices in which we engage.

Take it further, and we can see additional material practices that arise from this metaphorical relationship. Food is a commodity. In New York City people buy and sell and trade shares of corporations. In Chicago people buy and sell and trade food as a commodity. There is both a material and a symbolic chasm between humans as "inhabitants" of the planet and these "products" of the planet.

Another example of the manner in which symbolic constructs affect and shape the relationship between humanity and the earth can be seen in the role that economic theory plays in a number of social realms. According to Gore, classical economic theory, with its "faith" in the free-market system, is more than the official doctrine of our economic system; it is also, more importantly, the guiding perceptual filter[4] of our social life:

> The hard truth is that our economic system is partially blind. It "sees" some things and not others. It carefully measures and keeps track of the value of those things most important to buyers and sellers, such as food, clothing,

manufactured goods, work, and, indeed, money itself. But its intricate calculations often completely ignore the value of other things that are harder to buy and sell: fresh water, clean air, the beauty of the mountains, the rich diversity of life in the forest, just to name a few. In fact, the partial blindness of our current economic system is the single most powerful force behind what seem to be irrational decisions about the global environment. (p. 183)

Why is classical economic theory functioning in such a fashion, and how has this come to be? Gore offers a number of explanations. First, classical economic theory was formulated at a time when the natural resources of the earth appeared to be limitless, when economists did not feel a need to include the cost of natural resource depletion in calculating profit and loss. As a result, accounting practices used in these calculations count as profit the products constructed out of natural resources, but have no mechanism for determining the cost of waste produced in the construction process or the cost of lost natural resources. The price of obtaining the resource is a cost, but not the loss of that natural resource to the rest of the world. This accounting practice may, in fact, inflate the economic growth that we traditionally associate with the production of goods.

In addition, classical economic theories offer no method for calculating such intangibles as quality of life when figuring profit and loss. More important than this for the relationship of the economy and the ecology is the emphasis in classical economic theory on short-term consequences. According to Gore, the standard economic concept known as the "discount rate" that is used to calculate cost and benefit from the use of natural resources is heavily present-oriented. It "routinely assumes that all resources belong totally to the present generation. As a result, any value that they may have to future generations is heavily 'discounted' when compared to the value of using them up now or destroying them to make way for something else" (p. 191).

Although he offers few specific details here for remedying this situation, Gore argues that at the least we need to find some way to figure into the calculations such intangibles as quality of life. More important, we need to find some way to reduce the emphasis on short-term gains at the expense of long-term consequences, a practice Gore sees taking hold in at least some businesses and industries. In essence, we need to redefine what the term "progress"[5] means to contemporary society.

The role of classical economic theory as outlined by Gore functions as a Burkeian terministic screen. Screening the planet through the frame of a classic capitalist economy creates a world and humans that function according to the rules of that frame. Because this is not just one possible frame, but is instead the dominant frame, this screen offers not a perspective but a reality. This reality puts entirely different demands upon those people who wish to live in a different world. Basically, because capitalistic economic thinking is the dominant frame, people who oppose this reality are given two choices, neither of which is very attractive.

To oppose this screen requires that people either adopt the terminology, thinking, and practices of the screen (change the system from within) or create a new terministic screen from which reality may be created. Operating within this dominant system of symbolic and material relationships, while apparently easier, is fraught with dangers. To dispute with the system from within it requires the use of its symbols. The use of these symbols, unless it is managed carefully (and even then), has the possibility of reifying and strengthening the power of the dominant symbol system. Despite all postmodern protestations, it is not a simple matter of asserting that there is no necessary relationship between a symbol and a referent. Within a dominant symbol system, there is a necessary relationship. It is the relationship that has been developed over time, strengthened through actual practice, and supported by the internal logic of the dominant system. This dominant symbol system exists, and it has an impact upon those people operating within it.

The other alternative, to create a new (or re-create an old) symbol system, is also difficult. At the simplest level, it is necessary to construct the new screen, complete with its own history, practices, and internal logic, and then, in a sense, make people utilize or at least understand the new screen. This is the practice of articulation that Hall and Althusser call for, but it is also important to remember the warnings that come with that call. The current dominant symbol system will resist the change. It is not simply a matter of changing the symbols.

Another example of the manner in which symbolic communication has affected and shaped the relationship between the earth and humanity is found in the development of communication technologies. As Gore notes, it is not only the content of symbolic communication that influences human behavior, it is also the form in which this content is presented. He states that "information technology, like any technology, mediates our relationship to whatever we describe with it, because in the process of trying to capture the full meaning of a real phenomenon in a symbolic representation, we leave some features out and, by selective inclusion, distort the significance of others" (p. 202). For example, he continues, the use of the spoken word tends to reduce the distinction between the symbol and the thing referred to and reduces to direct experience what should be a far more complex referent.

He draws an analogy from this relationship between communication technologies and our relationship to nature. Just as communication can reduce a complex concept to a symbol, our understanding of nature as little more than a convenient place to find resources for consumption has reduced the feeling of reverence and awe that people once had for the natural world. As Gore puts it, "This is a primary reason that so many people now view the natural world merely as a collection of resources; indeed, to some people nature is like a giant data bank that they can manipulate at will" (p. 203). What's more, he adds, is that this reduction of nature to an object of manipulation is connected to (and simultaneously also influenced by) our belief in the scientific method—our ability to take a complex system, break it down into component parts, analyze these parts, and then understand (and improve) the whole system. Because of these intertwined symbolic responses to nature, we are unable to grasp the seriousness of the ecological crisis.

All of these symbolic relationships that humans have with nature, with our understanding of the ecology, and with our understanding of the place of humanity in the natural world are competing symbolic constructions, competing to be understood as the defining element of human existence. As Gore notes, "At the heart of every human society is a web of stories that attempt to answer our most basic questions: Who are we and why are we here?"[6] (p. 216). Gore offers a summary of some of these narratives that are used to define our existence and our relationship with the planet.

One narrative is that offered by a group of ecologically minded people Gore identifies as the "deep ecologists," those people who make up the membership of such groups as Earth First! This narrative views human beings as an unnatural part of the earth, as "pathogens" invading what would otherwise be a healthy body. Gore dismisses this metaphor as flawed in its inability to place humanity in any sort of positive or even necessary relationship with the earth. This is a narrative that has no possible happy or even workable conclusion.

Opposed to this narrative is the more familiar Cartesian narrative that depicts humanity as separate from the earth, as relating to nature only through an act of intellect. When we are separated from the earth in such a fashion, Gore argues, we search for a way to reconnect ourselves, and that way, because of our belief in a fundamental separation, becomes a dysfunctional relationship. Under the influence of the Cartesian narrative, our relationship to the earth can be seen only through the consumption of nature. Gore terms this relationship an "addiction," stating that

> our civilization is, in effect, addicted to the consumption of the earth itself. This addictive relationship distracts us from the pain of what we have lost: a direct experience of our connection to the vividness, vibrancy, and aliveness of the rest of the natural world. The froth and frenzy of industrial civilization mask our deep loneliness for that communion with the world that can lift our spirits and fill our senses with the richness and immediacy of life itself. (pp. 220–221)

This addictive relationship can be understood by yet another metaphor, Gore argues, that of the dysfunctional family. Just as families become dysfunctional when there is a gap between the internalized and traditional rules and a new situation, our consumer civilization suffers from a gap between our adherence to the Cartesian separation of the mind and the body (the rule) and the increasingly evident deterioration of the environment (the new situation). And the cycle continues. Dysfunctional families remain dysfunctional because of the near impossibility of questioning the rules. As Gore puts it, "[A]s in a dysfunctional family, one of the rules in a dysfunctional civilization is that you don't question the rules" (p. 230).

In this use of the metaphor of the dysfunctional family, we are able to see once again the power that symbolic construction has over our material actions. If this metaphor is a dominant one in shaping our relationship to the planet, as Gore suggests and as his evidence seems to support, then we are also once again left with two unattractive options. To operate within the narrative framework of the metaphor of the dysfunctional family is to continue both with this flawed narrative and with its material implications. The narrative provides us with the means to operate in the world, and those means are both symbolically and materially defeating. If we do not question the rules, the narrative cycle cannot be broken, and the material practices, the "consumption" of the earth, will continue unquestioned as well.

The other alternative, the creation and use of a new metaphor, contains all of the problems inherent in attempting to replace the terministic screen of the capitalist economy with a new screen. The other metaphors Gore cites, those of "people as pathogens" and "people as separate," are as flawed as the dysfunctional family metaphor.

What can we do about this flawed narrative? How can we repair the dysfunctional symbolic relationship that we have with the planet? The beginning of the solution, according to Gore, can be found in what he terms an "environmentalism of the spirit." Environmentalism of the spirit begins with the construction of a new perspective from which we can then view our relationship to the earth. This new perspective is built from a rereading of the traditional Judeo-Christian concept of stewardship (though Gore notes that similar concepts are found in nearly all major religious thought). In this perspective, stewardship is not just the simple relationship that places humanity in charge of the planet and all its resources—it is also a relationship of equality, care, and nurturance:

> Specifically, followers of this tradition are charged with the duty of stewardship, because the same biblical passage that grants them "dominion" also requires them to "care for" the earth even as they "work" it. The requirement of stewardship and its grant of dominion are not in conflict; in recognizing the sacredness of creation, believers are called upon to remember that even as they "till" the earth they must also "keep" it. (p. 243)

This reading of the concept of stewardship is at odds with the standard interpretations of the term, however, and has been lost by two conflicting interpretations that attempt to separate care from dominion. Gore argues that "politically conservative theologians and clergy," a group that would normally be in support of a traditional interpretation of the biblical concept of steward-ship, have been diverted from this interpretation because it has been linked with more politically liberal philosophies, such as statism and the removal from individual use of public property (p. 246).

At the same time, those who identify with a more liberal concept of Christi-anity, under such headings as the Social Gospel, have been more focused on the immediate and direct personal sufferings of human beings, those people Gore describes as "the poor, the powerless, the sick and frail, the victims of discrimi-nation and hatred, the forgotten human fodder chewed up by the cogs of industrial civilization" (p. 246). In this perspective, issues such as environmen-talism and the concept of stewardship, seen as long-term issues, have received less attention. Gore observes that "as an issue, 'the environment' sometimes seems far from the more palpable sins of social injustice" (p. 246).

Underlying all of this, creating an even wider schism between humanity and the planet, is the overriding belief in the separation of the mind and the body, the intellect and the physical world. This is the major symbolic relationship that has permitted, Gore argues, the wanton destruction of the environment. So long as we view ourselves as separate from the planet, we will continue to view the planet as just another stockpile of resources for our personal enrichment: "We have misunderstood who we are, how we relate to our place within creation, and why our very existence assigns us a duty of moral alertness to the conse-quences of what we do. A civilization that believes itself to be separate from the world may pretend not to hear, but there is indeed a sound when a tree falls in the forest" (p. 258).

CONCLUSIONS

Gore presents us with a compelling illustration of the symbolic construction of reality, of humans as agents and as constructs, and of the material effects of symbolism. Many may differ with Gore's specific political proposals, and many may also find flaws in his use of evidence. That is not what is at issue here. The essence of Gore's argument is that, as McGee and Burke have already noted, we live in a symbolically created world. The only meaningful relationship we can have with the material world is through symbol use. What Gore argues in his book is that we are playing out a no-win game by our failure to understand our symbolic relationship with the earth. The rules of the game have changed, as far as the planet is concerned. The problem is that we are still playing according to the old symbols and the old relationship in which we are placed by these symbols. Until we acknowledge the interdependence of the symbolic and the material, until we acknowledge that our symbols control our relationship with the material, and until we acknowledge that we can play an active role in the creation of new symbols and the reinterpretation of old, we will continue the degradation of the planet. No environmental program, no recycling campaign, no search for an alternative energy source—nothing will have an impact on the environment until our symbolic relationship with the planet is changed.

What can we learn from our analysis of this text, from our better understanding of the relationship between the symbolic and the material world? We learn that we cannot continue to separate the two, to believe that there is no relationship between the symbols that we use (and that use us) and the material world in which we live. There is no such thing as "mere" rhetoric. The language that we use is the only tool that we have for creating the material structures and practices by which we can change and improve the material world. If we are unable to correct the current dysfunctional relationship between the symbolic and the material or to create a better, more functional relationship, then there can be no material changes to the material world.

What both Gore and scholars such as Burke, McGee, Hall, and Althusser tell us is that we must practice symbolic change at the same time we work toward material change. Despite all the difficulties in creating (or renewing) a more positive symbol system for the relationship between humanity and the planet, that work must occur. To continue to operate within the current symbolic relationship will not allow real material change.

The battle over the environment is first and foremost a battle for the power to name. The winner in this battle sets the rules for the battle, the place for the battle, and the means by which a "winner" can be declared. If those who wish to create a more functional relationship between the earth and humanity fail to acknowledge the importance of the symbols that are used or fail to gain control of those symbols, then the earth and humanity will be left in the hands of those who have helped to create the dysfunction in the first place. This chapter cannot provide an explicit manual for how this change can be accomplished. But change is possible. We do not live in a world that operates without the consent of those who constructed it. Both the current symbolic relationship and the societal structures that have been created by this relationship and that help to maintain this relationship are the product of human action, and human action can alter this relationship. If there is one lesson to be learned from this analysis, it is this: The control of symbols is the control of social reality and the ability to make material consequences. Ignore rhetoric at your own (and the planet's) risk.

NOTES

1. The use of the term "balance" in the title offers a first illustration of the manner in which symbols influence and constrain interpretation. This term controls the structure and interpretation of all the findings in this book. The influence of this term, the belief in balance and equilibrium and homeostasis, makes any deviation seem wrong, if not sinister. If the term

"transition" had been substituted in the place of "balance," as in *Earth in Transition*, the entire tone of the book would be different, and the sense of crisis evoked by all these deviations would not be the same.

2. Throughout this chapter, a number of terms are used that depict the symbolic relationship between humanity and the planet. These terms include "metaphor," "narrative," "symbolic construct," "symbolic system," and "rhetorical construct" among others. It is not my intention to confuse readers, nor is it my desire to deny special meaning to specific terms within and outside of the communication discipline. But it is my contention that these terms all describe the same basic theoretical principle: the manner in which language and other symbols are used by people and the manner in which language and other symbols use people and create a social reality that functions as a material reality. Whether one wishes to call it a metaphor, a narrative, constitutive rhetoric, or an ideograph, these terms all describe the same basic phenomenon. The purpose of this chapter is not to argue for one set of preferred terminologies over another. While I am aware of the distinctions between these various approaches, I would argue that the similarities, especially for the purposes of this chapter, outweigh the distinctions. Those who are interested in the distinctions will find ample material elsewhere. I suggest starting with the following: Charland (1990); Cherwitz and Hikins (1990); Mailloux (1985); McKerrow (1989); W. Fisher (1987); Osborn (1967); Cox (1990); and Scott (1967, 1976).

3. Note the similarities here between Gore's description of the "culture of consumption" as an interlocking set of symbolic and structural elements and Hall and Althusser's earlier description of the role of social structures in constructing the human subject and in constraining human behavior.

4. For a very interesting discussion of the role of economic theory functioning as a terministic screen in other aspects of human relationships, see Posner (1992). His discussion of the Pareto concept in economic theory is especially insightful concerning Gore's call for a reconsideration of short-term and long-term cost-benefit analyses.

5. The use of the term "progress" as a justification for certain behavior, and even as a prompt for certain behavior, is an instantiation of McGee's concept of the ideograph. Richard Weaver has also written on the power of this specific term, progress, to call forth specific behaviors and responses (see Weaver, 1953, especially Chap. 9).

6. Gore's invocation of the term "narrative" as a method for explaining human behavior on a group and individual level is a familiar call for contemporary rhetoricians. Walter Fisher (1987) provides perhaps the best-known exploration of narrative in contemporary rhetorical theory. Perhaps most important for an understanding of narrative in the manner in which Gore is using the term is Fisher's concept of narrative rationality, which he defies as the process by which we decide which possible narrations, which possible constructions of the world and our place in it, make the best sense for us as individuals (p. 88).

CHAPTER EIGHT

Challenging the Dominion Covenant: The Preservationist Construction of an Environmental Past

Thomas R. Flynn

SINCE THE TURN of the century, American environmental policy and practice have been dominated by conservationism, a utilitarian ideology that perceives the physical world as a set of finite economic resources to be used in an efficient manner. With the emergence of the ecological crisis in the 1970s, the social dominance of conservationism has been challenged by preservationists,[1] who argue that economic and technological expediency can no longer be permitted to dominate environmental policy. Articulating an alternative perception of the relationship between society and the environment, preservationists seek to expand the range of values that inform environmental decision making to include aesthetic, historic, and ecological concerns and to bring about a corresponding change in social practice.

As communication scholars turn their attention to environmental discourse, we can anticipate the critical examination of legal and scientific discourses due to their centrality to the ongoing political maneuver that constitutes much of this current debate (for example, see Killingsworth & Palmer, 1992; Killingsworth & Steffens, 1989; Miller, 1981, 1984). While not as publicly prominent in this controversy, the significance and potential impact of historical discourse in bringing about public empowerment and change in environmental policy cannot be underestimated. A nation's historical consciousness constitutes "a consensus through time" which acts to reproduce a sequential social structure. As such, this consciousness is ideologically important because it shapes that culture's sense of identity (Kammen, 1991, p. 13). Cultural identity, produced through the articulation of past social reality, directs that society's recognition of (1) what has been and is "real," (2) its traditional norms and values, and (3) its sense of what is possible (Therborn, 1980, p. 18). This sense of identity, therefore, outlines the parameters of what is and is not acceptable. Social movements seeking change must engage in discourse that appears consistent with a society's sense of values and norms of behavior. Change that appears to violate these parameters is likely to be rejected as threatening social stability. Historical discourse presents a means by which social movements may transcend the parameters of present social practice by grounding their dialogue in the "historio-rhetorical mainstream of American social and political values" (Lentricchia, 1983, p. 33). By rooting itself firmly in the cultural milieu, such historical interpretation may self-consciously conserve social values while acting to negate those values that impede social change.

As such, historical discourse must be conceived not as merely a neutral vehicle that diffuses facts about the past,[2] but rather as a rhetorical form that converts perceived past reality into support for a particular vision of social order. Historical narratives represent material instantiations of ideology through which systems of social meaning are constructed, functioning as legitimating devices to create a "politically motivated production" of a particular perception of the past that may either affirm or subvert hegemonic social interests (Mumby, 1987, pp. 114, 119). Historical interpretations may articulate a conservative or orthodox perspective which represents the dominant social order as constituting the "natural order of things," past and present (Mumby, 1987, pp. 113–114). Other historical works may seek to bring about social change by contradicting or challenging dominant social assumptions through the articulation of an alternative value system. This divergence from dominant social assumptions and practices is motivated by the perceived unacceptable nature of present circumstances, the current ecological crisis for example, which renders a particular vision of social order and practice untenable. This results in the desire to alter the normative doctrines which shape the status quo through an altered understanding of the past. Historical discourse seeking social change, therefore, consists of language which, through its interpretation of the past, seeks to alter the hierarchy of values, assumptions, and ideas that dominate society so as to change the structure or direction of that society.

This chapter examines the ideological function of historical interpretation through the critical analysis of Frank Graham's (1978) *The Adirondack Park: A Political History*, focusing particularly on the question of how it constructs a particular interpretation of the past in support of a preservationist vision of social environmental practice. Graham's work traces the history of the Adirondack Mountains from their early exploration, through a long period of economic exploitation and environmental degradation, to their eventual protection by the "forever wild" clause of the New York State Constitution, which established the Adirondack Park. Graham believes that the unique means by which the lands within the Adirondack Park are protected present an object lesson to the present environmental debate. Graham contrasts what he perceives as the positive experience of the Adirondack Park under a preservationist model of wilderness protection with the conservationist-oriented practice of the National Park System and the national forests managed by the U.S. Forest Service, which he perceives to have been a failure. In short, Graham's history of the Adirondacks functions as an indictment of conservationism as inherently incapable of protecting American wilderness from economic exploitation, and he seeks to introduce an alternative ethic to direct social environmental practice.

The following sections provide context and a theoretical grounding for this analysis by (1) tracing the development of Western environmental practice and (2) examining the emergence of the current struggle concerning the nature and direction of that social practice. Next, based in the dramatistic theory of Kenneth Burke, the chapter identifies the questions directing this analysis and proposes an eclectic approach to these questions. This approach is then applied to the "preservationist" interpretation of the history of the Adirondack Park. Finally, the chapter concludes by offering social and rhetorical implications.

CONTEXT

The Dominion Covenant and Environmental Practice

All societies produce ideologies, which in turn act to facilitate cultural reproduction by serving as a template for the organization of society (Geertz, 1973, p. 220). Ideologies act not only to interpret and reflect social reality, but also to construct a preferred vision of that reality (Berger & Luckman, 1966, pp. 122–124). Social order is established and maintained when a particular set of values and beliefs becomes dominant. This ideological dominance, or hegemony (Gramsci, 1971, pp. 12–13, 80), is the result of a particular social group's success in persuading others as to the validity of its particular worldview. This worldview may permeate a society's collective consciousness to such an extent that its particular vision is considered objective reality and the natural order of things.

As with any body of social practice, the distinct behavioral patterns that mark our conception of the relationship between nature and society are culturally bound. In his seminal article, "The Historical Roots of Our Ecological Crisis," Lynn White (1973, p. 25) argued that the environmental practices developed by Western culture are derived from the Judeo-Christian conception of creation. This conception holds that since humanity was made in God's image, we share in God's transcendence of nature; it established the belief that we are separate from and hold dominion over nature. In short, it was God's purpose that we should use and enjoy the resources that nature and the earth provide.[3] Environmental practices developed slowly, however. The perceived purpose of life in early Christianity embodied a spiritual concept of progress, in which one moved through time toward eternal salvation. This spiritual conception of progress did not give way to a secular vision of the eventual perfection of human material existence for nearly a millennium.

The transition to a material perspective found culmination in the optimistic rationalism of Bacon (1960, pp. 87–89) and Descartes (1967, p. 119), which expressed the hope that the passage of time would witness increased material benefits through the application of scientific knowledge to the physical world. In addition to the development of science and technology, the emergence of capitalism completed the transition from pastoral, to agrarian, to commercial society. Under the market system, nature came to be perceived as potential instruments of wealth: as property, as natural resources to be used as one saw fit, or, in the case of water and air, as "free goods," objects without economic costs for use without regard to their purity or maintenance (Dahlberg, Soroos, Feraru, Harf, & Trout, 1985, p. 8).

The cultural dynamism of emergent science, technology, and capitalism and their concurrent impact on the environment have been clear since the Industrial Revolution, as forests have been decimated, resources depleted, and rivers, oceans, and the air increasingly polluted. Dahlberg et al. argue that any remaining cultural inhibitions, such as the frugality of the Protestant ethic, that may have "provided some restraint upon . . . the excessive use of resources" have been further weakened by "rampant individualism . . . advertising and consumerism" (p. 8).

The rapid population increases and urbanization brought about by industrialization resulted in an emerging nineteenth century social concern over public health issues and resource exhaustion. From 1890 through the turn of the century, early "environmentalists" in Europe and the United States proposed addressing these pollution problems in utilitarian terms, in short, by the "same principles of rational 'scientific' efficiency" that had governed mass industrialization (Petulla, 1987, p. 36). The primary American response to the environmental challenge from the late nineteenth century through the 1960s was an "economic perspective . . . broadly called the utilitarian approach to conservation," otherwise known as conservationism (Petulla, 1980, p. 26). Gifford Pinchot, recognized as the embodiment of early economic conservationism, declared in 1910 that conservation stood for "development," referring not only to the "husbanding of resources for future generations . . . but the use of natural resources . . . for the benefit of the people who live here now" (Pinchot, 1968, pp. 59–61). The premises of conservationism led to the creation, under Theodore Roosevelt, of the first federal programs and bureaucracies concerned with environmental issues, but pollution control and environmental management were left to regional agencies and to the state and local governments. Little emphasis was given to the protection of the quality of water and air, the preservation of wilderness, or even to the "protection of human health," as the nation's environmental policy at these various levels continued to emphasize the "efficient use of natural resources" (Petulla, 1987, p. 39). Because of conservationism, federal intervention into a variety of environmental problems would not begin until the 1970s, when rapid population growth, increased water and air pollution, and faster consumption of resources brought about greater national awareness of an apparent crisis.

Conservationism versus Preservationism

The current environmental debate, at its most fundamental level, represents a clash between opposing ideologies based in divergent perceptions of nature: the economic perspective of conservationism versus preservationism, which asserts that nature possesses a value unto itself. The emergence of the environmental crisis in the early 1970s raised questions among the attentive public as to the efficacy of an environmental policy dominated by conservationism. To many, this crisis demonstrated that "trusting in conservation alone would not enable us to survive indefinitely in surroundings which were growing more dangerous, ugly, and impoverished" (Scheffer, 1991, p. 3). In the 1970s, therefore, preservationism emerged as a strong alternative with widespread support among the American public. Grounding their argument in "the wilderness ethic," preservationists claimed "that nature has rights of its own, that it is good in and of itself, independent of its resource value" (Killingsworth & Palmer, 1992, p. 24).

What has come to be known as the modern environmental movement represents the rhetorical echo and popular emergence of the socially marginalized wilderness preservation movement of the nineteenth century. Adherents of this movement perceived the "value of nature" to reside in its ability to act "as the ultimate restorer and purifier of a humanity corrupted by civilization" (Petulla, 1980, p. 228). They were not so much interested in conserving the forests for utilitarian concerns, as they were in "preserving wilderness areas, which possess their own aesthetic, spiritual and moral values" (Petulla, 1978, p. 228). While the rhetoric of the nineteenth-century wilderness preservation movement gained no widespread public resonance in their era, the "high-minded transcendentalism of Thoreau, Muir, and their followers . . . came to serve the interests of the growing environmental consciousness of consumers" who "sought healthy environments in which to live and pristine environments into which they could escape from the routine grind of urban, industrial life" (Killingsworth & Palmer, 1992, p. 24).

The emergence of preservationism in the 1970s as the embodiment of public environmental values represents more than just a reawakening of the historical enmity between conservationists and preservationists, but rather a challenge issued by public advocacy groups such as the Sierra Club, the Wilderness Society, Greenpeace, and the Adirondack Mountain Club to the expert cultures of business, science, technology, and government that have dominated environmental decision making.[4] On one side of this struggle, leaders of government, business, science, and technology, preoccupied with economic growth, argue that environmental remediation will be brought about through market forces and technological innovation. Environmentalists, on the other hand, seek protection of endangered ecosystems, regardless of its economic consequences. Environmental advocates argue that effective remediation of the current crisis is impossible without both meaningful public participation in the formulation of environmental policy and an expansion of the value system that informs that policy. At its most fundamental level, the environmental debate represents the clash of divergent visions of the fundamental purpose of the natural world and society's relationship to that world. At stake in this debate is the question of the direction and control of future environmental policy.

CRITICAL PERSPECTIVE

Historical controversy is evidence of cultural struggle, involving the clash of opposing ideologies in which different visions of social order compete for cultural dominance. The critical examination of historical discourse, therefore, necessitates that attention be given to these questions: (1) How does a particular ideology inform the historical narrative's construction of past reality? and (2) How does that historical interpretation "function" ideologically? That is to say, how does its language act to influence collective historical consciousness through the articulation of a particular vision of past reality?

The instantiation of Burke's theories into the field of speech communication resulted in sweeping changes in the field's conception of the purpose and scope of rhetoric. Most significantly, the social power of rhetoric came to be seen as residing in the motivational power of symbolic form. Rhetorical critics came to realize that the forms that organize culture are not expressed in language, but rather that "social order is performed in language" (Klumpp & Hollihan, 1989, pp. 88–91) and that to recognize the "social significance of a work" the critic should focus "with all possible emphasis" on how a text "acts" (Lentricchia, 1983, p. 9). Motives are definitions of situations that express attitudes about reality and that serve as justifications for actions. Language, therefore, provides the means by which social life is organized.

Because society and beliefs are constructed through language, Burkeian criticism focuses on the way language induces the cooperation of an audience through the distorting or mystifying properties of language, which Burke refers to as the "resources of ambiguity." Criticism operates as a process of demystification, seeking to expose the mysteries and ambiguities contained within a particular discourse's terministic screen. Taking the inherent ambiguity of language as a starting point, Burkeian analysis engages in the systematic analysis of clusters or cycles of terms that are used again and again. Looking for terms that demonstrate a coherent pattern, we gain access to an inherent body of attitudes, values, and behaviors that serves to direct or inform that symbol usage, demonstrating the manner in which ideologies establish premises that structure a statement on social reality. By identifying these language patterns, we gain insight into the vision of society implied by that language. The attractiveness of this approach to criticism resides in the attention that it focuses on the rhetorical functioning of language.

This paper employs several terms from Burke's (1966, p. 54) concept of dramatistic screens—hierarchy/order, disorder, guilt, and purification—to analyze Graham's interpretation of past reality. Contained within discourse employed to describe social reality are statements which serve as "principles of governance." These statements operate as commandments, establishing exactly what does and does not constitute obedience to the preferred hierarchy. By identifying the principles that inform a vision of order, the critic is able to trace the manner in which the negativistic principle of guilt combines with the sacrificial principle of victimage, providing insight into that text's causes of disorder and its implicit remedies for the reestablishment of order (Burke, 1970, p. 314). By doing so, the critic is able to determine how a particular ideology informs the construction of past reality and how that historical interpretation functions ideologically to create support for a particular vision of social order.

RHETORICAL ANALYSIS

Analyzing Graham's vision of the past reveals the manner in which preservationism informs this historical interpretation and in which it creates support for a particular vision of social order. Contained within Graham's discourse describing past reality are statements that constitute the ontological and axiological foundations of his interpretation. The principles of governance contained within Graham's *The Adirondack Park: A Political History* are as follows:

1. The natural world possesses value beyond that of economic resource.

2. The economic perception of nature and the resultant social practice have created an environmental disaster.

3. Due to its subservience to the economic imperative, conservationism is unable to protect remaining American wilderness.

4. The history of the Adirondack Park demonstrates the efficacy of a preservationist model of wilderness protection.

The focus here will be to demonstrate briefly how these principles of governance (1) inform Graham's vision of order, (2) establish the means by which this interpretation perceives disorder, (3) attribute guilt for that disorder, and (4) construct the parameters of a preferred social order.

Hierarchy/Order

Graham's vision of order resides in society's need to maintain what he refers to as "a wilderness option" in reaction to encroaching civilization. Graham (1978, pp. 18–22) traces the development of the preservationist ethic as it parallels the history of the Adirondack Park. He finds support for his vision of order in the transcendentalists and also acknowledges the influence of George Marsh's concepts of man and nature in the ultimate establishment of the park (pp. 67–78) and of Aldo Leopold's "philosophy of wilderness," which led him to seek the establishment of "wilderness preservation areas in the national forests" (p. 103). Leopold's philosophy, according to Graham, asserts nature as a value unto itself. Graham writes that Leopold postulated "the 'rights' of the land as well as the animals and plants that lived on it," seeking to create "an ecological conscience in his fellow human beings" organized around "his ideas about wilderness" (p. 182).

Graham's assertion of nature's transcendent value reveals the first rhetorical function of his vision to be mystification. Mystery is a rhetorical quality infusing language, which seeks "to encompass conflicting orders of motivation . . . by finding a place for it in a developmental series" (Burke, 1950, p. 189). Mystification provides a "major source of persuasion," in that once an idea, person, or institution has been endowed with mystery, "you have set up a motivational appeal to which people spontaneously ('instinctively,' 'intuitively') respond" (Burke, 1952, p. 105). By establishing nature as the dominant term in his hierarchical vision, Graham elevates the value of nature to the status of "whatever is desirable for its own sake" (Burke, 1969, p. 292). His doing so also functions to place competing perceptions of nature, such as the economic, into a subordinate position in this hierarchical sequence. This rhetorical function plays out in three ways. First, Graham's history asserts that wilderness is an essential element of the American ethos, the preservation of which is necessary to the continued viability of our national identity. This assertion "acts" to elevate preservation beyond mere instrumental action to a spiritual necessity. Second, the transcendent value of nature functions to dominate the competing economic perception of nature, allowing Graham's interpretation to subsume particular material concerns, such as questions of property rights and the need for economic development. Third, the transcendent value of nature serves as the lens directing Graham's perception and evaluation of the environmental crisis, providing the means through which his historical interpretation establishes the causes and attributes the guilt for that disorder.

Graham firmly roots the transcendent value of nature in the mainstream of American social values, by establishing a connection between the development of the American identity and the wilderness. Immersion in the wilderness was perceived to have been the defining experience of the development of a distinctly American ethos. Perceived to be the first quintessentially American hero, James Fenimore Cooper's Natty Bumppo emerged as a "symbol of purity and excellence" due to his "lifetime exposure to the wholesomeness of the wilderness, separated from the evil habits of civilized [still European] settlers" (Petulla, 1978, p. 229). By intertwining American "rugged individualism" with the preservation of wilderness areas, Graham offers a compelling spiritual argument that elevates preservation beyond the level of instrumental action to the expression of American substance or identity. From a dramatistic perspective, Burke argues that "the connotations of 'to act' strategically overlap upon the connotations of 'to be' "; therefore, "action is not merely a means of doing but a way of being. And a way of being is substantial, not instrumental" (Burke, 1969, p. 310).

This rooting of the value of nature in the American ethic is significant for two reasons. First, if the value of nature is absolute and perceived to be an element of national identity, this value transcends material concerns. This enables Graham's interpretation to sublimate or subsume those aspects of preservationism that are perceived to clash with other American values, the most significant of which is the right of landowners to do what they wish with their property. Discussing a range of legal battles over this issue, Graham indicates that for the Adirondack Park Agency (APA), one of its "most satisfying victories came on a challenge to its authority to regulate on aesthetic grounds" (1978, p. 272). The court ruled that "aesthetic considerations alone generate a sufficient impact on the public welfare" to warrant regulation, arguing that because the Adirondack Park existed as a "unique and natural area," to act "to preserve the aesthetic and scenic value of the park" was by no means unreasonable (p. 273). Graham concludes, "That was exactly what the framers of the APA Act had in mind" (p. 275): the protection of the Adirondack Park from those "arrogant" and "purely selfish individuals," driven by an economic imperative, who would disregard the broader public interest and, in this case, the right of the citizens of the state of New York to a secure and aesthetically intact wilderness. By establishing nature as ascendant, through mystification, Graham's interpretation acts to subordinate those material or economic questions wherein preservationism might be perceived to contradict American values.

The second reason that the rooting of the value of nature in the American ethic is significant is the manner in which it establishes a perceptual lens that acts to evaluate "all policies in terms of means and ends alone" (Burke, 1969, p. 309). As such, the absolute value of nature serves as the criterion by which to evaluate the acts of significant agents and agencies within the historical drama constructed in Graham's interpretation. From this perspective, then, Graham perceives the causes of environmental degradation, attributes guilt for that disorder, and establishes parameters for a renewed social order.

Disorder

The Adirondack Mountains experienced a period of rapacious exploitation and environmental degradation between the 1850s and the early 1900s, a period that Graham (1978) characterizes as "the great age of extermination" (p. 22). By the 1850s, the "lumbermen were now dominant in the Adirondacks," having "pushed through the mountains" to cut into the "great primeval forest" (p. 15). Typically, the timber companies, after buying "the land cheap from the original speculators, . . . logged it, then let the ruins revert to the state for taxes" (p. 15). In addition to the lumbermen, the "charcoal industry had clear-cut vast areas . . . to fire the kilns of the local iron foundries" (p. 66). The tanneries had so depleted the area's stands of hemlock, a resource necessary to tanning, that the industry collapsed. Farmers seeking to plant crops in the "thin rocky soil" contributed to "the erosion that followed everywhere in the wake of the lumberman" (p. 67).

The advent of the Civil War spurred more rapid industrial growth, leading the timber interests to harvest "everything they could reach" (pp. 66–67). By the 1870s, much of New York State's forests had been "cut over or burned" and "abandoned by the owners" as "devastating fires swept over the carelessly cut woodlands" (pp. 74–75). The resulting erosion filled the once clear Adirondack streams with "malignant and deadly matter" (p. 104). In 1885, the New York state legislature reported that the Adirondack region had been reduced by "timber thieves, the lumbermen, and the railroads" to "an unproductive and dangerous desert" (p. 104). Graham indicates that by as early as the 1870s, with the demands of industry and the growing onslaught of tourists, what had been the "great northern wilderness" only a few years before was rapidly disappearing, as the "exploiters of the natural world" exhausted its supplies and as the "rusticators [campers] themselves" destroyed "the wilderness they came to find" (pp. 64–65).

The environmental disaster that constitutes the history of the Adirondacks in this period, writes Graham, neatly illustrates the fundamental question facing policy toward our remaining wilderness areas: "How can the wilderness . . . be preserved while at the same time making wilderness and its potential values accessible to a large public?" (p. 30). Contained within Graham's response to this question are the means by which his interpretation attributes guilt and reestablishes its vision of order through purification.

Guilt

Disobedience to the commands of hierarchy/order results in disorder and guilt, the realization that the principles which organize and direct a particular vision of order have been compromised. The recognition of disorder necessitates identifying the sources of disorder and the attribution of guilt (Burke, 1970, p. 314). Examination of the Burkeian concept of guilt, more fully than any other concept, reveals the manner in which Graham's preservationist interpretation functions ideologically. This chapter argues that disorder, in Graham's account, is constituted not only in the environmental disaster of the early industrial age, but in the continued acceptance of economic utilitarianism as the social lens through which nature is to be perceived in light of that disaster.

Since Graham seeks to alter present environmental practice through the negation of economic utilitarianism, the guilt must be attributed not only to past acts of environmental degradation, but to those present policies and bureaucracies based in economic utilitarianism as well. Graham's interpretation accomplishes this by equating the conscious environmental exploitation by commercial interests with the failure of conservationism to prevent that exploitation. Graham compares the development of the National Park System under conservationism with the experience of the Adirondack Park as protected by the "forever wild" clause of the New York State Constitution, which established in 1894 that state lands within the park were to be left as wild forest. This clause was expanded by the Adirondack Park Agency Act of 1971, which established a unified park of both public and private lands. Through this discussion, Graham identifies conservationism as the source of our current ecological crisis, for having created the illusion that the natural world can be "rationally" managed from an economic perspective. Conservationism is perceived to be inherently flawed because of its subservience to the economic imperative and because of the degree to which conservationist policy is open to political pressure and manipulation. These fatal flaws are best illustrated through the following two examples.

The first involves attempts by Pinchot's followers in 1895 to relax the "forever wild" clause to allow the resumption of forestry on state lands in the Adirondacks. Speaking in favor of this position, then Governor Frank Black argued that the state could sell timber, "reap a large revenue for itself, and still retain the woods" (Graham, 1978, p. 151). The Adirondacks would be protected through "scientific forestry." A state college of forestry was established under Bernhard Fernow, who perceived the duty of the school as the "utilization of the soil for the production of wood crops, and thereby of the highest revenue obtainable" (p. 153). Graham argues that the experiment was "doomed from the onset" (p. 152). The experiment in scientific forestry established a partnership between the Brooklyn Cooperage Company, which built wood alcohol and barrel-stave plants near the college, and a college-owned spruce nursery. The contract signed by Fernow resulted in his being forced to deliver "twice as much wood as he had planned each year, thus defeating his aim to operate the forest on a sustained-yield basis" (p. 152). The college was quickly beset by financial problems which led the state legislature to "condemn both present and prospective results" (p. 153). The experiment in scientific forestry reintroduced "aggressive cutting practices" into the Adirondacks, contributing to the outbreak of fire on the overcut college lands which quickly spread through the surrounding mountains (p. 153).

"The lesson was clear to preservationists all over the state," writes Graham: the Adirondacks' forest preserves must be "protected against the woodsman, under whatever guise he appeared" (p. 155). The "great experiment . . . failed to prove that scientific forestry could pay," rendering its fundamental premise—sustainability—invalid (p. 155). Greed, argues Graham, would always lead to overexploitation. Contributing further to the flawed nature of conservationism, in his perception, has been "the low reputation" of the politicians and bureaucrats charged with the administration of the decision-making process. Under conservationism, therefore, wilderness protection will always be subject to politicians responding to "local economic interests" and countless forms of "administrative decision or whim" (pp. 182–183). Graham strengthens the link between the historical causes of environmental disorder and the failure of current governmental policy to secure wilderness protection through his discussion of the attempt to merge the Adirondack Park with the National Park Service. He writes: "To many of the preservationists, the National Park Service seemed a frail fortress. . . . Congress has given little direction to the administrators of the national parks. . . . [These] administrators changed their policies in response to pressures from various political and economic forces in and out of government" (p. 224). Preservationists have learned, argues Graham, in this instance and others, that whatever wilderness protection is established through federal conservationist bureaucracies can be repealed by "administrative whim." Because it has been "made by Congress . . . Congress could also take it away" (p. 229).

Different material acts may be said to be similar if they are similar in proportion to an attitude they share (Burke, 1969, p. 276). Graham equates the failure of conservationism with economic exploitation: both cause environmental degradation due to their shared allegiance to economic utilitarianism. Graham's history of the Adirondacks, therefore, attributes guilt in two ways. First, it acts as an indictment of the commercial exploitation of natural resources that began in the 1850s and that has continued to this day. Second, by categorizing actions toward nature in terms of perceived effect rather than stated purpose, it also acts to indict conservationism. By placing the blame for the ecological crisis on the failure of conservationism to protect American wilderness from continued exploitation, Graham makes conservationism consubstantial with the cause of that exploitation, economic utilitarianism.

The manner in which this interpretation establishes conservationism as the scapegoat reveals a second rhetorical function, identification by antithesis. Antithesis is an extremely effective device that defines a policy in terms of what one is against, rather than in its own terms (Burke, 1989, p. 73). The use of the scapegoat is a "special case of antithesis" in which the social hierarchy creates a common enemy to establish identification and social unity by shifting the failure of social order onto a ritually perfected vessel (p. 281). In as much as present public consciousness rejects the continued exploitation of nature (Killingsworth & Palmer, 1992, p. 24), such an association may provide the rhetorical means to remove conservationism from its dominance of environmental matters.

Purification

In that disobedience to the commandments of order leads to disorder, the resultant guilt or social tension requires some form of resolution. Graham employs mortification, arguing that the resolution of the environmental crisis requires the purgation or alteration of some aspect of social life (Burke, 1970, p. 190). Preservation of remaining American wilderness requires that the economically determined perception of nature that informs our environmental practice be negated and that society's hierarchy of environmental values be expanded.

As Americans seek to "accommodate wild and viable green spaces," the history of the Adirondack Park presents a model of the means by which wilderness protection may transcend the inefficacies of conservationism (Graham, 1978, pp. 275–278). By employing mortification, therefore, Graham's third rhetorical function proposes not only to transform society's environmental ethic through the acceptance of the transcendent value of nature, but also to alter the means by which environmental policy is made. Whereas the conservationist approach is dominated by experts who are under economic pressure and open to political manipulation, the preservationist model presented by Graham bases wilderness protection in constitutional amendments at a state or federal level, secured by a broad public constituency (pp. 276–278). Such an approach, Graham argues, "makes it plain that only the people, by amendment to the Constitution, can permit the forest to be cut, sold, or significantly altered" (p. xiv).

SUMMARY AND IMPLICATIONS

Critical examination of *The Adirondack Park: A Political History* demonstrates the manner in which preservationism informs Graham's interpretation and construction of past reality. Analysis reveals that Graham's text "acts" to influence collective historical consciousness through these three rhetorical functions:

1. *Mystification.* Graham's vision asserts a transcendent value of nature that establishes wilderness as an essential element of the American ethos, the preservation of which is necessary to the continued viability of our identity. The transcendent value of nature subsumes particular material concerns and serves as a lens directing Graham's perception and evaluation of the present environmental crisis.

2. *Antithesis.* In that the public rejects environmental exploitation, Graham seeks to negate dominant environmental values and practices by making these consubstantial with the causes of environmental degradation.

3. *Mortification*. Graham proposes the alteration of society's hierarchy of environmental values and practices through the acceptance of the transcendent value of nature and through environmental policy based in public discourse and decision making.

Through these means, Graham's history of the Adirondack Park "acts" to transcend the boundaries of current social perception and practice and to create the possibility of social change through the negation of economic utilitarianism as society's dominant environmental lens and through the expansion of its hierarchy of environmental values.

The theoretical implications of this chapter derive from the insight provided into the ideological nature of historical interpretation, revealing it to be a language-based phenomenon that focuses on meaning as action. At its most fundamental level, language functions rhetorically, to assert values and to mystify reality. These findings not only contribute to our understanding of environmental rhetoric by providing insight into how one sociopolitical perspective involved in this debate employs language, but they also underscore the value of studying language irrespective of the field of discourse.

While the primary focus of this chapter has been analytical, the chapter nonetheless possesses significant implications for public empowerment in environmental matters. First, it underscores the potential of historical discourse to contribute to a deeper public understanding of those cultural forces that are at the heart of our current environmental crisis. Although scientific discourse has established the existence of this crisis and described its effects with impressive precision, it cannot explain why we find ourselves in this condition. Worster (1993) contends that "natural science cannot by itself fathom the sources of the crisis . . . for the sources lie not in the nature that scientists study," but in "human nature and especially in the human culture" that historians and other humanists study (p. 27). Addressing this crisis through public empowerment requires not only that we understand how ecosystems function, but that we understand how our perceptions of nature and social practices through time have brought about the crisis and how our ethical systems have failed not only to prevent it, but also to address it in any meaningful way.

Second, the analysis of Graham's *Adirondack Park* demonstrates the manner in which historical discourse in particular and humanistic rhetoric in general may further environmental empowerment. Not only does historical discourse present a means of creating public understanding, it also constitutes a powerful rhetorical form that can act to challenge and expand the range of values that direct environmental politics. The evolution of American environmental politics has created a division between expert and public cultures, resulting in policy and decision-making practices that are dominated by the values of science and economics to the exclusion of meaningful public influence (Killingsworth & Palmer, 1992, pp. 163–191). Remediation of the environmental crisis, we are told, will be found through technology and market forces. Katz (1992, pp. 269–273) argues that if technological expediency is allowed to have continued dominance over environmental policy, there will be no hope for the inclusion of other values in our decision-making processes or, ultimately, in the development of effective social responses to this crisis. Historical interpretation may function to create support for alternative visions of social order, seeking to alter the hierarchy of values, assumptions, and ideas that dominate society. The construction of an environmentally informed vision of the past presents one means of challenging the dominant economically based perception of nature and the social policies and practices that derive from that perception. That vision can be used in the attempt to create a new synthesis of technological knowledge and human values to inform our dialogue concerning environmental issues.

Third, Graham's history points to the Adirondack Park as an environmental success story, one which provides a potential model of preservationist wilderness protection. Through the constitutional protection of the "forever wild" clause, the Adirondack Mountains have recovered from intense environmental degradation to survive for more than a century as the largest remaining wilderness area in the eastern United States. The lesson we may derive from the continued existence of the Adirondack Park might be this: Wilderness protection must be based ultimately in the construction of a public consensus with the purpose of establishing similar social contracts to protect a wide range of values in nature. This would suggest that environmental groups engage in public persuasive campaigns in the attempt to secure wilderness protection in the form of constitutional amendments at the state and federal levels. While it is beyond the scope of this chapter, more research is needed into the valuable experience of the Adirondack Park to determine what implications this model holds for environmental empowerment and future wilderness protection.

NOTES

1. The term "preservationist" is employed to refer to the varying elements of today's environmental movement, subsuming for the purposes of this chapter the distinctions between the biocentric and ecologic perspectives recognized in Killingsworth and Palmer's continuum of perspectives on nature (1992, pp. 11–18). Preservationist is the term employed in Graham's *The Adirondack Park: A Political History* to refer to those perceiving nature to possess a value in itself and, more particularly, those in New York State who are active in the protection of the Adirondack wilderness.

2. We have the tendency as human beings to deny the interpretive nature of historical knowledge, that is, the necessity of human interaction with evidence to construct an account of the past, and the philosophical implications of this nature to historiography (Mink, 1987, pp. 92–99). The idea of such value-free inquiry has been undermined by scholarship emerging over the past three decades (Bochner, 1985; Burke, 1969, 1973; Geertz, 1980; Morgan, 1983; O'Keefe, 1975; Taylor, 1980; Toulmin, 1982). The integration of contemporary views of ontology and epistemology brings into question the extent to which historical explanation can qualify as an

objective account of past reality. It is the interpretive act that gives meaning to the past through the construction of the historical narrative.

3. See also Moncrief's (1973) "The Cultural Basis of Our Environmental Crisis," which constitutes a response to Lynn White's article. Moncrief acknowledges that the Judeo-Christian tradition has "probably influenced" the "forces of democracy, technology, urbanization, increasing individual wealth, and an aggressive attitude toward nature" that "seem to be directly related to the environmental crisis now being confronted by the Western world" (p. 39). He concludes, however, that to "assert that the primary cultural condition that has created our environmental crisis is Judeo-Christian teaching avoids several hard questions" (p. 40). Moncrief places greater emphasis on the influence of advanced capitalism and technology (pp. 40–41).

4. For more detailed discussion of the history, issues, and participants involved in the struggle over the control of environmental policy, see Killingsworth and Palmer (1992, pp. 1–51) and Scheffer (1991, pp. 3–15). See also Petulla (1980, 1987).

PART IV
ALTERNATIVE RHETORICS

CHAPTER NINE

In Search of Ecotopia: "Radical Environmentalism" and the Possibilities of Utopian Rhetorics

John W. Delicath

THE RHETORIC OF "radical environmentalism" represents a complex and diverse discursive field.[1] For two decades now, there has been a growing body of "radical environmental" thought. One strain of green thought that has been extremely influential and that is most commonly referred to under the banner of "radical environmentalism" is the rhetoric associated with the philosophy of deep ecology. The degree to which all "radical environmentalists" adhere to the principles of deep ecology is debatable. However, some of the most fundamental assumptions of this philosophy have been distilled into those positions that are described as "radical environmentalism." Notions of "interconnectedness," "biocentric equality," "inherent worth," "intrinsic value," and "oneness" with nature have infused radical green thought beyond the deep ecologists. Such deep ecological principles inform a variety of ideological approaches to "radical environmentalism."

The vision of "radical environmentalism" thus reflects a patchwork of ideas stitched together,[2] in various forms, out of the discourses of deep ecology.[3] Despite such differences, however, it is possible to discern some of the tenets central to "radical environmentalism." Kirkpatrick Sale (1993) explains that "despite differences, sometimes substantial, what generally united the radical environmentalists was an underlying criticism of the dominant anthropocentric Western view of the world and a feeling that the transition to an ecological or biocentric view had to be made with all possible speed" (p. 62). Thus the one central proposition on which "radical environmentalists" concur is that "human society, as it is now constituted, is utterly unsustainable and must be restructured according to an entirely different socioeconomic logic" (M. Lewis, 1992, p. 2). They are therefore often dismissed as "utopian."[4]

It would be a mistake, however, to dismiss "radical environmentalists" so easily. The accusation that "radical environmentalism" is utopian is a false one. To use the term "utopian" pejoratively, to describe "radical environmentalism" as naive fantasy and wishful thinking, represents a fundamental misunderstanding of "radical ecology" and the nature and possibilities of the utopianism. If one wanted simply to suggest that "radical environmentalism" represents an abstract ideal that cannot be obtained, the word utopian might be applicable. However, "radical environmentalism" is *not* utopian. This is not because "radical environmentalism" offers a realizable and welcomed ecotopia, but because its discourse is fundamentally anti-utopian.

While "radical environmentalism" expresses utopian yearnings, its rhetorics are not concerned with the project of utopia. I make this point because "radical environmentalism" needs to be utopianized. It is not now utopian, but it should be. "Radical environmentalists" need to consider the similarities that exist between ecological and utopian thought in order to construct a variety of ecotopian rhetorics capable of restructuring society along ecological lines. Martin Lewis may be correct to suggest that "the anarchic utopianism that marks the dominant strains of radical environmentalism stands little chance of gaining public acceptance" (1992, p. 18). Yet this need not mean that we should reject utopian rhetorics. Utopianism is uniquely relevant and important to "radical environmentalism's" struggle to reconstruct society along ecological lines. What is called for is a way to appropriate utopian discourse in a manner capable of mobilizing creative energies and offering empowering visions of an ecological future. For "radical environmentalists" to make the most effective use of utopian discourse it will be necessary to retheorize both utopian and ecological thought. It is my contention that utopia should be seen as a dialogue and that "radical environmentalists" must make a commitment to adopt utopian rhetorics.

A THEORY OF UTOPIA AS DIALOGUE AND THE COMMITMENT TO UTOPIAN RHETORICS

Traditionally, utopias have been defined on the basis of form, function, and/or content (Levitas, 1990). More recently, however, "there has been a revival both in Utopian thinking and practice, and in analytical approaches to the construction of Utopian aims and strategies, which has brought out the multifaceted nature of utopian thought and practice" (Atkinson, 1991, p. 116). In order to capitalize on the multifaceted nature of utopianism, I propose a theory of utopia as dialogue that seeks to transcend the focus on form, function, and content. Theorizing utopia as dialogue broadens the focus over form, content, and function to emphasize a process of public discoursing on the nature and direction of the ideal society. Rather than being concerned with any one particular dynamic of utopianism, utopia as dialogue is interested in social movement and the mobilization of the rhetorical in the effort to transform society. In this light, a theory of utopia as dialogue is consistent with Murray Bookchin's depiction of utopianism in *The Ecology of Freedom*, where he suggests that "[w]hether as drama, novel, science fiction, poetry, or an evocation of tradition, experience and fantasy must return in all their fullness to stimulate as well as to suggest. Utopian *dialogue* in all its existentiality must infuse the abstractions of social theory. My concern is not with utopistic 'blueprints' (which can rigidify thinking as surely as more recent governmental 'plans') but with dialogue itself as a public event" (1982, p. 334). It is in the sense of a conversation on the nature and direction of society that I develop a theory of utopia as dialogue.

A theory of utopia as dialogue allows us to place the goal of a utopia up for debate while allowing for a diversity of utopian forms, functions, and contents, all of which are designed, in one way or another, to facilitate the transformation of society. Utopia as dialogue would see the utopian project as one in the making. In Bookchin's words, it is "an interchange of utopian views that still awaits" (1982, p. 334). As a processual dialogue, utopianism would recognize a diversity of forms, functions, and contents. The search for ecotopia would embrace utopianism in a variety of forms, from motion pictures to political programs, in order to perform a range of functions, from consciousness raising to the critique and design of political and economic institutions, all of which would be promoted by a diversity of perspectives.

A theory of utopia as dialogue thus tackles the classical utopian dilemma of how to embrace diversity while promoting particular principles for an ideal society head on. "Radical environmentalism" has particular goals that it will not, and perhaps should not, relinquish. Infusing "radical environmentalism" with utopian thought immediately confronts the problem of how to keep utopian possibilities open and yet establish the principles necessary for an ecological society. In order to address this concern, a theory of utopia as dialogue promotes the idea of the future as a possibility, not a preset goal. Here, I draw upon Angelika Bammer's concept of utopia as process (1991, p. 48). As a process, utopia is continuously defined as dialogue, debate, and artistic creation. A theory of utopia as a process of dialogue presents the future as one in the making, being crafted by the cooperative interaction of humans with humans and of humanity with the natural environment. Such a conceptualization allows for a diversity of approaches while promoting certain goals because it holds them open for interpretation, definition, and a variety of strategies for achieving them.

A commitment to utopian rhetorics operates on the assumption that society is continuously transformed by the interaction of humans and their natural environment. Utopian rhetorics are premised on the idea that society can and does change.

Society and nature must be regarded as something to be made. We need a vision of utopia that will take us forward and make us active participants in an ecological future of our own making. This is the rationale behind a theory of utopia as dialogue and the commitment to utopian rhetorics. Establishing the search for ecotopia as the goal of "radical environmentalism" creates a unique context for effective Earthtalk. Utopian rhetorics not only serve as a reminder that society can change, but they also foster the belief that the future can be different than it is. Utopianism opens up the dialogue on the environment and makes possible the introduction of new issues into the debate. A utopian dialogue and the commitment to utopian rhetorics shift the grounds of the debate in such a way that emphasizes both the desire for and the possibility of an ecological society. By operating on the assumption that restructuring society is not only a possibility, but a necessity, utopian rhetorics move the discussion to one that concerns the nature and direction of an ecological society. To provide a further explanation of the need for utopian rhetorics, it is necessary to return to an examination of "radical environmentalism" and the anti-utopian dimensions of this discourse.

"RADICAL ENVIRONMENTALISM" AND THE VISION OF ECOTOPIA

It is important to remember that "radical environmentalists" advance a variety of critiques and offer a diversity of perspectives on what constitutes an ecological society. The descriptions I offer here can only be generalizations. Not all "radical environmentalists" agree upon the same principles, offer similar visions, or utilize the same rhetorics. While there are other forms of "radical ecology," I limit my critique to an ever fragmented cluster of discourse most closely related with, but not limited to, deep ecology.[5]

Despite the difficulties of isolating which lines of thought can adequately represent "radical environmentalism," there is a set of characteristics that we may speak of as being central to the ideas that fall under this banner. Martin Lewis (1992) postulates that the most "dominant version of radical environmentalism rests on [these] essential postulates: that 'primal' (or primitive) peoples exemplify how we can live in harmony with nature (and with each other) [and] that thoroughgoing decentralization, leading to autarky, is necessary for social and ecological health" (p. 3).

In general, "radical environmental" discourse glorifies a primordial past. People who lived in small-scale hunter-gatherer societies are praised both for living a more sustainable life and also for possessing a more acute sense of ecological awareness. "Radical environmentalists" hold up as ideals the primordial societies and native peoples that supposedly lived (and continue to live) in greater harmony with the natural environment. As Dave Foreman (1991), a cofounder of Earth First!, suggests, we can see that "life in a hunter-gatherer society was on the whole, healthier, happier, and more secure than our lives today as peasants, industrial workers, or business executives" (p. 28). It is a return to some form of small-scale communal societies that most radical environmentalists endorse. While this view ranges from returning to the very "primitive" and loosely knit bands of hunter-gatherer societies to living in decentralized, bioregional communities linked together as part of an ecofederation, radical environmentalism insists on a return to living closer to nature. "Eco-radicalism tells us," M. Lewis (1992) explains, "that we must dismantle our technological and economic system, and ultimately our entire civilization" (p. 251). Indeed, as "radical environmentalist" Christopher Manes (1990) argues, we need to "unmake civilization."

A second dominant theme of "radical environmentalism" is the need for an alternative to the dominant paradigm. "Radical environmentalists" seek to promote a shift in worldviews. This is reflected in Earth First!'s commitment to "help develop a new worldview, a biocentric paradigm, an Earth philosophy. To fight, with uncompromising passion, for Earth" (Foreman, 1991, p. 18). From this perspective the environmental crisis is a crisis of culture. "Radical environmentalists" suggest that it is because humanity has failed to see itself as a part of nature that we have destroyed the environment. "Radical environmentalism" calls for the development of an ecological awareness that recognizes humanity's place in the natural world. In searching for an alternative to the dominant paradigm, "radical environmentalism" requires an ecological awareness that embraces the principle of "biocentric egalitarianism" (Devall & Sessions, 1985). From this standpoint, all species are equal because they all exist in a complex set of interrelationships with one another. Dave Foreman (1991) describes the notion of biocentric equality as "the idea that all things are connected, interrelated, that human beings are merely one of the millions of species that have been shaped by evolution for three and a half billion years" and suggests that "all living things have the same right to be here" (p. 3). Recognizing humans' status as beings that are inherently connected with all other forms of life is supposed to offer humanity a perspective which promotes humbleness and restraint in our outlook on and our use of the environment. However, "radical environmentalists" often speak of an even "deeper" connection with the environment.

This call for a deeper connection argues that humans must recognize their status as an animal that is physically and spiritually connected to the earth. Often this comes in the form of calls for a mystical "oneness" with nature.[6] The descriptions of humans' place in the natural order are often described in mystical detail. Jonathan Porritt, a leading spokesperson for the British Ecology Party, suggests that "[a]ll thinking worthy of the name must now be ecological. [Ecological] in all its biocentric, holistic fullness, seeing humankind as just one strand in a seamless web of creation, not above or outside creation but miraculously incorporate within it" (1985, pp. 221–222). Ecological awareness is both spiritual and intuitive. Dave Foreman (1991) suggests that "[w]e must get back in touch with the emotional, intuitive right hemisphere of our brain, with our reptilian cortex, with our entire body. Then we must go beyond that to think with the whole earth" (p. 5).

"RADICAL ENVIRONMENTALISM" AND ANTI-UTOPIAN DISCOURSE

Despite the fact that "radical environmentalism" requires revolutionary changes in society, it often turns out to be regressive, conservative, and somewhat mystifying. While "radical environmentalists" develop a number of important perspectives on the environmental crisis, the dominant theme represents a crude ecological reductionism that abstracts humanity, nature, and the vision of an ecotopia. "Radical environmentalism" relies on a combination of functional rationality and spiritual mysticism that puts it distinctly at odds with ecological utopian thinking. There are three characteristics of "radical environmental" discourse that are at odds with a commitment to utopian rhetoric.

Ecotopia: Future Horizon or Primordial Past?

A utopian vision is one of the future.[7] Mythical visions of the past and future describe the end and destiny of the world, as well as the standpoint of history, as immutable and are, therefore, too rigid for the vision of a utopia. Utopia exists as a reconciliation in the future. As Plattel (1972) declared, the "critical portrayal of the future is the essence of the utopia" (p. 44). "Radical environmentalist" attempts to unmake civilization and return to an ecologically harmonious past thus conflict with utopias' focus on a future horizon.

The "radical environmentalist" vision of the primordial past is not only anti-utopian; it is a path to ecological disaster. As "radical environmentalists" look to the past they see smaller groups of people living in closer contact with the land and enjoying the fruits of their labor in a manner that was sustainable. To suggest, however, that we could unmake civilization and return to such ways of life is absurd.[8] The notion that we can or should return to the land, living in hunter-gatherer societies that tread more softly on the earth, is a regressive fantasy that both romanticizes primordial societies and ignores the problem and potential involved with decentralization. This is compounded by the fact that few "radical environmentalists" have attempted to outline a sustainable program for scaling back institutions and localizing economies and politics.[9] In this context, the rush to embrace nature would have grave ecological consequences.[10]

"Radical environmentalists" must resist the tendency to romanticize primordial cultures and native peoples as the source of our ecological salvation. While a utopian dialogue must rely upon an understanding of the past, it must also posit the future as one of our making. "Radical environmentalists," however, undermine such an attempt to construct an ecological future by determining the nature of the utopian horizon and limiting the potentialities of human vision. The problem here is that the rhetoric of "radical environmentalism" is antihumanist while utopia is an inherently humanistic discourse.

Ecotopia and Antihumanism

Utopia is a distinctly humanistic enterprise. Utopias maintain faith in the ability of humanity to construct an ideal society. They are founded in the belief that the future is ours for the making. Indeed, the utopia often holds humanity responsible for the task of constructing the future. Matthew Plattel (1972) argues that "the utopian imagination is born from man's desire to bring about his own happiness by his own creative endeavors. Utopian thought is essentially humanistic insofar as it implies an act of faith in man and doesn't start from the premise that man's life is immutably fixed" (p. 26). "Radical environmentalists" speak an antihumanist rhetoric that affords priority to the natural world over human interests. On this level of antihumanism, the radical environmental line is fairly consistent. As Carolyn Merchant (1992) suggests, "[F]or Earth First!ers, many Greenpeace activists, and deep ecologists, the welfare of wilderness and other species has priority over, or is equal to, the welfare of humans" (p. 181). The problem with "radical environmentalist" commitment to nonanthropocentrism is threefold: antihumanistic discourse is rhetorically uncompelling, ethically dangerous, and politically debilitating.

First, as a rhetorical strategy, the notion that other species have value equal to that of humans runs the risk of alienating humanity from nature. Suggesting that all species have an equal right to exist is not likely to inspire people to embrace an ecological self. As humans are told they are of no more importance than deer, salmon, or tsetse flies, they often react with a hostility that further distances them from nature.

Second, nonanthropocentrism is not only an unattractive rhetoric, it is perhaps more importantly an ethically dangerous way of seeing and valuing human life. The hands-off posture and restraint in the face of nature promoted by biocentrism can lead to extreme forms of antihumanism and a deference to nature that would allow some questionable acts of letting nature run its course. David Pepper argues that "privileging non-human nature seems to lead towards a slippery slope—either to middle-class elitism or to plain misanthropy" (1993, p. 246). "Radical environmentalism" in its commitment to nonanthropocentrism threatens to dissolve an abstract humanity into an even greater, more abstract nature, leaving us with no ground upon which to make ecological decisions.[11] A resolute commitment to biocentric equality would make it impossible to act in the environment. Biocentrism and notions of intrinsic value immediately run into problems because humans must inevitably act upon and manipulate the environment. "Radical environmentalists" recognize this and are quick to suggest that we must recognize trade-offs and encroach upon the natural world only to the point to which it is necessary. Ultimately, "radical environmentalists" suggest that these principles should serve as ideals to move us in the direction of an ecotopia. However, the first retreat from the absoluteness of the principle of biocentric equality and intrinsic value sets the stage for a barrage of questions demanding that we choose between nature and humanity. In this sense, the very rhetoric of nonanthropocentrism may serve to reinforce the dialectic between humanity and nature.

More important, as soon as a qualifier is placed on how humans may intervene in the natural world, it becomes our obligation to determine what types, and what levels, of intervention are appropriate. And it is as an "obligation" that we should read the fact that humans are inherently connected with the environment. This is more theoretically sound than to conclude, from a reductionist logic, that the interconnectedness of all living things makes them equal. Indeed, to suggest that because humans are inherently connected with the earth and other life-forms they are in essence no different from them is a move that abstracts specificity and diversity from both human and nonhuman life.

Essentially, "radical environmentalists" draw the wrong conclusions from so-called ecological principles. To recognize that humans are fundamentally animals that must respect the natural world for what it is as nature implies that we have a responsibility to maintain biological diversity and ecological stability, not that we succumb to the forces of nature. Our connection to the natural environment gives humanity an obligation to protect nature and serves as a justification for intervention into the natural world. As ecological agents, we must make decisions based on the fact that we are part of nature and therefore have an obligation to it. According to Bookchin (1987), we have no other choice. "If there is to be anything that approximates a 'biospheric democracy' in the nonhuman world, it will be shaped by human empathy, which presupposes the rational and ecological intervention of human beings into the natural world" (p. 38). We must recognize that humans are moral and ecological agents that inevitably must make tough decisions about the necessity of interventions into the environment.

The antihumanism of "radical environmentalism" undermines the ecotopian project because it ignores the social and institutional forces behind environmental crises. Bookchin (1990b) argues that "the divisions between society and nature have their deepest roots in divisions within the social realm, namely, deep-seated conflicts between human and human that are often obscured by our broad use of the term 'humanity' " (p. 32). "Radical environmentalists" are misguided when they indict other approaches for their humanism. Humanism is not the dominant mode of thinking behind existing environmental crises. It is not simply because we fail to see ourselves as part of nature that we face environmental catastrophes. While this is certainly a factor, the root cause of environmental crises lies in the institutions and practices humans developed to mediate their relationship with the natural world. We must change institutions and practices as well as worldviews. It is therefore essential that a utopia be tied to politics. Unfortunately, the perspective offered by "radical environmentalists" does little to forward a vision of a political ecological utopia.

Ecotopia and Politics

From a utopian perspective, environmentalists must be concerned with practical politics. Unfortunately, "radical environmentalists" are not. Ecological thought, as it is applied by "radical environmentalists," does not provide the institutions or practices on which to construct an ecological society. The ecological insights provided by deep ecology function primarily as a critique of existing conditions, but they do not provide the basis for making choices. Constituting harmony with nature as the raison d'être of a society is not enough to establish an ecotopia. The utopian yearnings for reconciliation with nature cannot by themselves constitute the basis of an ecological society. Utopias are necessarily political and it is only through politics that utopia can be realized (Goodwin & Taylor, 1982; Moos & Brownstein, 1977).

"Radical environmentalists" must promote a unique approach to politics, one that synthesizes a variety of ecological and utopian thought. A vision of utopia as dialogue is consistent with what Moos and Brownstein (1977) call a "political ecological utopia" (p. 271). According to Moos and Brownstein, an ecotopia would (1) arise out of a diverse and collective process, (2) reflect a broad participatory process, and (3) have an appropriate social base with concrete historical goals. I will briefly examine each of these as they relate to the theory of utopia as dialogue and the search for ecotopia.

To suggest that utopia should arise out of a collective process requires that a host of utopian rhetorics be spoken with a variety of functions in mind, in a variety of forms, from a diverse range of perspectives. A collective process would establish a commitment to utopian rhetorics and the transformation of society as goals to be promoted by a diversity of opinions and approaches. Different disciplines and movements, institutions and practices, are necessary to engage in a truly utopian dialogue. In this light, "radical environmentalists" must confront the forces of ecological destruction on a number of levels. Robyn Eckersley (1992) is correct to suggest that "[t]he [ecocentric] Green movement needs idealists and pragmatists, creativity and critical analysis, grassroots activity and institutional support if it is to achieve its long-term aims" (p. 186). "Radical environmentalism," however, remains limited to concerns with wilderness preservation and the tactics of direct action and civil disobedience. While the effort to save wilderness and the tactics of nonviolent direct resistance are necessary components of a radical ecological movement, "radical environmentalists" must not limit their political efforts to such approaches. At least three issues demand immediate attention.

First, "radical environmentalists" can no longer simply avoid politics. A viable ecology movement requires action within existing structures, something that "radical environmentalists" have so far rejected in their refusal to compromise. The movement needs to direct its attention to when and where to compromise. Even utopian politics recognizes the need to engage in existing political processes. The very fact that one must move individuals to want a utopia necessitates working out some instrumental means of getting to ecotopia. Any such instrumentality involves using politics that remain this side of utopian. An excellent example of this is the need for a radical environmental voice on global issues that must inevitably require action on the part of the nation-state. Dealing with crises like global warming and the depletion of the ozone layer requires international action and the responses of governments in the form of effective energy, defense, trade, and foreign policies.

Second, "radical environmentalists" must critically examine their calls for decentralization and participatory democracy. In light of the global nature of many ecological crises, it would be a mistake to operate solely upon a commitment to bioregionalism and face-to-face political participation. "Radical environmentalism" requires a more holistic approach. An effective "radical environmentalism" requires both a local and an international focus. Its efforts must be directed toward decentralization, regional cooperation, and local politics as well as international action. In addition, "radical environmentalists" have yet to critically reflect upon their commitment to participatory democracy and face-to-face politics. These political ideals do not guarantee ecologically sound policies. "Radical environmentalists" must continue to theorize and discuss institutions and practices capable of making an ecological society desirable and feasible. In this context, utopianism is a vital discourse for exploring the possible institutions and practices of an ecotopia. In a variety of discursive forms, those committed to an ecological society can propose, debate, and work out the practical and ethical dynamics of ecotopia.

Third, it is necessary for "radical environmentalists" to address the issue of agency. While there has been much talk of new social movements, with the middle class, the unemployed, and the underemployed as revolutionary candidates, no one group is likely to establish a viable ecotopia. Given the connections that exist between ecological crises and issues of health, labor, and reproduction, "radical environmentalists" must seek to establish connections between ecological issues and the concerns of race, class, and gender. "Radical environmentalists" must point to the common interests behind grass-roots movements and seek to mobilize people along a range of interconnected issues. "Radical environmentalism" must therefore clarify its connectedness with emerging political and social forces. As an important practical concern, the discourse of "radical environmentalism" must make connections with society's growing interest in postindustrial values. By articulating an effective and compelling critique that recognizes the connections among a variety of issues mobilizing people to act in the status quo, "radical environmentalists" can incorporate these transformative energies in the direction of more responsive and efficient institutions and more sustainable ways of life.[12] David Levine observes that "there are creative opportunities within the radical ecology movement for building alliances and connections across community, issue, race, gender, class, and political lines" (quoted in Chase, 1991, p. 5). Unfortunately, much of the rhetoric of "radical environmentalism" is incapable of constructing such linkages.

To restructure society along ecological lines requires that "radical environmentalists" come up with specific institutions, practices, attitudes, and sensibilities. At some level, "radical environmentalists" must offer visions of a "concrete utopia." Bloch (1986) defined a concrete utopia as one that offers a well-articulated critique of existing conditions, a constructive vision of an alternative, and evidence of its practicality and feasibility. The differing strains of radical green thought have long articulated a well-developed and insightful critique of industrial civilization. Their ability to offer a viable alternative, however, remains limited to demands for decentralization, a reenvisioning of humanity's relationship with nature, and the commitment to live in accordance with ecological principles. Thus arises the problem of how to develop specific characteristics of a utopia and yet allow for a diversity of voices and a multiplicity of approaches. To address such problems Angelika Bammer (1991) describes and argues for a concept of utopia as "concrete possibility" (p. 159). This is consistent not only with a theory of utopia as dialogue, but also with an ecological conceptualization of utopia. Utopianism, when informed by ecological thought, can be seen as evolutionary. An evolutionary approach that views utopia as a process of dialogue serves as a check against absolute and dogmatic principles, whether they be a commitment to economic growth and industrialism or a commitment to interconnectedness and biocentric equality.

Finally, the commitment to ecotopia must have a concrete historical basis and be attached to specific historical objectives. The historical basis for a utopian "radical environmentalism" rests in the existing symbolic and material conditions. The conditions of late Western industrialism create the space necessary for the utopian voice to be heard and a climate in which it can be inspiring. Utopianism may be uniquely relevant in the postindustrial context (see Bammer, 1991; Frankel, 1987; Kumar, 1991). Indeed, some believe that current conditions call for utopias.[13] In this context, a utopian dialogue may be more than an appropriate response to the fragmented and alienated conditions of late Western capitalist societies. Radical greens must find a critique and discourse capable of addressing the angst of society and mobilizing people to act in light of the potential of a radical alternative. While a general sense of social fragmentation and alienation coupled with increasing threats to the environment may produce the "crisis conditions" frequently at the source of utopian thinking, there must be a more adequate incentive to act than the impending doom of ecological catastrophe. Green utopianists must point to the possibility and potentiality of creating the future.

It is here that specific historical objectives become necessary. Robyn Eckersley has quite eloquently expressed concern for concrete political practices. According to Eckersley (1992), "To be realized, the aspirations released by utopianism must be critically related to one's knowledge of the present, thereby uniting desire with analysis and leading to informed cultural, social, and political engagement" (p. 186). A major shortcoming of the politics of "radical environmentalism" is that it views the commitment to ecological principles and the recognition of humans' interconnectedness with the natural environment as the necessary and sufficient conditions for establishing an ecological society. While such a perspective is wise in suggesting that we bridle human arrogance toward the natural world, it does not provide the basis for action; it operates merely as a principle for restraint. At best, a "radical environmentalist" view of politics suggests ways to resist dominant practices. It does not offer a sense of empowerment to change political and economic institutions.

A utopia, however, cannot be solely a political project. Andrew Dobson has accurately observed that the task of reconstructing society along ecological lines "is an infinitely more difficult process than simply putting environmentalism on the political agenda" (1990, p. 170). "Radical environmentalists" must construct rhetorical strategies capable of offering compelling visions of an ecotopian future. A necessary component of such visions lies in the cultivation of cultural sensibilities that are consistent with ecological concerns.

Ecotopia and Culture

An integral dynamic of any attempt to transform society along ecological lines must involve the construction of utopian cultural rhetorics. It is therefore important that "radical environmentalism" develop a concern with how cultural sensibilities shape how we see and value nature. A utopian dialogue necessitates the attempt to critique "nature" in cultural products and to create cultural products for the mutually reinforcing goal of infusing culture with natural sensibilities and developing a cultural sensibility capable of protecting nature. "Radical environmentalism" must break down the dichotomy between culture and nature, a dichotomy that denigrates nature and legitimates its domination by humans. For this to happen, the relationship between humanity and nature must become part of a more general public discourse on environmentalism.

More specifically, "radical environmentalists" must develop rhetorical strategies that utilize the forces of culture to promote ecological sensibilities. Promoting ways of seeing nature are as important as transforming institutions and practices and in some ways are a precondition for such changes. All of this is hardly new to utopianists. Cultural rhetorics have long been uniquely relevant in the context of utopianism. Utopias were traditionally expressed in cultural forms like literature, art, music, and, more recently, film. Ecotopian visions cannot ignore cultural sensibilities and aesthetic representations. "Radical environmentalists" must be responsive to the fact that how we define and value nature is mediated by a variety of cultural rhetorics. Any attempt to make nature part of culture again must include attempts to cultivate ecological sensibilities through art, literature, and the mass media.

Such a move is made extremely urgent given the fact that "radical environmentalists" have largely ignored cultural dimensions of the ecological crisis. In my opinion, "radical environmentalists" have done little to explore the political dimensions of culture. While "radical environmentalists" often describe the ecological crisis as a crisis of *culture*, they hardly exhaust a meaningful analysis of this concept. "Radical environmentalists" may claim to examine society's cultural attitudes toward nature, but they rarely examine cultural products, especially those of the mass media, or their influence on how we see and value the natural environment. An adequate understanding of the cultural dimensions of the ecological crisis requires investigations like Alexander Wilson's (1992) attempt "to understand how nature is lived with and worked with, copied and talked about in contemporary society" (p. 12). Wilson's work, *The Culture of Nature: North American Landscape from Disney to the Exxon Valdez*, suggests (and examines) a plethora of cultural products, representing "a long human tradition of investing the natural world with meaning," a tradition often articulated in "popular cultural forms" (1992, pp. 128–129). "Radical environmentalism" would benefit greatly from investigating everything from Ansel Adams calendars to theme parks like Disneyland for their potential to both reflect and shape how we see and value nature. The many dynamics of humans' relationship with nature permeate all sorts of cultural products.

"Radical environmentalists" must turn their critical insights toward television and film and examine everything from nature programs, documentaries, and news coverage of environmental issues and groups, to weather reports, commercials, advertisements, and representations of nature in popular movies and television shows. Also ripe for exploration are dynamics of the landscape that reflect the interaction between humanity and the environment, between nature and culture. Here, everything from landscape design and architecture to recreation, tourism, theme parks, and national parks and monuments are potential sources for inquiry. The list could go on. Literature, poetry, clothing styles, music, science journalism, acts of ecological restoration, and incidents of ecological destruction are all important sites where humanity's relationship with nature is worked out. "Radical environmentalists" must join in an emerging dialogue that seeks to understand such dynamics of the relationship between nature and culture.

Alexander Wilson's work has been especially informative for a growing number of thinkers in the arena of cultural studies. Indeed, there is an important dialogue emerging within this area of scholarship about "environmental matters" (Berland & Slack, 1994). These scholars remind us that nature is culturally and rhetorically constructed and is therefore open to definition and interpretation. Efforts in cultural studies can further open the door to challenge dominant conceptions of nature. "Radical environmentalists" must seek to learn from and participate in these discussions. While "radical environmentalists" have intervened in ecological discourse in politics, economics, and the sciences, they have done less to disrupt dominant ways in which nature is "promoted." Both utopian cultural criticism and cultural production are necessary to counter this deficiency.

In terms of cultural production, however, "radical environmentalists" have been notably quiet. There are, however, poignant examples of cultural rhetorics that express ecological sensibilities. It would be wrong to suggest that "radical environmentalism" is bereft of cultural rhetorics. Nature writing, both literature and poetry, has been a very important component of radical green thought. Edward Abbey, Wendell Berry, Aldo Leopold, and Gary Snyder, as well as Thoreau, Whitman, and Emerson, have long been sources of inspiration and reflection for "radical environmentalists." In addition, there are important examples of ecotopian novels written by Ernest Callenbach, Ursula K. LeGuin, and Kim Stanley Robinson. More efforts like these are needed if "radical environmentalism" is to promote adequate ecological sensibilities.

To construct cultural products capable of challenging, resisting, or otherwise contesting the meaning of nature, "radical environmentalists" must invest greater energy to create literature, poetry, art, films, and documentaries that stimulate a discussion of ecotopian possibilities. Adrian Atkinson (1991) has done well to emphasize the need to mobilize culture in the direction of ecotopia, arguing that "whilst social theory remains largely the esoteric province of academe, it is literature and other aesthetic media which are far more effective in broadcasting the underlying notions to society at large" (p. 117). Utopian cultural rhetorics therefore hold emancipatory possibilities not just because they stimulate the imagination or raise consciousness, but because they often work out the practical and political dynamics of utopian institutions and practices.[14]

"Radical environmentalists" cannot afford to overlook these sites of meaning production, political theorizing, and institution building. They must work in these cultural forms to perform a variety of functions. The creation of cultural products that question, challenge, and explore alternatives to the dominant rhetorics and representations that sustain humanity's domination and exploitation of the earth is essential if we are to reach ecotopia.

CONCLUSION

What is perhaps most significant about utopian rhetorics is that they open up possibilities, serve as a reminder that institutions and practices can change, and provide a sense of hope that things can be different than they are. It may be the sense of hope and possibility offered by utopia that is its most important function. In the context of ecological discourse, utopianism would provide a much needed alternative to the gloom-and-doom rhetoric often characteristic of the movement. Far from being a diversion, utopian rhetorics can be the source of inspiration that will mobilize the forces capable of radically restructuring society.

As Murray Bookchin laments, "It will be an unpardonable failure in political creativity if a green movement that professes to speak for a new ecological politics in this country indulges in a 'hate America' mood or thinks and speaks in a political language that is unrelentingly negative or incomprehensible to the majority of the American people" (quoted in Chase, 1991, p. 85). I suggest that if the hope of "radical environmentalists" for an ecological society is to survive, they must embrace the inherently utopian character of their project and establish the construction of ecotopia as the driving force behind the movement. Rather than eschew the label "utopian," "radical environmentalists" must promote the cultivation of utopian sensibilities. Indeed, if "radical environmentalists" are to address the rhetorical challenges confronting the movement, the insights of ecological thinking must now be infused with the creative potential of utopian cultural and political rhetorics.

NOTES

1. Indeed, it is for this reason that the term "radical environmentalism" will appear in quotation marks throughout this essay. Using quotation marks will serve as a reminder of the problematic nature of the term "radical environmentalism." The label "radical environmentalism" is problematic as it ignores a fairly accepted distinction between ecology and environmentalism. In "radical ecological" literature, another problematic label, environmentalism serves to denote a brand of activism that is reformist and piecemeal. Radical ecologists (social ecologists, political ecologists, and some deep ecologists) instead use the term "ecology" to denote those positions that call for more fundamental and widespread changes in response to environmental crises. According to this line of thought, the term "radical environmentalism" is a misnomer. Environmentalism is by definition not radical. It accepts the existing system and attempts to work within it. I find this distinction useful and will attempt to extend it here. When I use the term "radical environmentalism," it will remain in quotation marks and will refer to the rhetorics, philosophies, and tactics commonly described as "radical environmentalism," despite the fact that I would describe them as "radical ecology." I make this observation because many authors dealing with "radical ecology," that is, revolutionary and not reformist activism, often describe those philosophies and tactics as "radical environmentalism." That not everyone who deals with radical ecology recognizes a distinction between "radical environmentalism" and "radical ecology" is evident in the recent work of Peter List (1993), who deals with the philosophies and tactics of groups committed to radical politics yet whose book is entitled

Radical Environmentalism: Philosophy and Tactics. Indeed, there seems to be a general problem with establishing what the terms "radical environmentalism" and "radical ecology" encompass. This is evidenced by the recent works of two major environmental and ecological thinkers. In Carolyn Merchant's (1992) most recent book, *Radical Ecology,* she includes a discussion of mainstream environmental organizations as a part of radical ecological thought. In Kirkpatrick Sale's (1993) most recent work, *The Green Revolution: The American Environmental Movement 1962–1992,* bioregionalism, deep ecology, and ecofeminism are described as overlapping approaches that constitute "radical environmentalism."

2. The result is that "radical environmentalism" often incorporates multiple, inconsistent, and often contradictory positions. Murray Bookchin (1987) cites this as one of the most troubling aspects of "radical environmental" discourse.

3. My point here is twofold. I want to pinpoint my criticism, making it clear that my critique of "radical environmentalism" is not limited to deep ecology, but it does not apply to other forms of radical ecology like ecofeminism, ecoanarchism, or ecomarxism. Indeed, as I argue later, a few radical ecologists have examined the relevance and significance of utopianism (Atkinson, 1991; Bookchin, 1971, 1980, 1982, 1990b; Cotgrove, 1976, 1982; Dobson, 1990; Pepper, 1993). The second reason for this discussion is to make a point about the nature of "radical environmental" discourse and to site its fragmentary and often inconsistent character as a problem for the vision of radical ecology.

4. A good example of this was the charge by Michael McCloskey, a former director of the Sierra Club, that the "new more militant" environmentalists are "just utopian. We may be 'reformist' and all, but we know how to work within the context of the institutions of the society—and they're just blowing smoke" (quoted in Sale, 1993, p. 61).

5. The point is that deep ecology's influence extends beyond the theorizing of ecophilosophers and has informed many different "radical environmental" positions. Manes (1990) suggests that deep ecology has served as "the banner under which radical environmentalism has rallied its forces" (p. 61). Indeed, Peter List (1993) reports in his survey of "radical environmental" philosophies and tactics that "deep ecology has now become a very influential means of interpreting the earth's environmental crisis in the environmental movement. It is clearly one of the leading contenders for philosophical belief in the radical wing of this movement" (p. 9). Groups that hold deep ecological positions, beliefs, attitudes, and sensibilities or who otherwise appropriate the rhetorics of deep ecology include bioregionalists, ecofeminists, spiritual ecologists, Earth First!ers, Green Party and Green Movement members, the Sea Shepherds, and even members of Greenpeace. Not all activists embrace the same view of deep ecology. German and British Green parties have many sympathies with deep ecology and espouse principles very similar to the rhetoric of deep ecology. Rudolph Bahro, a former member of the German Green Party, left the Greens over the issue of animal experimentation, which he "vehemently opposed for what are recognizably deep ecological reasons" (Dobson, 1990, p. 70). Deep ecological rhetorics are also central to the U.S. Greens. Carolyn Merchant (1992) suggests that many U.S. Greens "espouse deep ecology and an ecocentric ethic" (pp. 170–171). Finally, the rhetorics of deep ecology that permeate radical ecology have also made their way into "ecocentric" political theory (Eckersley, 1991; Pepper, 1993) and the ecological sciences like conservation biology.

6. I do not use the term "mystical" in a derogatory manner. Notions of consciousness and spirituality are inherently subjective. They may be no less material than the earth that inspires them, but they are nonetheless abstract, and that is why I use the term mystical.

7. Most descriptions of utopia and its form and content consider utopianism oriented toward the future (Bammer, 1991; Bloch, 1986; Kumar, 1991; Levitas, 1991; Mannheim, 1936; Moos & Brownstein, 1977; Plattel, 1972).

8. Indeed, there is a good case to be made that these past societies did not live in peaceful coexistence with the natural environment or each other. M. Lewis (1992) makes a good case

about the unsustainability of primal societies, pointing to a number of examples of ecologically destructive and violent societies in anthropological and geographical literature.

9. One notable exception here is Brian Tokar's (1987) *The Green Alternative*.

10. Such consequences would not simply be the result of the lack of a program for decentralization. The sheer numbers of the human population will not allow us to unmake cities and disperse people into the environment. For an engaging theorization of decentralization that incorporates concerns for the sustainability of cities, see Murray Bookchin (1992), *Urbanization Without Cities: The Rise and Decline of Citizenship*.

11. Dobson explains that "radical environmentalists" often abstract nature by speaking as though there is a pristine nature and it is this "untouched nature that receives the movement's greatest concern" (1990, p. 181).

12. Here, it is possible and important to point to the connections being made between ecology and feminism. While the body of work on ecofeminism is much too diverse to discuss here, it is worth noting Kumar's (1991) argument that many feminist utopias make the critique that male domination also results in destroying the environment: "Feminism and ecology are therefore often to be found conjoined in the same utopian works for much the same reason" (p. 103). As well, Levitas suggests that emerging utopian yearnings are establishing connections among ecologists, feminists, and marxists (1990, p. 170).

13. See Krishan Kumar (1991). Kumar specifically cites the popularity of ecological and feminist concerns as evidence of society's utopian yearnings.

14. Excellent examples of this can be found in the ecotopian works of Kim Stanley Robinson: *Pacific Edge* (1988) and parts of his Mars trilogy—*Red Mars* (1993) and *Green Mars* (1994).

CHAPTER TEN

Two Rivers, Two Vessels: Environmental Problem Solving in an Intercultural Context

Susan Mallon Ross

IN RECENT COMMUNICATION scholarship, an oxymoronic theme appears—a claim that the communication professorate is isolated or alienated from discourse upon public issues (e.g., Flynn & Ross, 1995; Wartella, 1994). Following Jacoby (1989, p. 274), the claim can be seen as part of a larger phenomenon, the transformation of public intellectuals into academicians. One socially significant outcome of this transformation is "that the scholar ceased to function as a social critic. The decline of the intellectual, therefore, has created a vacuum in public discourse" (p. 5).

By ignoring our roles as social critics, since we "cannot not communicate" (Watzlawick, Beavin, & Jackson, 1967, p. 51), we may be seen as choosing a particularly conservative political stance. As Wartella (1994) observes, by not serving "the public at large" with our research we leave ourselves vulnerable to the accusation that we are "wittingly or unwittingly supporting the status quo and the society's dominant institutions" (p. 58). More specifically: "If we in communication do not address the pressing public questions about communication and the quality of life ... we are shirking our responsibilities. ... In particular, I would be pleased if ... [future] communication research were directed to the ... public at large and not just to policymakers or institutional elites. ... I would hope we could empower the disempowered with knowledge and understanding" (p. 59).

This chapter takes Wartella's challenge very seriously. In focusing upon communication practices related to environmental protection and remediation, it addresses questions about communication and the quality of life. In so doing, it also seeks to demonstrate how communication practices in environmental decision making forums can be reformed to "empower the disempowered."

Effective communication involving all concerned is fundamental to formulating environmental protection and remediation policy that balances concern for the natural ecology and the economic geography of a region. However, in a 1991 article, a colleague and I describe the forums in which environmental policy is typically deliberated as "non-congruent sites of discourse" (Ross & Karis, p. 247). We observe that in those forums, members of several professional communities, with differing ("non-congruent") expectations about principles and procedures, are parties to the deliberations and must interact not only with each other but also with the general public. This results in a struggle to adapt to each other's discourses and create new "rules" for debate not linked solely to one disciplinary matrix. Such rules would include, for example, constraints on what may be talked about, who may speak, and what form concepts and theories must take to be considered valid (Foucault, 1972, pp. 50–52).

In two more recent essays, the model is refined (Ross, 1992, 1994). Those essays argue that a modified version of Habermas's *Theory of Communicative Action* (1981, 1987) could provide new rules for environmental debate. Communicative action is ethical argumentation on normative (justice) questions motivated only by the search for agreement (consensus). All communicatively competent speakers may participate in this discourse (see, for example, Habermas, 1990, pp. 86–89, 178). The criterion for valid consensus is "universalization," the willingness (without compulsion) of each participant "to apply a proposed norm equally to [himself or herself] and to others and to go on applying [it] in interpersonal situations when the roles are reversed" (Mackie, 1977, pp. 84–85).

The modifications to communicative action that I have suggested (Ross, 1994) are consistent with Gilligan's (1982, 1987) and Benhabib's (1987) scholarship, legitimizing not only the ethic of justice that guides Habermas's model but also an ethic of responsible care. To illustrate this more inclusive perspective I use two controversies involving a rural county in New York and a Mohawk reserve. For while Gilligan and Benhabib argue for the legitimization of an ethic of care to empower female voices, I have noted—gender politics aside—that an ethic of responsible care is also fundamental to the Mohawk worldview. In this worldview, moreover, an ethic of responsible care is inextricably woven together with an ethic of balance. Legitimizing a care perspective may be only the beginning to inclusiveness, and European and European American feminist ethical insights may ultimately empower not only women from cultures of European origin but also women and men of many other cultures.

CASE ONE: REMEDIATION EFFORTS RELATED TO A ST. LAWRENCE RIVER SUPERFUND SITE

In 1990, a front page article in the *Wall Street Journal* read, in part:

The building of the St. Lawrence Seaway in the 1950s gouged out the [Mohawks' long-time] fishing grounds and changed a way of life forever. The new channel and cheap hydroelectric power induced GM, Reynolds and . . . Canadian companies to build shoreline factories [joining] Alcoa, which had long had a plant on . . . a St. Lawrence Tributary. . . . With environmental law enforcement still primitive, the Mohawks' corporate neighbors poured industrial wastes into riverside lagoons and landfills and sometimes the river itself. (Tomsho, 1990, p. A1)

Because hazardous industrial waste, such as polychlorinated biphenyls (PCBs), had polluted a section of the river near a General Motors (GM) plant, in 1983 the Environmental Protection Agency (EPA) added the GM site to its Superfund cleanup list, a list of sites where the danger to public health from pollution warranted highest priority in developing and implementing cleanup plans. Women of childbearing age and children who lived on the Akwesasne ("land where the partridge drums") reserve along the river were advised to stop eating the fish, and interstate markets were closed to Mohawk commercial fisheries (Tomsho, 1990, p. A1).

Furthermore, when a snapping turtle was found on the reservation with 835 parts per million PCBs in its fat, it represented a blasphemous outrage to the Mohawks, in light of the Iroquois tradition that the entire earth is built on the back of a turtle. While this could be recorded in official reports as "bioconcen-tration," there was no place to acknowledge the deep cultural outrage.[1]

The potential danger to unborn and infant children if pregnant or nursing mothers ate PCB-contaminated fish was of particular concern to the Mohawks, who were under the leadership of Katsi Cook, a traditional midwife and a scientist at the State University of New York (Martin, 1992, p. 1). Previous studies indicated that high levels of PCBs in mothers "can cause subtle neuro-logical problems at the time of birth [and] babies who are born with less muscle tone than expected for newborns" (Martin, 1992, pp. 1-2). Therefore, Cook initiated (and is listed as an author of) a breast milk study. The study involved analyzing (1) a sample of breast milk and (2) answers to interview questions concerning demographic characteristics, lifestyle factors, and reproductive and dietary histories. The first results of that study indicate that the Native American mothers' levels of PCBs were not higher than the levels of mothers in a control group. Researchers also discovered that local fish consumption had declined significantly since the community had been warned about the dangers to babies from PCB-contaminated fish.

Midwife-scientist Cook spoke to the local daily newspaper when the study was released. She commented: "The [Mohawk] mothers were relieved to hear our levels were not higher than the control group. But they did send a strong message that we need remediation to protect our future generations" (Martin, 1992, p. 2). She explained that women had to change their diets and native lifestyles to protect their infants, and then said: "They expressed anger at always being the one to have to make adaptations. We have a human right to have access to our environment and the natural resources within it" (Martin, 1992, p. 2). Later in the article, the Mohawk mothers and others expressed concern that the study's results would be interpreted as showing that there is no need for the polluting companies to clean up the river because the mothers' "voluntary" dietary changes prevented potential harm. Indeed, the final remedy selected by the EPA to clean up the site was far less than the Mohawks wanted.

In a December 1990 decision, the EPA decided that the cleanup should involve excavating and permanently treating contaminated sediments in the St. Lawrence River, contaminated sediments and soils on the Mohawk reserve, and contaminated soils in a disposal area on the site of the contaminating industry. The polluting company would be responsible for this cleanup. However, on April 6, 1992, the EPA announced that the company would not have to excavate and decontaminate the remainder of the site but could cover [the area] with five feet of soil and build an underground wall around it to separate it from the river (reportedly less than thirty feet away) and the native reserve. Homes on the reserve are reportedly within one thousand feet of the site (Akwesasne Task Force, 1992, p. 8).

In reporting the decision, a Mohawk newsletter wrote, in an article entitled "EPA Sells Out Mother Earth":

> Our traditional values teach us that we must respect Mother Earth. . . . We have a duty to look seven generations into the future to ensure that our decisions will have no negative effects on the seventh generation. (p. 1)

After describing Mohawk obligations to Mother Earth, the article describes the EPA approach to studying a hazardous waste site and deciding what remedial action to take at the site:

> When EPA studies a hazardous waste site, they examine the health impacts on people (Health Risk Assessments), determine how the contamination is impacting the bloodlines (groundwater and surface water) of Mother Earth, and how our brothers and sisters (animal and plant life) are being impacted through fish and wildlife studies. However, when it comes time to make a decision on cleaning up a hazardous waste site, cost becomes

more important than the environment. Risk is calculated, not on the future, but on the number of cancer deaths. Animal and plant life are considered expendable as long as society progresses. (p. 1)

The report then uses the literal criterion of cancer risk in a poignant metaphorical way, describing covering up the contamination as knowingly leaving "a cancer" on Mother Earth rather than removing the cancer so "Mother Earth will become healthy again." This neglect is then characterized as a failure to meet humanity's obligations "as set out by the Creator" (p. 1). The authors of the report write:

The Creator made people physically the weakest of Mother Earth's children. However, we have been given an intellectual capacity to compensate for this weakness. When we don't use it or don't use it wisely, then we are selling out Mother Earth and ourselves. EPA isn't using it wisely. (p. 1)

CASE TWO: PROTECTION EFFORTS RELATED TO A (PROPOSED) ST. REGIS RIVER SOLID WASTE LANDFILL SITE

On April 5, 1993, a site in the town of Brasher was chosen by the Solid Waste Disposal Authority (SWDA) of St. Lawrence County, New York, as the preferred site for a new solid waste disposal landfill for the county. Less than one month later, county residents and their Mohawk neighbors were embroiled in controversy over SWDA's designation. However, in the summer of 1993, St. Lawrence County was offered an alternative to building its own landfill—exporting the solid waste to an already constructed facility in the town of Rodman in nearby Jefferson County. St. Lawrence County ultimately selected that option. However, what role the controversy outlined below played in that decision remains unclear and warrants further study.

Prior to the decision to export St. Lawrence County's solid waste to another county's landfill, the solid waste disposal problems of St. Lawrence County had been of ongoing concern since the state ruled that the county's existing landfill sites must be closed by the mid-1990s. In 1990, a proposed incinerator was voted down by the county legislature. Instead, the county government commissioned the county's Solid Waste Disposal Authority to select a suitable site for a modern landfill. Controversy accompanied each step in the site selection process. For example, in 1992 the executive director of the Solid Waste Disposal Authority left his position after conflicts with the county legislature, and SWDA was nearly disbanded. Additionally, various local residents mounted campaigns to discourage the county from choosing sites near their homes. Those opposing specific sites included, for example, a university student, whose home was near one of the three "final" sites, who argued that social factors as well as engineering and economic factors should be included among site selection criteria (see Day,

1992); Amish residents, who opposed placing a landfill on prime agricultural land or near land they'd used as a burial ground; and a grass-roots organization called Save Our River, which opposed the site along the St. Regis River eventually selected as the preferred site by SWDA.

After the announcement that site 123 in Brasher was the preferred site for the landfill, Mohawk opposition became a significant element in the ongoing controversy. One news report (Reagen, 1993, p. 1) suggests that Mohawks were unaware of how close site 123 was to the St. Regis River and the Akwesasne reserve until that site had been designated the preferred site. Once it was realized that site 123 was less than one mile from the reserve, Mohawks feared that the landfill would leak and pollute their best remaining river. For example, Ken Jock, Mohawk tribal environmental director, said that landfills always leak eventually (Reagen, 1993, p. 1). Alma Ransom said the Mohawks have been told "the truth" many times only to discover twenty years later that their land has been polluted (Reagen, 1993, p. 1).

At issue, repeatedly, in the ensuing debate was how to select appropriate criteria for choosing the landfill site—criteria that would strike a wise, just, and responsible balance among technological, economic, ecological, and social criteria—allowing the communities involved to grow, prosper, and progress without undue harm to the human and natural environment. Opponents to building the landfill on the chosen site included a strong coalition of several Mohawk factions that seldom agree (Lanphear, 1993a, p. 32), as well as nonnative opponents. Commenting upon this unusual coalition, traditional chief Jake A. Swamp said: "It's better if we all cooperate. Usually politicians don't listen to Indians on anything, but when it is a concerted effort involving non-natives we may find a workable solution" (Lanphear, 1993b, p. 25). However, another opponent to building the landfill on site 123, a Mohawk named Philip Tarbell who lives near the site, summarized many opponents' perceptions succinctly when he said, "We have no voice" (Reagen, 1993, p. 2).

Mohawk and non-Mohawk opponents felt their concerns for quality-of-life issues such as maintaining the scenic beauty, quiet, and fecundity of the proposed landfill site were ignored. Indeed, these considerations were lumped by the acting SWDA director under the category of public opposition, and opponents were told that public opposition—or lack thereof—was not a selection criterion (Hill, 1993a, p. 2). While proponents' positions were phrased strictly in terms of economic advantages and technical feasibility, these concerns stood in stark contrast to the aesthetic and ethical concerns opponents raised. At least one opponent, Mohawk subchief Hilda Smoke, saw ethical implications at the life-or-death level. Of the landfill, she said: "All my great great grandchildren will die from it. I'll be gone. How will I protect them? I think you're putting the landfill next to us so you can genocide us again" (Reagen, 1993, p. 1).

But public opposition was not one of the criteria to be used in site selection. Hilda Smoke's pleas fell upon the ears of people such as James H. McFaddin,

chair of St. Lawrence County's legislature, who said that although he understood the Mohawks' distrust of the county because of past problems with
industrial contamination, "the Mohawks also generate waste and they should
be treated the same as the rest of the residents of the county. We all produce
waste" (Mende, 1993b, p. 13). McFaddin also expressed the belief that, this time,
problems would be avoided. He said that "people will be protected. Strict
construction regulations will be followed and all concerns will be satisfactorily
answered" (Mende, 1993b, p. 13).

It seems likely that McFaddin meant all concerns related to officially stipulated criteria which would have been taken into account during the process of
developing an environmental impact statement (EIS) for the site—had the
selection process proceeded. However, as noted, the selection process was
abandoned prior to the EIS development process.

During the siting debate, economic criteria were dominant in news reports
(e.g., Mende, 1993d; Webb, 1993b). However, some reports referred to the fact
that a lawyer had been hired to represent Mohawk interests and that a lawsuit
was expected if county officials pursued the Brasher option (e.g., Lanphear,
1993c).

Both the environmental ethics and economic interests of the Mohawk people
led to their opposition to building a landfill along the St. Regis River in Brasher.
Their lawsuit, however, appears to have been considered as an economic factor
in the cost-benefit analysis of Rodman vis-à-vis Brasher (Webb, 1993a, p. 30).
Still, it is possible that the ethical arguments of the opponents of the Brasher
landfill were heard and considered—that the Rodman option was chosen not
only for the officially announced economic reasons but also because it allowed
the county to tacitly yield to opponents' ethical concerns.

RELATED LITERATURE

Environmental Risk Communication and Environmental
Policy Making

Environmental problems, such as waste management, are often most easily
understood in terms of balancing benefits and risks. Perceived risk of harm to
natural and human environments leads both to proposing environmental
cleanup and to opposing waste disposal. Recently, scholarship related to risk
communication, particularly environmental risk communication, has greatly
increased. As detailed review of this literature is available elsewhere (e.g.,
Belsten's work in this book, chap. 2; Hirst, 1993), I will summarize only a few
contributions cited in analyzing the cases.

Covello, von Winterfeldt, and Slovic (1986a) defined risk communication as
"any purposeful exchange of scientific information between interested parties
regarding health or environmental risks" (p. 222). It is important to note that

their definition excludes all but scientific information from the category of risk communication, a bias that persists today. Klapp (1992) reviews legislation and court cases that show how that scientific bias developed. Under the Administrative Procedures Act of 1946, "an agency must state the source of its scientific information and the relationship between that information and the solution it proposes" (p. 18). This law has been judicially interpreted to mandate full disclosure of this information (*Wellford v. Hardin*, 1970), even if the information would be incomprehensible to ordinary citizens (*Robles v. Environmental Protection Agency*, 1973). The decision in another case (*U.S. v. J. B. Williams*, 1975) stipulated that full disclosure means including all purely factual information. This case has sometimes been interpreted to mean that any information not indisputably certain may be excluded from review.

More specifically, a distinction has been made between how national and state agencies may treat scientific information through judicial interpretation of the National Environmental Policy Act of 1969 (NEPA) and the State Environmental Quality Review Act of 1976 (SEQRA), respectively. Because of judicial interpretations of these laws, the (national) Environmental Protection Agency may choose which scientific evidence to use to reach a decision and which to dismiss from review, owing to uncertainty; however, states must consider all available scientific information (Klapp, 1992, pp. 19–20).

However, scholarship has suggested that the public does not limit its assessments of risk to scientific factors. For example, Sandman (1988) writes: "To the experts, risk means annual expected mortality. But to the public . . . risk means much more than that. Let's redefine terms. Call the death rate (what the experts mean by risk) 'hazard.' Call the other factors, collectively, 'outrage.' The public pays too little attention to hazard; the experts pay absolutely no attention to outrage. Not surprisingly, they rank risks differently" (p. 236).

Slovic also discusses conflicts between experts and the public concerning what constitutes a "rational" approach to defining and communicating about environmental risks. He writes that scientifically oriented experts have labeled public perceptions of risk "irrational" because "[e]xperts define risk in a narrow, quantitative way, while the public has a wider view, which is qualitative and complex, incorporating value-laden considerations such as uncertainty, dread, catastrophic potential, and controllability into the risk-benefit equation" (Slovic, 1991, p. 7).

In an attempt better to understand differing perceptions of meaningful risk, Krimsky and Plough (1988) sought to identify specific social, political, and cultural factors in the process of environmental risk communication. Krimsky and Plough state, for example, that there are two fundamental approaches to the meaning of risk. One views risk as a technical concept, a problem that requires expert direction to solve. This perspective seeks economic efficiency in dealing with risk so defined and uses quantitative measures and statistical evaluation of risk. The other emphasizes social and cultural aspects in dealing with risk and seeks morally just and responsible solutions through participatory decision making. This approach tends to prefer qualitative methods to quantitative ones, which are seen as reducing people to statistics.

The situated environmental debates upon which this chapter focuses include participants representative of each perspective that Krimsky and Plough describe. Therefore, analysis of their communicative confrontations adds concreteness to our understanding of the conflicting values that underlie their opposing viewpoints.

In proactive protection efforts, the primary communicative practice established under the National Environmental Policy Act of 1969 is the environmental impact statement (EIS). Killingsworth and Steffans's (1989) claim, however, is that although the EIS was intended to ensure "careful study of possible effects of projects involving public lands" (p. 155), as currently used, the EIS development process is used to defend decisions already made and to ward off possible lawsuits. Killingsworth and Palmer (1992) characterize environmental impact statements as scientific by stipulation rather than by method.

Killingsworth and Steffans (1989) also note another rather paradoxical problem with the EIS process, which includes a provision for public responses to the official document to be appended to the final EIS verbatim: "Part of the democratizing rhetoric of the EIS is that these responses are included verbatim in the final EIS. But the respondents' complaints about the lack of review time, the scientific deficiencies of the study, their own lack of expertise and their disadvantage in the face of the army of . . . bureaucrats, indicate their tacit recognition that their voices will have little effect" (p. 170).

Following C. Miller (1984), Killingsworth and Steffans (1989), and Killingsworth and Palmer (1992), a colleague and I have argued (Ross & Karis, 1991; see also Ross, 1992, 1994) that actual debate, including all interested parties, is preferable to the processes of remediation plan development and EIS construction that generally have substituted for and preempted full debate at the present time. Analysis of the two cases that were introduced earlier will be used to support this argument. However, before the cases are considered, a selection of philosophical writings that could be used to reform current practice are reviewed and critiqued, focusing (1) upon Habermas's model of communicative action, as modified by several other scholars, and (2) upon Mohawk communication and environmental ethics and practices.

Communicative Action/Needs Interpretation: Debate, Not Dogma

Habermas claims that the potential for modern societies to substitute democratic, ethically oriented deliberations ("communicative action") for authoritarian, self-serving fiat ("strategic action") contrasts with the actual course of capitalist modernity. Habermas says that when action is coordinated by money and power, that action "objectifies" or "reifies" people, treating them like things, merely factors that may impact on actors' "success or failure in an attempt to manipulate a state of affairs" (Habermas, 1981, p. 88). This kind of action is oriented to the ends of success, not of morality, and is called "teleological" or "strategic" action (in contrast to the communicative action—the democratic, ethical debate—he proposes). Normative questions consider what justice demands in particular situations, and communicative action is motivated only by the desire to reach agreement about what is universally applicable to all concerned (Habermas, 1990, p. 62). In pursuit of universalized consensus through communicative action, each participant (1) may call any proposal into question, (2) may introduce any proposal into the discourse, and (3) may express attitudes, wishes, and needs (see Habermas, 1990, pp. 86–89, 100–102, 120, 178).

Habermas not only helps us understand the oppressive dynamics of current environmental policy making, but he also has created the groundwork for reforms. Habermas argues that in contemporary capitalist societies science sets norms that in other societies have been set by religion. Habermas thinks that through this privileging of science, contemporary capitalist societies have traded one form of dogma for another rather than trusting people to use communicative action to solve their problems (see S. White, 1988, p. 116).

If we accept Habermas's assessment, it issues important challenges to those of us who would like to democratize environmental decision making by substituting debate for dogma. We are challenged not only to explain the dynamics of privilege and oppression in the present system of environmental policy making but also to create an alternative process that represents inclusiveness and empowerment. Furthermore, we need to demonstrate advantages of the alternative process over the present one. These are difficult challenges but are important ones for communication scholars and teachers to pursue, as we seek to demonstrate our "moral engagement" (Flynn & Ross, 1995) "in service to the society" (Wartella, 1994, p. 57).

Our first step may be refining Habermas's vision to remove hidden barriers to inclusiveness that it contains. Benhabib (1987) builds a model of "communicative need interpretations" upon the foundation of Habermasian communicative action but splits with Habermas over two crucial aspects of Habermas's philosophical basis for communicative action: (1) that there is a single path of human moral development, with an ethic of justice near its top (Habermas, 1990; Kohlberg, 1981, 1984) and (2) that what is just in situated, ethical debate (actual, not imaginary, interaction) can be determined by assessing what is fair to all, as if it were unknown at the time of deliberation what individual roles would be occupied by which participants in the debate.

As I have discussed the Gilligan–Kohlberg debate and relevant implications elsewhere (Ross, 1994),[2] I will review only essential points concerning ethical development before moving on to the second issue, universality. Lack of communicative competence, partially assessed in terms of moral competence[3] in Habermas's conceptualization, would exclude those who argue from a care orientation from debates conducted under Habermas's model of communicative action. It is that disempowering exclusion that Benhabib questions. Habermas has argued that one way modern capitalist economies have oppressed women, and truncated their moral development, has been assigning them to caregiving roles for male convenience (Habermas, 1987, pp. 393–394). This culture-specific claim depicting caregiver oppression becomes relevant to my argument for inclusiveness as it contrasts with the culture-specific rationale for caregiver leadership in Mohawk culture (explained in the next section of my literature review).

Benhabib (1987) expresses her concern with Habermas's concept of universalization in this way: "A definition of the self as a generalized other becomes incoherent and cannot individuate among selves. Without assuming the standpoint of the concrete other, no coherent universalizability test can be carried out, for we lack the necessary . . . information to judge my moral situation to be 'like' or 'unlike' yours" (p. 167). Benhabib suggests that such assessments require considering a concrete rather than a generalized other, that is, not presupposing that "I should act in such a way that I would also be willing that all others in a like situation would act like me" (p. 167), but acknowledging that other perspectives might exist within which my action would be considered undesirable. Rather than presupposing one path of development and one universally superior set of norms, Benhabib would like ethical debate to begin without such preconceptions. Such initial inclusiveness, it seems to me, is especially important in intercultural situations, as the following discussion of Mohawk (Iroquois) culture demonstrates.

MOHAWK TRADITIONS: RESPONSIBLE CARE, BALANCE, AND PEACE

Mohawk Female Leadership

As pointed out by traditional clan mother Audrey Shenandoah (1992), Iroquois women are seen as caregivers to their people: "Through a person's life from the time they are conceived, from the time they are born to the time they leave this earth their care is . . . in the hands of the women, the mothers of our nation and that is a sacred trust" (p. 38). Awareness of this principle, as well as the fact that the responsibility extends "unto the seventh generation," allows us to understand the cultural basis of maternal leadership in Mohawk environmental protection and remediation efforts as well as frequent explicit and implicit references to the "seventh generation" criterion itself in Mohawk argumentation.

Although in looking at the oppressive dynamics of capitalism, Habermas sees caregiving as a disempowering role, in Mohawk society caregiving—in light of the above—is a leadership role. Female leadership is hardly surprising within a society with equal rights for women, established by a messianic figure, the Peacemaker (Lyons, p. 31), and a matrilineal tradition (Shenandoah, p. 38). Indeed, Shenandoah says that in her culture, there is no need for a feminist movement: "As a woman within my own society, I have never had the desire or the feeling to join . . . conclaves of women who are trying to get what I guess they call equal power. They all have the power; they only need to assert themselves. You don't need permission from anyone to do what your inner person tells you you must do" (p. 41).

Mohawk Communication Practices and Principles

Traditional Mohawk communication practices and ethics stand in stark contrast to current U.S. government policies for environmental deliberations. Mohawk communication ethics emphasize consensus building, maintaining balance, and appreciation for the "fine arts" of speaking and listening. Each principle is briefly explained below.

Ceremony plays a major role in maintaining the consensus orientation among Mohawks in deliberations important to their community. For example, each Mohawk gathering is begun by a recitation called the Thanksgiving Address. The Thanksgiving Address acknowledges "the full circle of creation" (Barreiro, 1992, p. 10), including people, "our Mother, the Earth," the entire universe, and the Creator (see Thomas, 1992b, p. 11). After each acknowledgment, the community members give a short utterance which means, "Yes, I agree with what you are saying" (Thomas, 1992b, p. 11). This can take hours to recite but is "always given" as "a preamble to our way of life . . . to help human beings living in society to achieve what the Iroquois call 'one-mindedness,' " from which basis "a human gathering can be set to work consentually toward unanimity" (Barreiro, 1992, p. 10).

The concept of balance is a key philosophical foundation for Iroquois communication practices. Shenandoah (1992) explains that "everything has to be balanced" and that responsibility for monitoring balance is an essential charge of the female elders of the Iroquois who, like her, are clan mothers. Clan mothers "perpetuate the ways of our people" by teaching them to the young people, by monitoring community and nationwide affairs, by providing help for clan members in trouble, by recommending candidates for chief, and by choosing times for ceremonies by watching the moon and the stars. Shenandoah (1992) says: "The balance is what allows us to continue to be. We breathe the air, we use the water, we share the space, and the balance must be looked at very carefully" (p. 40).

Among the Iroquois, where oral tradition transmits culture from one generation to another (Barreiro, 1992, p. 4), both speaking and listening are valued (Shenandoah, 1992, p. 41). Indeed, one qualification for chief is the ability to speak loudly and clearly (Porter, 1992, p. 18). Also valued is listening well "to the people who have the good things to tell us" (Shenandoah, 1992, p. 41), for example, chiefs and elders who speak in the longhouse. Part of the traditional training of children is to learn to sit and listen with respect in the longhouse, so that when their elders have died, they may carry on tradition (Porter, 1992, p. 14).

Some of the ethical values associated with the communicative arts of speaking and listening are compassion, yearning for the welfare of their people, peace, equity, justice, the power of the "good minds" (the chiefs, whose authority comes only from the respect given them by their people), and having "a skin seven spans thick" to endure under pressure (Lyons, 1992, p. 32).

Separation of church and state, entrenched in the U.S. Constitution, is not found in the Mohawk nation. One Haudenosaunee (the word is Iroquois for "people who build") speaker put it this way: "Everything is together political and spiritual because when the Creator . . . made this world he touched the world altogether and it automatically became spiritual and everything that comes from that world is spiritual and so that's what leaders are. They are both the spiritual mentors and the political mentors of the people" (Posner, 1992, pp. 18–19).

When asked to describe the effect of the white man's[4] culture upon their own, Mohawks are likely to say "we're still here" and to assess their survival as "a miracle" (see, for example, Porter, 1992, p. 13). These indigenous people realize that the eurocentric notions brought to their continent by the white man are different from their own in key ways—ways that seem likely to be pertinent to their differing perspectives in environmental debate. For example, Jose Barreiro (1988) writes: "The eurocentric notion universalizes the idea of the Man-God connection as primary and despiritualizes the natural world, assigning inanimity to all non-human beings. Where it [eurocentrism] has run up into Native beliefs and religions, it has worked to invalidate them through concepts of 'paganism, primitivism, and savagism' " (p. 12). However, there has been growing acknowledgment[5] in recent years that Iroquois culture in the seventeenth and eighteenth centuries had well-developed democratic principles and practices, which were admired and in some cases adopted by the founders of the U. S. government (Barreiro, 1988, pp. 2–3).

Principles brought to the Iroquois by a spiritual leader, the Peacemaker, led to the founding of the Great League of Iroquois Nations. Traveling from nation to nation, the Peacemaker delivered a message that Mohawk (1992) summarized as follows: "He said that peace is arrived at through the conscious and energetic struggle by human beings to use their intelligence to negotiate a place in which all injustice has been spoken to, and all persons feel they have been treated fairly" (p. 23). The teachings of the Peacemaker have been passed down through Iroquois oral tradition to this day, and those teachings, the Great Law of Peace (Kayanesha 'Kowa in Mohawk), take eight days to recite (Thomas, 1992a, p. 44). Under the Great Law of Peace, Lyons (1992) asserts, "the . . . Peacemaker established a government of absolute democracy" and [the Iroquois] "became a nation of laws" (p. 32). Mohawk interprets the spirit of the Great Law as follows: "The Iroquois tradition of law is a tradition of responsible thinking. . . . [T]he questions that have to be put before the people are *what is the thinking? Is the thinking right?*" (p. 23, emphasis in original). He continues: "When we create a reality . . . in which all people can say that no one in their society is abused, we will have reached a state of peace. Then our job would be to extend that ideal to all the peoples of the world and there would be peace among nations and peace among clans and peace between individuals. There would be peace across the earth" (p. 23).

The cases summarized and analyzed in this paper focus on intercultural environmental controversy related to two rivers. The two cultural traditions represented in the controversies have long been characterized, from the Iroquois perspective, as two vessels afloat on the "river of life," one the boat of the Euro-Americans and the other the canoe of the native peoples (Lyons, 1992, p. 33). Iroquois tradition holds that this vision of intercultural relations is recorded in the "two-row wampum" which Lyons (1992, pp. 33–34) describes as a record of the first treaty between European settlers and natives, near Albany, New York, in 1613. The design of the belt features two lines of purple beads and a background of white beads.

R. Hill (1992, p. 156) cites an Iroquois interpretation of the belt in which one of the two purple lines signifies the white man's laws and beliefs, and the other signifies those of native people. The white background signifies "purity, good minds and peace" as well as noninterference "with one another's views."[6] R. Hill says that the two-row wampum has become a symbol of the preferred relationship of the Six (Iroquois or Haudenosaunee) Nations to other nations (such as Canada and the United States)—"separate, but equal" (p. 159). However, pursuit of this relational goal remains a struggle and continues to meet with resistance from a society that tends to see separate as inherently unequal.[7]

TWO RIVERS: MOHAWK RHETORIC RELATED TO ENVIRONMENTAL REMEDIATION AND PROTECTION EFFORTS

Communicative Action/Needs Interpretation in the Superfund Case

As envisioned by Habermas and modified by Benhabib, communicative action/needs interpretation would require an open forum for face-to-face ethical debate, to be conducted prior to policy making on an issue. Such a forum, per se, did not exist in this case. Instead, procedural law privileged scientific criteria and the expertise of scientists. The Mohawks attempted to work within this system although it ignored some of their important concerns. Since no face-to-face forums for predecision ethical argument existed, Mohawks used the press as a forum for their ethical positions.

The press, however, has limitations as a forum for ethical argument. Newspapers tend to be event oriented. Therefore, it takes an event, such as the release of results from a scientific study, to obtain press coverage. When the Mohawks used coverage of that specific event to communicate their ethical positions (Martin, 1992, p. 1), a headline read, "Mohawk Breast Milk Said Safe," a message potentially counterproductive to their reason for seeking coverage.

After the EPA decision was announced, the Mohawks' community newsletter concluded that the EPA had used the cloak of scientific certainty to privilege the polluting industry's economic interest over all but their right to remain alive— their increased risk of death from causes (e.g., cancer) directly related to the pollution. Quality-of-life concerns—even long-term health consequences—the newsletter claimed, were disregarded. It was to emphasize this point that they compared the cleanup plan to leaving a cancer on Mother Earth.

Consistent with the Mohawk ethic of responsible care, responsibility arguments dominate their discussion. They argue for maintaining systemic balance to allow long-term survival. However (whether it's because they understand the privilege "enjoyed" by the justice ethic in Euro-American philosophy or not), they make at least one justice claim. Specifically, Katsi Cook argued, "We have a human right to have access to our environment" (Martin, 1992, p. 1). However, even justice claims were considered only within a preconstructed framework with narrowly defined criteria for legitimate claims (e.g., proven increase in cancer risk).

Environmental Risk Communication in the Landfill Case

In making perhaps the most passionate Mohawk plea in the landfill site selection process, Hilda Smoke, ironically, was alone in claiming harm substantially consistent with scientific risk assessment. She characterized landfill placement near the Mohawk reserve as a life-and-death issue. However, because only direct (and short-term) risks are acknowledged in the most stringent risk assessment regulations, Smoke's long-term perspective would probably serve to "disqualify" her claim.

This case also provides a concrete example of both the technical and social perspectives on risk communication. SWDA used scientific and technical criteria; opponents (both Mohawk and non-Mohawk) emphasized human factors. In the debate that began when the preferred landfill site was announced, people were promised by county officials that all of their concerns would be dealt with during the EIS development process (e.g., Mende, 1993b, p. 13). But the research reviewed earlier (Killingsworth & Palmer, 1992; Killingsworth & Steffans, 1989) suggests that the EIS process historically has dealt with public concerns in a proforma fashion: recording and appending them, but not seriously considering them. Indeed, the Mohawks initiated a lawsuit challenging whether legally correct procedures had been followed prior to the anticipated EIS development process (Lanphear, 1993c, p. 27). One might speculate that both county and Mohawk officials had an understanding of how the EIS process operated; therefore, the county wanted to initiate the process as soon as possible, and the Mohawks wanted to forestall it.

Communicative Action/Needs Interpretation in the Landfill Case

St. Lawrence County officials overtly attempted instrumental (or teleological) action as described by Habermas (1981, p. 88) instead of anything approaching communicative action. They decided to exclude public opposition as a decision-making factor prior to the EIS stage of the process. Rather than deferring policy making until ethical norms had been established, county officials were goal-driven to site a landfill and used science as a cloak of authority to pursue that goal.

As SWDA sought to use science as a cloak of authority, an elected county official (McFaddin) put faith in science as a protector (Mende, 1993b, p. 14). This appears consistent with Habermas's claim that scientific and technological arguments have, in contemporary capitalist societies, assumed the authority that religious dogma has enjoyed elsewhere.

Additionally, the same official, in assessing the "just" thing to do in this situation, constructed what Benhabib would see as a "generalized other" when he claimed that all roles are interchangeable because everyone involved in the debate produces waste. As I discuss in more detail elsewhere (Ross, 1994), this contrasts with Smoke's appeal, which implies that the Mohawks' situation should be assessed in the context of their history as a people—people who have long perceived themselves threatened by extinction, through death or assimilation. Smoke wanted to be empowered as a "concrete other" who wishes to protect future generations in a situation wrought with ongoing, salient threat. McFaddin's view, consistent with Habermas's model, pursues universalized justice; Smoke's view, consistent with Benhabib's model, attempts to fulfill a personal responsibility.

Mohawk Communication Ethics in the Landfill Case

In this case, Smoke represents the maternal voice of responsibility and employs the traditional multigeneration criterion. Similarly, Jake Swamp represents the voice of the Peacemaker, calling for cooperative action to attain consensus—a communication ethic quite compatible with communicative action/needs interpretation.

The significance of Tarbell's claim of having no voice is also better understood by someone aware of Mohawk communicative traditions. In the longhouse, just sitting and listening is the role of children (Porter, 1992, p. 14). Hence, in being silenced, Mohawk adults may feel as if they are being treated like children.

Mohawks did have an opportunity to express their views at a public comment session related to the landfill site selection process. However, this occurred after the preferred site had been announced. Still, the session was a relatively open forum attended by all concerned. Ironically, and tellingly, however, when the local press reported on this heated but peaceful debate, the article's headline read, "Landfill War Begins" (Mende, 1993a, p. 1). This spin seems consistent with the journalistic principle "win-lose is news."[8] To be fair, responsible, and balanced, it should also be noted that when Jefferson County officials offered to permit St. Lawrence County to use their landfill, the headline referred to it as a "win-win situation" (Mende, 1993c, p. 2). Perhaps, from a Mohawk perspective, which prefers consensus building to confrontation, this is a hopeful sign.

CONCLUSION AND IMPLICATIONS

These case studies have focused on Mohawks' attempts to have their ethical arguments heard, understood, and accepted in two environmental controversies in northern New York. There is some evidence these attempts were at least sometimes successful. For example, the draft edition of one study related to the GM site remediation plan concludes by giving credit to "native peoples for expressing the idea that prevention at the source, not cleanup after the event, is the only practical and effective approach to the problem of maintaining the integrity of the ecosystem" (Sloan & Jock, 1990, p. 25).

Whether or not this acknowledgment was a harbinger of meaningful changes may be better measured once we have more closely studied the deliberations over the landfill site selection process in St. Lawrence County. It is currently unclear whether prevention of harm to the ecosystem was a primary consideration in deciding to use an existing out-of-county landfill rather than constructing one in St. Lawrence County. Had a forum existed for public ethical debate prior to policy making, such a study would probably be unneeded.

I believe that deliberations dedicated to resolving controversies such as the two described in this chapter should include opportunities for what a colleague and I have elsewhere called "full, ethical debate" (Ross & Karis, 1991, p. 249). Such debate includes those who are currently silenced or whose ethical concerns are considered illegitimate in contemporary environmental decision making, including current EPA deliberations and those of local officials such as the St. Lawrence County legislature and the Solid Waste Disposal Authority it created. With Benhabib (1987), Habermas (1990), and C. Miller (1984), I believe that actual debate should be allowed to occur rather than being preempted by impact statements or entrenched regulatory criteria. I believe we should reform the ways in which our public debate on environmental issues takes place so that—as nearly as possible—we follow Habermas's rules for communicative action (1981, 1987, 1990), in which all participants may call any proposal into question, introduce any proposal into the discourse, and express any attitudes, wishes, and needs—in pursuit of consensus.

Furthermore, with Benhabib, I would open the philosophical foundations of communicative action themselves to debate, especially with respect to universality and the privileging of an ethic of justice as always and everywhere the most "mature." Indeed, we may have begun to realize that the moral voice of indigenous survivors deserves to be heard because of what it represents: survival. As Mohawk (1992) has commented:

> I've heard in the last ten years, people saying that we have to think about the faces of coming generations, we have to think about the ideas of Mother Earth. Those are . . . part of the language of America, trying to rethink what it means to live on this planet . . . using language that finds its way back . . . into the North American forest to those people who could have been standing on the shore when Columbus found his way across the ocean. (p. 27)

That speaker continues, characterizing the "language" he referred to as follows:

> [It is the language of] our responsibilities as human beings to one another, our responsibilities to the people of the future, and our responsibilities as human beings when we create institutions to remember those institutions must respect and reflect on the rights and the sacredness of the individual. (p. 27)

Through empowering full, ethical debate—using our best thinking concerning environmental issues—we could, perhaps, accomplish just and responsible peace (consensus) and maximize our chances for long-term survival. This point is consistent not only with European and Euro-American scholarship discussed in this chapter, but also with traditional Haudenosaunee thought.

NOTES

1. Ross and Karis (1991, p. 250) also make this point; the "turtle island" tradition is discussed in detail in Bruchac (1991) and its relationship to this case, in Ross (1994).

2. Readers are also referred to Benhabib's own discussion (1987, pp. 167–169).

3. Communicative competence has only been sketched out by Habermas, but as envisioned it would include cognitive, linguistic, and interactive (including socioethical) dimensions. Moral competence is included in the interactive category (Habermas, 1990, pp. 29–40; S. White, 1988, p. 29).

4. It has been suggested that the term "white man" was chosen as conscious recognition that Euro-American males oppressed females. For a discussion of this issue, see Wagner (1992).

5. This interpretation is somewhat controversial. See Barreiro (1992, pp. 6–7).

6. R. Hill also notes other interpretations (1992, pp. 149–159).

7. Perhaps the most famous example is the *Brown v. Board of Education* decision.

8. Once when I was covering a controversy (not in New York) over relocating a community's water system because of highway construction, I took copious notes at an open forum held before a decision was reached. When I called the paper for whom I was a stringer, the editor declined to print anything, since no decision was reached that night. "Nothing happened," the editor said. The following night, when the state government had listened to the community members and decided to accept their position, the editor decided to print part of my story with this headline: "State Bows to [Town Name] on Water System." To my editor, ethical argument was "no news" and achieving consensus ("win-win") was given a "win-lose" spin.

CHAPTER ELEVEN

Constructing a Goddess Self in a Technological World

Trudy Milburn

CURRENT INTEREST IN Goddess spirituality can be described as a reaction to technological society. Within technological society, people become passive components of a system too large and incomprehensible for one to control. Goddess-based spirituality can be understood as a way to reclaim one's power with others to affect change in the system as a whole. As we expose key features of what has come to be known as technological society, its ideological implications for ourselves and our world become clearer. Once these premises are laid out, the rise of Goddess-based spiritual practices within this technological society will be explored.

As technological society and Goddess spirituality are examined through an ethnorhetorical[1] analysis, both belief systems will be described according to the key terms that define central concepts which create meaningful actions. The key terms operate within distinct discursive systems. These systems will provide clearer answers to questions about how one can rightfully act toward one's world based on a particular meaning system. Until the premises upon which systems of meaning function are explicated and until our individual "selves" are understood in relation to these meaning systems, we may live our lives mindlessly and will continue upon the present rate of environmental destruction.

This chapter addresses these questions:

1. What is the definition of technological self?
2. What is the definition of Goddess self?
3. What are the implications for environmental action based on these definitions?

Through this analysis, these views are discussed and treated as related but distinct systems of meaning. A careful analysis of the connections between the two systems focuses on questions of power and action. Finally, I draw out some implications for empowered environmental action.

THE TECHNOLOGICAL SOCIETY

Our society has been described by a variety of scholars as characteristically technological (Barrett, 1978; Ellul, 1964; Hickman, 1990; Mumford, 1934; Pacey, 1983). Today we hear phrases such as "high technology," "medical technologies," "biotechnologies," "technologies of the body," and so on. These phrases speak to the pervasiveness of technology in our society. New inventions, such as interactive music systems (CDi) and virtual reality, are generally seen as representative of our evolving technological culture. Yet the assertion that "our society is a technological society" (Ellul, 1990b, p. 348) encompasses more than just these few technologies.

Not only are modern inventions[2] considered technology, but so are the activities we pursue and the way we live our lives. As Hickman (1990) has argued, technology "conditions and permeates virtually every human experience" (p. 1). All of our experiences are tied inextricably to technology. For Mumford (1934), technological society grew out of the notions inherent in the Industrial Revolution. However, Ellul (1964) critiques this notion as valid only if technique is equated with the machine (p. 42). Expanding the definition of technology to include more than machines would lead to a definition of technological society that is composed of at least two main components: technology and technique. William Barrett (1978), for example, described technological society through the use of the hyphenated term "technique-technology" (p. 21).

Method

To describe the technique component of technological society is to describe a method. If technology is a machine or instrument, technique is the know-how to use it. In other words, technique can be described as the means. In Ellul's (1964) definition, technique itself is the quest for the best means, and he argues that this quest itself takes primacy over the quest toward an end. In this sense, then, technique began as *a* way and became *the* way[3]. Technique is considered no longer an instrument, but a force which determines its own destiny (Ellul, 1964, p. 159).

One implication of this distinction would be that when technique becomes all-encompassing, we can speak of society as technological.[4] William Barrett (1978) describes the social influence of technique through a discussion of Wittgenstein's philosophy, which incorporated all aspects of modernism (p. 18).

Hence, the social influence of any technique was the logic used. Barrett describes this logic as a technique of philosophy, but it has become all-encompassing. Ellul (1964) used the term technique[5] to argue that we have all become subjects of this way of being. Individuals in technological society conform to the goals of "progress."[6] Technology itself becomes the agent directing society to make more, consume more, strive for more and better things.[7] Technological society is in this regard closely related to capitalism.[8]

With people so busy passively conforming to a system so set in motion, they lack any personal control over it because they lack knowledge about the system as a whole (Ellul, 1964, p. 162). What this society needs are technicians (Ellul, 1964, p. 84). Those with the know-how to use the machines will be valued. Other individuals within this society play passive roles.[9]

Ellul (1990c) defines our relationship with technology as one in which our actions contribute to the values and ends of technology itself. Metaphorically speaking, people act as a single cog in the machine of technology. This machine directs its functions without any adjustment to its individual parts (p. 60). Yet the individual parts, not knowing how it functions, act to perpetuate its operation. Pacey (1983) describes this "technology-practice" as one that involves all things working for the system (p. 6).

Ideology/Organizing Structures

Technology has become an overarching ideology. The structure of technology includes all the technologies and techniques within it. In this way, the structure is inseparable from the technology. Donna Haraway (1993) draws on postmodern thought when she describes technology as producing binary opposition by producing meaning (p. 205). Global technology leads people to experience the separation of text from context (Haraway, 1993, p. 203). According to the postmodern theorist Lyotard, we can consider the language game of technology to have overtaken the former grand narrative.[10] In this way, progress is perpetuated ahistorically. The technological society is made up of not only machinery and organizing structures, but also the practices of people within the society. Within this perspective, technology becomes valued by the people who created it and these values, in turn, become reasons for continuing technological practices (Milburn, 1992).

Given technology's pervasiveness, we can include its influence to encompass our definitions of self. Within technological society, individuals live technological lives and come to see themselves within its frame.

Social Construction of Identity

Considering ourselves as intertwined within this technological society implies that our identity itself must be linked with the components of the technological society. One can conceptualize identity as being formed through interaction. Berger and Luckman (1966) describe identity as being formed by and in a dialectical relationship with society (p. 173). Identity is reified in the process of the dialectic. Reification can be described as the process where, for example, something is said and then we act toward the statement as if it were an object. Words become parts of our reality when statements are reified. This process occurs between people, but it can also occur about people.

Reification occurs when one objectifies self and others. When this happens, Berger and Luckman (1966) argue, there is "a total identification of the individual with [his or her] socially assigned typifications" (p. 91). This is a crucial step for arguing that an individual's self-identity is socially constructed. By acting toward self as an objectified entity, we reinforce society's construction of us and thereby legitimate the society.

In order to examine the impact of the larger society on self-identity we must first examine the society itself. Recognizing that reality is socially constructed, we can look to our definitions or labels of the technological society and its corresponding characteristics for evidence of what we have constituted as reality (Milburn, 1992).

Technological Self

Being immersed in technological society changes people's self-concepts and the categories they use to interpret their selves and their experiences (Hickman, 1990, p. 169). One way of characterizing technological society is by its autonomy. This autonomy refers to technological society obeying its own laws and renouncing all tradition (Ellul, 1964, p. 14). If society is autonomous, then the people within it will come to see themselves as separate and disjointed parts of a system that cannot be influenced by any one part. When this definition of self is taken on, people will not feel personal responsibility for an autonomous, self-determining society (Ellul, 1990a, p. 335).

Ellul's (1990a) pessimistic assessment of the relationship between humans and technique culminates in the view that people merely obey technology. Furthermore, people only recognize their successes within this system by becoming the objects and products of their interactions with technology (p. 342). Within this separating system, people come to bond with one another through understanding reality in the same way and participating in the same "means" (Ellul, 1964, p. 131). He argues that "when technique enters into every area of life, including the human, it ceases to be external to [people] and becomes [their] very substance" (p. 6).

Need for the Sacred

Ellul (1990a) considers humans to possess a need for the sacred. However, the technological society operates without pretense, without mystery. Technology explains and reveals everything people once believed was mysterious or sacred. Furthermore, people within this society operate autonomously, without others, and do not collectively gather in rituals which create mystery. Because people need the sacred and because technology cancels out the very factors that define the sacred, they come to regard technology as sacred (pp. 339–340).

Ellul (1964) poses the paradox of the sacred within technological society by describing technique as sacrilegious and sacred (p. 141). At the same time, he says, "technique is in every way sacred; it is the common expression of human power" (p. 145). The mystery used to lie in the connection between what people did and the outcomes that came from those actions. Now, however, causality has been explained fully by scientific theories and techniques. Hence, the mystery has been taken out of actions. Yet Ellul (1964) also posits that "those who have preserved some of the notions of magic both admire and fear technique" (p. 143). These people preserve the mystery of causality even though they recognize their link with actions and outcomes.

In conclusion, technological society is composed of machines, method, and structure. Predictability, routine, exactness, and autonomy are valued within this society. It is an all-encompassing closed system that is self-determining, necessary, and irreversible. Furthermore, technological society functions ideologically to define the people within it. Through technological practices, people internalize it and act in ways to perpetuate progress.

Recognizing that not only do we live within technological society, but that it fundamentally constitutes who we are, a description of an alternate way of being within this society seems warranted. Goddess spirituality allows for the possibilities of alternate ways of being.

GODDESS SPIRITUALITY

Judging from the increasing number of books written about the Goddess,[11] this belief system is an important place to begin a search into alternate ways of being and knowing within what has come to be seen as an all-encompassing ideology (technological).[12]

In her book, *The Elements of the Celtic Tradition*, Caitlin Matthews (1989) asserts that the Goddess has recently become a prominent spiritual principle (p. xi).[13] How does this Goddess spirituality spread awareness of its particular consciousness within the technological system, which robs people of the sacred?

Goddess spirituality as an ideology seems to follow its own premises while operating within technological society. To uncover these different premises, the relationship between components of the technological belief system and the Goddess-based spiritual belief system should be examined.

Active versus Passive

One way to contextualize Goddess spirituality would be to consider it as a reaction to technological society. Starhawk (1982) attributes our alienation from our own bodies to "our economic systems, our science and technology" (p. 137). Just as we are alienated from technological society because of autonomy, we are alienated from our bodies which function to keep the system moving. Because of our bodily detachment, as well as our detachment from other components of the system and the system itself, we become passive components. Therefore, rather than viewing one's self as a passive component of the system, from the Goddess perspective one recognizes one's impact within the world.

A focus on one's impact upon the world is a different rhetorical strategy, as Foss and Griffin (1992) point out. They state that Starhawk uses interconnection as the context for her rhetoric of inherent value (p. 333).[14] They explain that Starhawk creates a rhetoric that speaks of mystery, ritual, and "power-with." Starhawk's rhetorical strategies are based on a context whereby the connections between people are highly valued.

The rhetorical strategies of technological ideology fall on the opposite side of the fence from those of Goddess ideology. Technology is artificial by definition. It is invention, the creation of machines and of people as workers. Goddess spirituality is considered natural, a state prior to invention, the proverbial Garden of Eden. Goddess spiritualists seek to live in "harmony with nature" (Adler, 1976, p. 4). Their spiritual practices center on the forces in nature and belief in nature symbols as discursively powerful representations. For example, during rituals one invokes the four elements: earth (as represented by salt, for example), air (incense), fire (candle), and water (chalice of water). These elements bring nature into the discursive realm where the corresponding directions, north, east, south, and west, are invoked as well. In this way, one combines nature and desire to produce magic.[15] In other words, nature symbols are used to create a conscious discourse that constructs the reality of the participants.[16]

These two rhetorical strategies hold fundamentally different consequences for action. If everything can and should be made new and more advanced, then progress will continue on its path without resistance because people have internalized this discourse. However, when Goddess discourse promotes the idea that what is good is what is natural, then the rhetorical force of "progress for progress' sake" will not be valued.[17]

The rhetorical strategies used in Goddess spirituality are dealt with more directly in a discussion of naming.

Naming

Naming serves a particular rhetorical function for both Goddess spirituality and technological society. Naming is a way to assert control. In the technological realm, trees, water, oil, plants, and so on are named "resources." These resources serve the larger purposes of new technology. Because of this way of naming, we act toward our environment as if it were "merely" a resource to be used (used up) for technology (whatever form it takes).

Goddess spirituality uses naming in a similar way but with a different purpose. Goddess spirituality is not a discourse that is self-perpetuating; it is consciously, intentionally perpetuated. The notion of naming can be thought of in two stages: the name given to the deity (deities) or "Goddess" figure(s), and the naming which creates a manifestation of desires, hopes, or wishes through spell casting.

The first act of recognition of what Goddess spirituality encompasses begins with the act of naming. In labeling what the Goddess is for each person, one begins to name her characteristics. Starhawk (1982) describes the Goddess through ancient symbols such as "birth-giver, weaver, earth and growing plant, wind and ocean, flame, web, moon and milk" (p. 4), which all bespeak the connection to nature. These names are purposefully given and their connotations clearly understood. In Starhawk's (1982) conception, the Goddess connotes connectedness, sustenance, healing, and creating (p. 4). One names purposefully and responsibly by recognizing the power naming evokes.

Self-Determining Principles

When technology is considered self-determining or as a self-perpetuating structure, it operates ideologically. Goddess spirituality creates a space in this ideological structure by unbinding its limitations. Whereas technological society operates by imposing strict regulations, "the rule of the Goddess is that there are no rules" (Matthews, 1989, p. 19). While there may not be definitive rules to live by, one can find basic principles which guide this belief system. The first tenet of magic, termed the witches "reed," is if "it harm none, do what you will" (Coppigan, 1992, p. 2). Furthermore, Edwards (1991) discusses seven principles, or characteristics, of the Goddess. She describes the Goddess as dark and light, life and death, planet and selves, desire, destruction, feminine, and ancient herstory (pp. 3–4). These terms may at first glance seem like the very same dualistic notions found in technological thinking. However, these terms are used to illustrate the range of characteristics that the Goddess represents.

The principles which seek to bridge dualistic premises can be illustrated in Goddess therapeutic work. Bolen (1984) and Matthews (1989) argue that stories and symbols of the Goddess can be used to heal the mind/body and the rational/intuitive dualisms. These dualisms, which are pervasive categories in technological society, are played with as paradoxically[18] existing within the Goddess and within the same individual.

The principles in Goddess spirituality seem to contain quite a diverse set of characteristics. This diversity is not only welcomed but also celebrated. The Goddess belief system is an inclusive system, where different emotions and ways of being are appreciated. Furthermore, these differences, which at first seem at odds with each other within a technological, rational-logical mindframe, are accepted as coexisting within each of us. Goddess spirituality considers paradox a natural state. "Natural" is accordingly valued as part of this discourse.

Edwards (1991) considers our paradoxical relationship with the Goddess as varied as the characteristics people use to describe her (p. 12). In addition to a paradoxical relationship with the Goddess, one's self is also a paradox and this is celebrated. Bolen (1984) explains how one can use different goddesses to describe people's actions as paradoxically both highly developed and unconscious (p. 11). Bolen observes that using the Goddess to describe women is a more inclusive, holistic theoretical framework for women to organize their experiences (p. 23).

Values

Because Goddess spirituality takes place within technological society, some parts overlap. The concept of Goddess spirituality being transcendent or somehow outside the realm of technological society can be witnessed in the practice of drawing the circle[19] during rituals. The circle is drawn and creates a space between worlds. In this realm, magic occurs. Using this rhetorical, albeit socially constructed, device, Goddess spiritualists are able to take either a more holistic perspective of the events in our world or a more deeply focused concentration at one small aspect of this world or themselves. These two can occur simultaneously. For example, in a magic spell, one can focus on a specific desire one has, for example, to attain inner harmony. At the same time, however, an overall gestalt of the world—including others' desires—comes into awareness and links a specific strand with the web of interconnections.

Goddess spirituality creates a way to look at the system, technological society, in the circle which is space between worlds. This circle is usually cast during rituals. During other moments of their lives, Goddess spiritualists live within the boundaries of and are affected by the very logic that guides technological society. However, while most Goddess spiritualists have experienced early socialization based on technological logic and organization, they are now trying to create a new logic. The logic they are trying to foster can be thought of as a logic that includes paradox. The logic Goddess spiritualists try to employ is cyclical, like a spiral, rather than linear. Yet perhaps this different logic can only be witnessed within the technological framework itself.

Technological society is autonomous with regard to values. The values inherent in the system serve to perpetuate the system—progress, technology for technology's sake, and so on. Goddess spiritualists hold inner beliefs, attitudes, and values according to their relationship with the Goddess. One's relationship with the Goddess, if thought of as monotheistic, could be thought of as one form of perpetuating technological society. The relationship perpetuates the system. However, in the space between worlds, Goddess spiritualists transcend their ties with the technological system by creating a different discourse which expands the boundaries of reality and opens it to more potentials. Furthermore, Goddess spiritualists recognize and foster adherence to divergent beliefs. By recognizing different aspects of the Goddess, monotheism is not a trap, but one way to celebrate. S. Fox (1989) refers to this celebration by describing different beliefs within Goddess spirituality. She states that it is pantheistic that the divine is seen everywhere. It is animistic in that all humans, animals, and other natural forms contain a Divine Spirit. It is monotheistic, honoring the divine unity, and polytheistic, honoring many gods and goddesses.

Autonomy does not have the same impact for Goddess spiritualists as it does for others operating within technological society. Goddess spirituality assumes interconnected relationships (Edwards, 1991, p. 13). The quality of separateness and isolation that pervades technological society is overcome in Goddess spirituality, where all parts are described as a web of interactions. Edwards describes the operation of the system as a cycle where energy regenerates in another part of the system from the operation of one part (p. 13). Goddess spirituality reveres this cycle of connection with all.

These conceptions within Goddess spirituality match the notion of interrelated parts which defines technological society. Is this point of similarity a weakness in Goddess spirituality? Is Goddess spirituality merely conforming to technological society itself? Occurring within technological society, and understanding this as an ideological system, we can recognize that while all things may be interrelated, in technological society a single individual does not have the same awareness as does the individual Goddess spiritualist.

The Sacred

The everyday experience is spiritual. Edwards (1991) describes daily living practices as spiritual. Being conscious of what one consumes is a spiritual matter, and "[c]omposting and recycling become religious practices" (p. 14). All actions are viewed with reverence.

Mindfulness might be the key difference between technology and Goddess spirituality. Within the technological belief system, people passively respond to the quest for progress that is technology's main goal. Being agents of technology robs people of actor status. Goddess spirituality creates the space for people to become aware of themselves and their actions. Within this space, with this awareness, the sacred is lived.

Starhawk (1982) asserts that people (otherwise mindless agents of technology) can make a choice. They can choose to change their attitude. People can act in and toward the world with an attitude that all creatures and the meaning of life are sacred (p. 11): not sacred in the passive, awestruck sense that everything is too big and incomprehensible, but sacred in the sense that everything matters and that everything is connected—sacred in the sense of reverence.

Goddess spirituality, as opposed to other religions which command our actions, offers a philosophy which challenges one to consider how an individual's needs and desires fit into context with others' hopes, dreams, circumstances, and responsibilities (Edwards, 1991, p. 14).

Power and Control

The concepts of control and power are valued differently according to each belief system. In the technological society, power and control operate through the patriarchal, hierarchical structures. Through these structures, the ones at the top have the power to socially construct and define those at the bottom. These concepts operate within technological society to maintain the status quo and keep those on the lower rungs of the ladder passive. The concepts themselves therefore take on relative associations and values depending upon your position on the social ladder.

Given these current structures and values, to discuss concepts like control and power at all runs the risk of adhering to the same belief system and inferring that the value is inherent within the concept. However, I am offering a discussion of these concepts through a different belief system. Recall the first and only guideline, that if "it harm none, do what you will" (Coppigan, 1992, p. 2). Given this, one necessarily must take into account all others before one acts in the world. Power, then, is a very different concept (has a different rhetorical use) in Goddess spirituality than does power in technological logic. For Goddess spiritualists, power can be seen as similar to the term "empowering," where individuals are aware of their actions and yet understand the responsibility that goes along with any action.

Power is energy that shapes reality. This type of power cannot be "assumed, inherited, appointed, or taken for granted" (Starhawk, 1979, p. 51). One person cannot have power over another, nor can one's power diminish another's. Through this concept of power we can understand how energy is negotiated among individuals. Starhawk (1982) discusses the concept of "power-from-within," which she likens to the growth in a seed, similar to the Latin word *podere* ("to be able"), in contrast to "power-over," which she considers domination (p. 3). Power-from-within can manifest as stories one creates. Stories structure and shape our thoughts, our images, our actions. When we create and name our own stories, we have a certain power. Starhawk (1982) reminds us that "it is a magical principle that knowing something's name gives us power—not over it, but *with* it" (p. 23). In this way, power is a shared story, a cocreated story.[20]

Creating stories that structure our world and naming concepts give us power. However, this conception of power must be understood with the other components of Goddess spirituality. Specifically, recalling the notion of our interconnections with others and, furthermore, recognizing the power-within each entity in the world pull the focus from the individual into the web of relations.

Edwards (1991) recounts the power she feels from her experience with Goddess spirituality:

> Today, Earth-centered spirituality has given me back the night, the dark, blood, Crone, under, and lower. It has given me back surrender, too. Earth-centered spirituality focuses on the truths—however murky and contradictory—of my body, partnership, and the Planet. Today, I can say that I picture surrender not as a rape or an invisibility, but as the awe I feel when I allow myself to accept—not fix or dominate—the endlessly shifting facts of existence. (pp. 139–140)

Edwards's experience describes passivity as a conscious choice. She describes the other side of the control coin. If control no longer points to power-over others, then passivity does not indicate being at the mercy of this larger system. Rather, passivity is a state of harmony with all other things in the system.

Coming to the conclusion that Goddess spiritualists are passive may seem contradictory to the initial definition of Goddess spiritualists as active. Yet within this discourse the emphasis is placed upon the active choice to take a passive stance and to live in harmony with the world. Within this system, the choice is an action. One acts consciously and with awareness of one's power to name. One understands that all actions require responsibility.

CONCLUSION

Biehl (1991) and others may argue that Goddess spirituality is based on ancient patriarchal hierarchical systems and therefore cannot be a way for women, or others, to feel honored and spiritually free. However, understanding Goddess spirituality as postmodern creates space to view the potential of this perspective. Postmodern concepts allow the continual creation of meaning within the practices of Goddess spiritualists as they have defined themselves.

If we recognize that postmodernism can only be perceived within modernist thought, then the historical link is no longer problematically tied to the present practice in the same way. For example, critics such as Biehl have a commitment to describing Goddess spirituality through historical lenses as a "modern" development, adhering to scientific norms. However, that perspective is overly simplistic and does not take into consideration the complexities and incommensurability of this alternate belief system. Perhaps the connection to historicity appeals to those who, in technological society, feel they have lost any connections to the past because the present is always based on progress. This appeal makes sense when we consider Lyotard's (1984) proposal that science has destroyed the grand narrative, with an accompanying loss of history. Yet postmodern notions of multiplicity through which Goddess spirituality operates may give us new local stories that create ties to the past without sacrificing the future. These ties are created through a different narrative and fit in with Sarup's (1993)definition of poststructuralism, which promotes the idea that " 'reality' is a purely discursive phenomenon" (p. 168).

The implications for Goddess-based spiritual practices within the technological society are manifold. Because Goddess spirituality is practiced within a technological society, some people will take note of their similarities. Like Biehl, they will overlook the context and local meaning. While technological society is patriarchal, Goddess spirituality tries to create a space for other potentials through the concept of power-with.

Other limitations within the current structure for adopting this new system include the notions that technology is autonomous and self-determining. These components call for a continuation of its structure through passive participants who re-create and perpetuate the system. However, because the technological system is made up of the individuals within it, when individuals become aware and conscious, then we can jointly begin to re-create a world where each individual person is responsible for using his or her talents for the good of the whole system. All living things will be considered a part of the whole and will not be taken advantage of for one group's benefit. Perhaps even technology will be considered differently. Rather than constituting an all-encompassing social system, the tools and techniques created will serve a spiritual function.

While Ellul (1964) was sure that technique cannot be put to good use, he made this assertion from the vantage of one who was immersed within the system. Perhaps the circle between the worlds, the corresponding invocation of "natural" symbols, the recognition that one creates one's reality and with that creation comes responsibility, all contribute to a different system. Perhaps this system can use techniques, when these "ways" are understood as the sacred creation of discourse.

When Ellul (1964) explained or made predictions based on his perception of technological society, he did recognize that certain factors may come to pass that would upset the current flow of events. One of the factors he agreed might change the course of technological society was "if an increasing number of people become fully aware of the threat the technological world poses to [people's] personal and spiritual life, and if they determine to assert their freedom by upsetting the course of this evolution, my forecast will be invalidated" (p. xxx).

Within this modern world of technological society, people have proposed the postmodern as the opening up of potentials. Paula Treichler (1993) points out that "our names and representations can nevertheless influence our cultured relationships to the disease [AIDS] and, indeed, its present and future course" (p. 286). She made this statement as an argument for attending to our linguistic constructions of the world, whether or not they had any direct link to the physical world (so-called reality). In describing why the distinction between reality and social construction of reality is not the focus, Treichler shifts our focus to what we can do with our language once we recognize how we use it to describe our world and our relationship to that world.

Understanding Goddess spirituality as a discourse within technological society creates a new starting point. Ethnorhetorical studies seek to examine the meanings people attribute to the symbols they use to create their world and themselves. This study has attempted to explicate the assumptions behind facets of our technological society as well as tenets of Goddess spirituality. These meanings come to be known through practice. This study, while not overtly analyzing a specific practice, has stepped closer to lived beliefs by describing the way these practices come to be fashioned into a distinct belief system through authors who live them and describe them to others.

This chapter speaks of Goddess spirituality. Yet any similar notion of spirituality that considers the same principles important would fit within this framework. This chapter is meant as a beginning, an attempt to connect two seemingly unlike ideologies. For it is in the similarities that we come to understand how concepts, and people, can work together to form a more integrated whole. Awareness is the first step. Becoming consciously aware of our place in this technological society is the only way to come to personal responsibility.

The implications for our environment can be guessed at based upon each of these ideological systems. However, as a first step these belief systems have been sketched out to aid local communities as they decide what actions to take based on a clearer understanding of their place within technological society. Based on the premise that only those who bear the consequences should make decisions, Starhawk (1982) has proposed a vision: "It is interesting to try to envision a large society based on this principle. At first, one is struck by how much less would get done. . . . We would have to transform our technology, our economy, our entire way of living. Instead of damming a wild river to provide electricity, we might need to construct a windmill for every house" (p. 36). This vision gives us one place to start envisioning new alternatives for interacting with our environment. A vision for a better relationship with the environment centers on our awareness of how our discourse shapes our reality and the attendant consequences of this action. In a world of hierarchical rankings and power-over, one person's vision may seem to overtake and dictate how others can act toward the environment. However, Goddess spirituality reminds us that we have power to choose our actions. Furthermore, we must choose together to build a discourse that begins with premises that value nature. Such a discourse may assert that the four sacred things, earth, air, fire, and water, are essential for life and must be cared for (Starhawk, 1993, p. 72). Yet this is only a beginning.

NOTES

1. Donal Carbaugh suggested the use of the term "ethnorhetorical" to describe this type of study.

2. Ellul (1964) describes this as the phenomenon of inventions (p. 23).

3. Ellul (1964) defines technique as "the totality of methods rationally arrived at and having absolute efficiency" (p. xxv).

4. For Ellul (1964), the word "technique" points to its social influence more clearly than "technology." Henceforth, when I employ the word "technique," I will be referring to the overall encompassing aspect of the technological society.

5. In the foreword to Ellul's *The Technological Society* (1964), Robert Merton explains that technique refers to "any complex of standardized means for attaining a predetermined result" (p. vi).

6. Ellul (1964) notes two laws of technological progress. First, technological progress is irreversible. Second, it acts according to a geometrical—not arithmetic—progression (p. 89). These two concepts of progress illustrate its constancy and its multiplication.

7. Ellul (1964) discusses technological production and consumption as being out of the consumer's control (p. 93). Furthermore, he describes this process in a discussion on economics in general (p. 221).

8. Ellul (1964) notes that Marx was correct in suggesting that the power of production dominates over ideas and theories (p. 153).

9. Ellul (1964) describes our passive situation as "[w]hen man [*sic*] himself becomes a machine, he attains to the marvelous freedom of unconsciousness, the freedom of the machine itself. . . . He does not feel himself an object, but he is" (p. 226). In this way, people take on the automatic processes formerly associated solely with machines. Barrett (1978) agrees, noting that "[a] machine is, logically speaking, an embodied decision procedure" (p. 23). In this way, people are no longer creative, but follow specific routines while they thoughtlessly pursue their goals.

10. Initially observing that "[s]cience has always been in conflict with narratives" (p. xxiii), Lyotard (1984) explains that "[t]he grand narrative has lost its credibility" and that "the decline of narrative can be seen as an effect of the blossoming of techniques and technologies . . . which has shifted emphasis from the ends of action to its means" (p. 37).

11. Creating an inclusive bibliography would be a monumental task. However, in compiling bibliographies from just two sources, Sjoo and Mor (1987) and Gadon (1989), I found at least 350 related published sources.

12. This type of spirituality does not exclude honoring gods as well as goddesses. Here I refer to Goddess spirituality, but many types of pagan beliefs and practices would fit this description as well.

13. Many others, including Margot Adler (1979) in *Drawing Down the Moon*, speak of this current interest in Goddess spirituality.

14. Starhawk (1979) created one of the most prominent early discourses outlining Goddess spirituality for our time.

15. These elements have been described in a variety of sources including Medici's *Good Magic* (1988, pp. 55–68) and Coppigan's *The Portal Book: Basic Teachings of Celtic Witchcraft* (1992, pp. 14–16). Though these elements have been used as symbolic representations of nature in magic rituals, Starhawk (1993) presents them as sacred because they are limited resources. These elements remain things no one can own or control.

16. This argument is not the same as that which Susan Griffin (1979) has made. For Griffin, women are equated with nature. Goddess spiritualists do not exclude men in this same way. The rhetoric of Goddess spirituality does not equate gender with nature, but uses nature symbolically to signify ways of being human, ways of acting, and so on. Furthermore, this move is made to redefine and emphasize the connections people have with their world.

17. The natural concept does not deny its mythic creation (Barthes, 1972, pp. 109–159, and Schwichtenberg, 1989).

18. Adler (1979) expands on the notions of play and paradox for other pagan spiritualists, such as Druids, Discordians, and Erisians (pp. 319–337).

19. Information about drawing the circle or casting the circle can be found in many books about magic rituals, including *Drawing Down the Moon* (Adler, 1979, pp. 470–472), *The Portal Book* (Coppigan, 1992, pp. 28–29), *Good Magic* (Medici, 1988, pp. 64–69), and *The Spiral Dance* (Starhawk, 1979, pp. 69–89).

20. Starhawk (1982) describes the connection between power and language when she explains that "[n]aming the stories, we can see how they shape us, and awareness is the first step toward change. When we talk about stories, we are talking about language. Language shapes consciousness, and the use of language to shape consciousness is an important branch of magic" (p. 23). The recognition of language as power, explicitly in magic rituals, relates to this explication of the discourses as a necessary step toward future action.

BIBLIOGRAPHY

Activist Solangel Rodriguez reflects on need for diversity in enviro movement. (1993, January 17). *Boston Globe*, p. 2.

Adler, M. (1979). *Drawing down the moon: Witches, druids, goddess-worshippers and other pagans in America today*. Boston: Beacon Press.

Akwesasne Task Force on the Environment. (1992, Fall). EPA sells out mother earth. *Akwesasne Task Force on the Environment Newsletter*, pp. 1, 8.

Alexander, C. (1992, February 3). Gunning for the greens. *Time*, pp. 50–51.

American Heritage Electronic Dictionary [Computer program]. (1990). Cambridge, MA: Houghton-Mifflin.

Amway supports environmental action [Advertisement]. (1991, December 30). *Time*, pp. 76–77.

Amy, D. (1987). *The politics of environmental mediation*. New York: Columbia University Press.

Angus, I. (1984). *Technique and enlightenment: Limits of instrumental reason*. Washington, DC: Centre for Advanced Research in Phenomenology and University Press of America.

Angus, I. (1989). Lectures for "Media, technology, and culture." Graduate course in the Department of Communication, University of Massachusetts.

Arbuthnot, J. (1974). Environmental knowledge and recycling behavior as a function of attitudes and personality characteristics. *Personality and Social Psychology Bulletin, 1*, 119–121.

Aristotle. (1991). *On rhetoric: A theory of civic discourse* (G. Kennedy, Trans.). New York: Oxford University Press.

Arnold, R. (1980). *Ecology wars*. Bellevue, WA: Free Enterprise Press.

Arnold, R., & Gottlieb, A. (1993). *Trashing the economy: How runaway environmentalism is wrecking America*. New York: Merril Press.

Atkinson, A. (1991). *Principles of political ecology*. London: Belhaven Press.

Bacon, F. (1960). *The new organon* (F. Anderson, Ed.). Indianapolis, IN: Bobbs-Merrill.

Bacon, L. S., & Wheeler, M. (1984). *Environmental dispute resolution*. New York: Plenum Press.

Bailey, R. (1993). *Ecoscam*. New York: St. Martin's Press.

Baker, F. (1990). Risk communication about environmental hazards. *Journal of Public Health Policy, 11,* 341–359.

Baldwin, D. (1993). The forest or the trees. *Old Oregon, 72,* 14–15.

Bammer, A. (1991). *Partial visions: Feminism and utopianism in the 1970s.* New York: Routledge.

Barreiro, J. (1992). Introduction. In J. Barreiro (Ed.), *Indian roots of American democracy* (pp. 1–10). Ithaca, NY: Akwekon.

Barret, M. E. (1990, December 14–16). Peddling the planet. *USA Weekend,* p. 5.

Barrett, W. (1978). *The illusion of technique.* Garden City, NY: Anchor Books.

Barthes, R. (1972). *Mythologies.* New York: Noonday Press.

Bateson, G. (1972). *Steps to an ecology of mind.* New York: Ballantine.

Begley, S., & King, P. (1992, May 4). War among the greens. *Newsweek,* p. 78.

Benhabib, S. (1987). The generalized and concrete other: The Kohlberg-Gilligan controversy and moral theory. In E. F. Kittay and D. T. Meyers (Eds.), *Women and moral theory* (pp. 154–177). Totowa, NJ: Rowman and Littlefield.

Benjamin, S. L., & Belluck, D. E. (1990). Risk feedback: An important step in risk communication. *Journal of the American Water Works Association, 82,* 50–55.

Berger, C. R. (1986). Uncertainty outcome values in predicted relationships: Uncertainty reduction theory then and now. *Human Communication Research, 13,* 34–38.

Berger, C. R., & Calabrese, R. J. (1975). Some explorations in initial interaction and beyond: Toward a developmental theory of interpersonal communication. *Human Communication Research, 1,* 99–112.

Berger, P., & Luckman, T. (1966). *The social construction of reality: A treatise in the sociology of knowledge.* New York: Anchor Books.

Berland, J., & Slack, J. D. (1994). On environmental matters. *Cultural Studies, 8,* 1–4.

Biehl, J. (1991). *Rethinking ecofeminist politics.* Boston: South End Press.

Biesecker, B. (1992). Michel Foucault and the question of rhetoric. *Philosophy and Rhetoric, 25,* 351–364.

Bingham, G. (1986). *Resolving environmental disputes: A decade of experience.* Washington, DC: Conservation Foundation.

Birds and the trees. (1993, April 5). *Newsweek,* p. 53.

Bitzer, L. (1959). Aristotle's enthymeme revisited. *Quarterly Journal of Speech, 45,* 399–408.

Blue Line Council. (1994, Winter). APA shows true colors on permits. *The Blue Line,* p. 1.

Bloch, E. (1986). *Principle of hope.* Oxford, England: Basil Blackwell.

Bochner, A. (1985). Perspectives on inquiry: Representation, conversation, and reflection. In M. Knapp and G. Miller (Eds.), *Handbook of interpersonal communication* (pp. 27–58). Beverly Hills, CA: Sage.

Bolen, J. S. (1984). *Goddesses in everywoman: A new psychology of women.* New York: Harper & Row.

Bookchin, M. (1971). *Post-scarcity anarchism.* Montreal: Black Rose Books.

Bookchin, M. (1980). *Toward an ecological society.* Montreal: Black Rose Books.

Bookchin, M. (1982). *The ecology of freedom: The emergence and dissolution of hierarchy.* Palo Alto, CA: Cheshire Books.

Bookchin, M. (1987). Thinking ecologically: A dialectical approach. *Our Generation, 18,* 3–40.

Bookchin, M. (1989, August 22). Death of a small planet. *The Progressive,* pp. 19–23.

Bookchin, M. (1990a). *The philosophy of social ecology: Essays on dialectical naturalism.* Montreal: Black Rose Books.

Bookchin, M. (1990b). *Remaking society: Pathways to a green future.* Boston: South End Press.

Bookchin, M. (1992). *Urbanization without cities: The rise and decline of citizenship.* Montreal: Black Rose Books.

Bowers, J., Ochs, D., & Jensen, R. (1993). *The rhetoric of agitation and control* (2nd ed.). Prospect Heights, IL: Waveland Press.

Braile, R. (1994, Fall). What the hell are we fighting for? *Garbage*, pp. 28–35.

Breech, R. (Segment producer). (1992, October 14). L.A. Law episode. In S. Sheslow (Executive producer), *L.A. Law*. New York: NBC.

Brock, B. L., Scott, R. L., & Chesebro, J. W. (1990). *Methods of rhetorical criticism: A twentieth-century perspective* (3rd ed.). Detroit, MI: Wayne State University Press.

Broughton, J. (1982). About environmental gossip. In A. C. Schoenfeld (Ed.), *Interpreting environmental issues* (pp. 78–79). Madison: University of Wisconsin Press.

Brower, D. (1995a, April 5). *CPR* for the earth! (*conservation, preservation, and restoration)*. Speech presented at the University of Denver, Denver, CO.

Brower, D. (1995b). *Let the mountains talk, let the rivers run*. San Francisco: HarperCollins West.

Brown, M., & May, J. (1991). *The Greenpeace story*. New York: Dorling Kindersly.

Bruchac, J. (1991). Otstungo: A Mohawk village in 1491. *National Geographic, 180*, 68–83.

Burke, K. (1950). *A rhetoric of motives*. New York: Prentice-Hall.

Burke, K. (1952). *Counter-statement* (2nd ed.). Berkeley: University of California Press.

Burke, K. (1957). *The philosophy of literary form*. New York: Random House.

Burke, K. (1966). *Language as symbolic action: Essays of life, literature, and method*. Berkeley: University of California Press.

Burke, K. (1969). *A grammar of motives* (3rd ed.). Berkeley: University of California Press.

Burke, K. (1970). *The rhetoric of religion* (2nd ed.). Berkeley: University of California Press.

Burke, K. (1973). *The philosophy of literary form* (3rd ed.). Berkeley: University of California Press.

Burke, K. (1989). *On symbols and society*. (J. Gusfield, Ed.). Chicago: University of Chicago Press.

Campbell, H. (1994, March). Outdoor recreation: An endangered tradition? *Popular Science*, pp. 7–10.

Campbell, K. K. (1972). Critique of Spiro T. Agnew: An exercise in Manichean rhetoric. In K. Campbell (Ed.), *Critiques of contemporary rhetoric* (pp. 94–110). Belmont, CA: Wadsworth.

Carless, J. (1992). *Taking out the trash*. Washington, DC: Island Press.

Carpenter, S. L., & Kennedy, W. J. D. (1988). *Managing public disputes: A practical guide to handling conflict and reaching agreements*. San Francisco: Jossey-Bass.

Carragee, K. M. (1990). Interpretive media study and interpretive social science. *Critical Studies in Mass Communication, 7*, 81–96.

Carragee, K. M. (1993). A critical evaluation of debates examining the media hegemony thesis. *Western Journal of Communication, 57*, 330–348.

Carson, R. L. (1962). *Silent spring*. Boston: Houghton-Mifflin.

Cathcart, R. (1980). Defining social movements by their rhetorical form. *Central States Speech Journal, 31*, 267–273.

Charland, M. (1990). Rehabilitating rhetoric: Confronting blindspots in discourse and social theory. *Communication, 11*, 253–264.

Chase, S. (Ed.). (1991). *Defending the earth: A dialogue between Murray Bookchin and Dave Foreman*. Boston: South End Press.

Chavis, B. (1993, January 25). Environmental racism harms social justice. *Sacramento Bee*, p. B13.

Cherwitz, R. A., & Hikins, J. W. (1990). Burying the undertaker: A eulogy for the eulogists of rhetorical epistemology. *Quarterly Journal of Speech, 76*, 73–77.

Chiras, D. (1990). *Beyond the fray*. Boulder, CO: Johnson Books.

Chrislip, D., & Larson, C. E. (1994). *Collaborative leadership*. San Francisco: Jossey-Bass.

Christensen, E. (1988). Risk communication: A surprise package for the chemical industry? *Toxic Substances Journal, 8,* 261–280.

Claus, G., & Bolander, D. (1977). *Ecological sanity.* New York: David McKay.

Cockburn, A. (1995, March 25). *Phoenix Gazette,* p. B9.

Cohn, D. (1990, March 2). NE dispute outgrowth of Earth Day group's dilemma. *Washington Post,* p. C3.

Cohn, V. (1989). *News and numbers: A guide to reporting statistical claims.* Ames: Iowa State University Press.

Colglazier, E. W., Cox, T., & Davis, K. (1991, December). *Estimation of resource requirements for NPL sites.* Knoxville: University of Tennessee, Waste Management Research and Education Institute.

Commission on the Adirondacks in the Twenty-First Century. (1990). *The Adirondack Park in the twenty-first century.* New York: State of New York.

Companies go green as environmental coalition gains influence. (1995, March 15). *Rocky Mountain News,* p. 36A.

Cooling down on global warming [Editorial]. (1995, April 9). *Washington Post,* p. C6.

Cooperstein, B. (1990, April 22). Earth Day: Color it green. *Los Angeles Times Book Review,* p. 15.

Coppigan, I. (1992). *The portal book: Basic teachings of Celtic witchcraft.* Salem, MA: Association for Consciousness Exploration.

Cotgrove, S. (1976). Environmentalism and utopia. *Sociological Review, 24,* 23–42.

Cotgrove, S. (1982). *Catastrophe or cornucopia: The environment, politics and the future.* New York: John Wiley and Sons.

Covello, V., & Mumpower, J. (1985). Risk analysis and risk management: An historical perspective. *Risk Analysis, 5,* 103.

Covello, V., von Winterfeldt, D., & Slovic, P. (1986a). Communicating scientific information about health and environmental risks: Problems and opportunities from a social and behavioral perspective. In V. Covello, L. Lave, A. Moghissi, & V. Upulur (Eds.), *Uncertainty in risk assessment, risk management, and decisionmaking* (pp. 221–239). New York: Plenum Press.

Covello, V., von Winterfeldt, D., & Slovic, P. (1986b). Risk communication: A review of the literature. *Risk Abstracts, 3,* 171–182.

Cox, R. J. (1990). On "interpreting" public discourse in post-modernity. *Western Journal of Speech Communication, 54,* 317–329.

Creighton, J. L. (1992, October). *The new challenge for decision makers.* Colorado Center for Environmental Management Conference, Snowmass, CO.

Crowfoot, J. E., & Wondolleck, J. M. (1990). *Environmental disputes: Community involvement in conflict resolution.* Washington, DC: Island Press.

Dahlberg, K., Soroos, M., Feraru, A., Harf, J., & Trout, T. (1985). *Environment and the global arena: Actors, values, policies, and futures.* Durham, NC: Duke University Press.

Dao, J. (1993, June 24). Blazing a power trail in the Adirondacks. *New York Times,* pp. B1, B8.

Davenport, J. (1970, February). Industry starts the big cleanup. *Fortune,* pp. 114–117.

Davis, G. G. (1993, November/December). Baikal, bring us together. *American Forests,* 38–41, 55, 56.

Day, K. (1992). Proposal for heavier emphasis on socio-economic criteria in the St. Lawrence county landfill siting process. Submitted to the St. Lawrence County Solid Waste Authority, December 30.

Day, S. M., Zeinelabdin, E., & Whitford, A. (1991, December). *State and private sector cleanups.* Knoxville: University of Tennessee, Waste Management Research and Education Institute.

de Certeau, M. (1988). *The practice of everyday life.* Berkeley: University of California Press.

DeFleur, M. L., & Ball-Rokeach, S. (1989). *Theories of mass communication.* White Plains, NY: Longman.

D'Elia, A. N. (1979). *The Adirondack rebellion.* Onchiota, NY: Onchiota Books.

Descartes, R. (1967). Discourse on method: Part VI. In E. Haldane & G. Ross (Trans.), *The philosophical works of Descartes.* Cambridge: Cambridge University Press.

Devall, B. (1988). *Simple in means, rich in ends: Practicing deep ecology.* Salt Lake City, UT: Peregrine Smith.

Devall, S., & Sessions, G. (1985). *Deep ecology.* Salt Lake City, UT: Peregrine Smith.

Dobson, A. (1990). *Green political thought.* London: HarperCollins Academic.

Dowie, M. (1994, April 18). The selling (out) of the Greens. *The Nation,* pp. 514–518.

Doyle, J. (1991, Spring). Hold the applause! Says FOE of Du Pont. *Friends of the Earth,* p. 5.

EarthWorks Group. (1990). *50 simple things you can do to save the earth.* Berkeley, CA: Earthworks Press.

Easterbrook, G. (1989, July 24). Cleaning up our mess. *Newsweek,* pp. 27–42.

Eckersley, R. (1991). *Environmentalism and political theory: Toward an ecocentric approach.* Albany: State University of New York Press.

Edwards, C. M. (1991). *The storyteller's goddess: Tales of the goddess and her wisdom from around the world.* San Francisco: HarperCollins.

Ehrlich, P. (1968). *The population bomb.* New York: Sierra Club–Ballantine.

Ehrlich, P., & Ehrlich, A. (1991). *Healing the planet: Strategies for resolving the environmental crisis.* New York: Addison-Wesley.

Elkington, J., Hailes, J., & Makower, J. (1990). *The green consumer.* New York: Penguin Group.

Ellul, J. (1964). *The technological society.* New York: Alfred A. Knopf.

Ellul, J. (1990a). The autonomy of technology. In L. A. Hickman (Ed.), *Technology as a human affair* (pp. 333–342). New York: McGraw-Hill.

Ellul, J. (1990b). The present and the future. In L. A. Hickman (Ed.), *Technology as a human affair* (pp. 343–357). New York: McGraw-Hill.

Ellul, J. (1990c). The technological order. In L. A. Hickman (Ed.), *Technology as a human affair* (pp. 59–72). New York: McGraw-Hill.

Emery, C. E. (1995, March 23). Environmental leader assails GOP. *The Providence Journal-Bulletin,* p. 11D.

English, M. R., Gibson, A. K., Feldman, D. L., & Tonn, B. E. (1993, September). *Stakeholder involvement: Open processes for reaching decisions about the future uses of contaminated sites.* Knoxville: University of Tennessee, Waste Management Research and Education Institute.

Environmental laws on hit list. (1994, December 30). *Rocky Mountain News,* p. 30A.

Fink-Eitel, H. (1992). *Foucault: An introduction* (E. Dixon, Trans.). Philadelphia: Pennbridge Books.

Fisher, A. (1991). Risk communication challenges. *Risk Analysis, 11,* 2–17.

Fisher, W. (1987). *Human communication as narration: Toward a philosophy of reason, value, and action.* Columbia: South Carolina University Press.

Fiske, J. (1987). *Television culture.* New York: Routledge.

Fitzgerald, E. F., Hwang, S., Brix, K. A., Bush, B., Quinn, J., & Cook, K. (1992). *Draft: Chemical contaminants in the milk of Mohawk women from Akwesasne.* Albany: New York State Department of Health.

Flynn, T. & Ross, S. (1995). Reconciling theory and teaching: Meeting the moral challenge of a rhetorical epistemology. In J. Hanser & R. Somer (Eds.), *New Dimensions in Communication VII: Proceedings of the 51st Annual New York State Speech Communication Association Convention* (pp. 5–12). Clinton, NY: Hamilton College.

Foes of gold mine predict environmental damage. (1991, November 4). *Rocky Mountain News,* p. I6.

Folz, D. (1991). Recycling program design, management and participation: A national survey of municipal experience. *Public Administration Review, 51,* 222–231.

Folz, D., & Hazlett, J. (1991). Public participation and recycling performance: Explaining program success. *Public Administration Review, 51,* 526–532.

For civility in Adirondacks [Editorial]. (1990, May 22). *Schenectady Daily Gazette,* p. A1.

Foreman, D. (1991). *Confessions of an eco-warrior.* New York: Harmony Books.

Foss, S. (1989). *Rhetorical criticism: Exploration & practice.* Prospect Heights, IL: Waveland Press.

Foss, S., Foss, K. A., & Trapp, R. (1991). *Contemporary perspectives on rhetoric* (2nd ed.). Prospect Heights, IL: Waveland Press.

Foss, S. K. (1986). Ambiguity as persuasion: The Vietnam veterans memorial. *Communication Quarterly, 34,* 326–340.

Foss, S. K., & Griffin, C. L. (1992). A feminist perspective on rhetorical theory: Toward a clarification of boundaries. *Western Journal of Communication, 56,* 330–349.

Foucault, M. (1970). *The order of things.* New York: Vintage.

Foucault, M. (1972). *The archaeology of knowledge* (A. M. Sheridan Smith, Trans.). New York: Pantheon.

Fox, S. (1989). *An introduction to the Wiccan religion.* Mt. Horeb, WI: Circle Sanctuary.

Fox, W. (1990). *Toward a transpersonal ecology: Developing new foundations for environmentalism.* Boston: Shambhala.

Frankel, B. (1987). *The post-industrial utopians.* Cambridge, MA: Polity Press.

Fumento, M. (1993). *Science under siege.* New York: William Morrow.

Gabriel, T. (1990, November 4). If a tree falls in the forest, do they hear it? *New York Times,* pp. VI: 34, 58–62.

Gadon, E. W. (1989). *The once & future goddess: A symbol for our time.* New York: Harper & Row.

Galbraith, J. K. (1994, Fall). The living industry and the environment. *EPA Journal,* pp. 41–43.

Gallagher, W. (1993). *The power of place.* New York: HarperCollins.

Gates, C. T. (1991). Making a case for collaborative problem solving. *National Civic Review, 80,* 113–119.

Gates, D. (1993, March 29). White male paranoia. *Newsweek,* pp. 48–53.

Geertz, C. (1973). *The interpretation of cultures.* New York: Basic Books.

Geertz, C. (1980). Blurred genres: The reconfiguration of social thought. *The American Scholar, 49,* 165–182.

Gerdts: Cuomo is a "criminal," women and kind "property." (1992, April 11). *Glen Falls Post-Star,* p. A1.

Gergen, K. J. (1978). Toward generative theory. *Journal of Personality and Social Psychology, 36,* 1344–1360.

Gibbs, L. (1982). *Love Canal.* Albany: State University of New York Press.

Gibbs, L. (1993, February). Celebrating ten years of triumph. *Everyone's Backyard, 11*(1), 2.

Gilligan, C. (1982). *In a different voice.* Cambridge, MA: Harvard University Press.

Gilligan, C. (1987). Moral orientation and moral development. In E. F. Kittay & D. T. Meyers (Eds.), *Women and moral theory* (pp. 19–33). Totowa, NJ: Rowman and Littlefield.

Glendinning, C. (1990). *When technology wounds: The human consequences of progress.* New York: William Morrow.

Golding, D., Krimsky, S., & Plough, A. (1992). Evaluating risk communication: Narrative vs. technical presentations of information about radon. *Risk Analysis, 12,* 27–33.

Goodwin, A. (1992). *Dancing in the distraction factory.* Minneapolis: University of Minnesota Press.

Goodwin, B., & Taylor, K. (1982). *The politics of utopia: A study in theory and practice*. London: Hutchinson.

Gore, A. (1992). *Earth in the balance: Ecology and the human spirit*. New York: Houghton-Mifflin.

Gottlieb, A. (1989). *The Wise Use agenda*. Bellevue, WA: Free Enterprise Press.

Gouran, D. S., & Hirokawa, R. Y. (1986). Counteractive functions of communication in effective group decision making. In R. Y. Hirokawa & M. S. Poole (Eds.), *Communication and group decision making* (pp. 81–90). Beverly Hills, CA: Sage.

Graham, F. (1978). *The Adirondack Park: A political history*. Syracuse, NY: Syracuse University Press.

Gramsci, A. (1971). *Selections from the prison notebooks* (Q. Hoare & G. Smith, Eds. and Trans.). New York: International Publishers.

Grass roots: Greens see access; wise use sees money. (1993, March 3). *Greenwire*, p. 1.

Gray, B. (1989). *Collaborating: Finding common ground for multiparty problems*. San Francisco: Jossey-Bass.

Gray, B., & Wood, D. J. (1991). Collaborative alliances: Moving from practice to theory. *Journal of Applied Behavioral Science, 27*, 3–21.

Greenberg, M., Sachsman, D., Sandman, P., & Salomone, K. (1989). Risk, drama, and geography in coverage of environmental risk by network TV. *Journalism Quarterly, 64*, 267–276.

Greider, W. (1992). *Who will tell the people*. New York: Simon and Schuster.

Griffin, S. (1978). *Woman and nature*. New York: Harper & Row.

Gronbeck, B. (1992, August). *Rhetoric, ethics, and tele-spectacles in the post-everything age*. Paper presented at the International Conference on Academic Knowledge and Political Power, University of Maryland, College Park, MD.

Gronbeck, B. E. (1978). The rhetoric of political corruption: Sociolinguistic, dialectical, and ceremonial processes. *Quarterly Journal of Speech, 64*, 155–172.

Grossberg, L. (1993). Can cultural studies find true happiness in communication? *Journal of Communication, 43*, 89–97.

Habermas, J. (1981). *The theory of communicative action: Vol. 1. Reason and the rationalization of society* (T. McCarthy, Trans.). Boston: Beacon Press.

Habermas, J. (1987). *The theory of communicative action: Vol. 2. Lifeworld and system: A critique of functionalist reason* (T. McCarthy, Trans.). Boston: Beacon Press.

Habermas, J. (1990). *Moral consciousness and communicative action* (C. Lenhardt & S. Nicholsen, Trans.). Cambridge, MA: MIT Press.

Hall, J. S., & Weschler, L. F. (1991). The Phoenix Futures Forum: Creating vision, implanting community. *National Civic League, 80*, 135–157.

Hall, S. (1980). Encoding/decoding. In S. Hall, D. Hobson, A. Lowe, & P. Willis (Eds.), *Culture, media, language* (pp. 128–138). London: Hutchinson.

Hall, S. (1982). The rediscovery of "ideology": Return of the "repressed" in media studies. In M. Gurevitch, T. Bennett, J. Curran, & J. Woollacott (Eds.), *Culture, society and the media* (pp. 56–90). New York: Methuen.

Hall, S. (1985). Signification, representation, ideology: Althusser and the post-structuralist debates. *Critical Studies in Mass Communication, 2*(2), 91–114.

Hamilton, N. (1995, March/April). Open season on the environment. *Sierra*, pp. 13–14.

Hammond, W. F. (1993, July 11). Fund is compromise for environmentalists, Adirondackers. *Schenectady Daily Gazette*, p. A1.

Haraway, D. (1993). The biopolitics of postmodern bodies. In L. S. Kauffman (Ed.), *American Feminist Thought at Century's End: A Reader* (pp. 199–233). Cambridge, MA: Blackwell.

Harris, M. (1990). *Embracing the earth*. Chicago: Noble Press.

Harris, R. A., & Milkis, S. M. (1989). *The politics of regulatory change*. New York: Oxford University Press.

Hart, R. (1990). *Modern rhetorical criticism.* Glenview, IL: Scott, Foresman.

Heath, R., & Nathan, K. (1991). Public relations' role in risk communication: Information, rhetoric and power. *Public Relations Quarterly, 35,* 15–22.

Hebert, H. J. (1995, March 26). Babbitt draws equal fire from opposing sides. *Los Angeles Times,* p. A16.

Heidegger, M. (1977). *The question concerning technology and other essays.* New York: Harper.

Henneberger, M. (1993, April 12). Adirondack hamlet defies time, and help. *New York Times,* pp. A1, B8.

Hickman, L. A. (1990). *Technology as a human affair.* New York: McGraw-Hill.

Hill, M. (1993a, April 7). Violence predicted over landfill. *Potsdam (New York) Daily Courier-Observer,* p. 1–2.

Hill, M. (1993b, April 8). Official says Brasher to benefit: Not everyone opposes landfill. *Potsdam (New York) Daily Courier-Observer,* p. 1.

Hill, R. (1992). Oral memory of the Haudenosaunee: Views of the two row wampum. In J. Barreiro (Ed.), *Indian roots of American democracy* (pp. 147–159). Ithaca, NY: Akwekon.

Hirokawa, R. Y. (1985). Discussion procedures and decision-making performance: A test of a functional perspective. *Human Communication Research, 12,* 203–224.

Hirokawa, R. Y. (1988). Group communication and decision-making performance: A continued test of the functional perspective. *Human Communication Research, 14,* 487–515.

Hirokawa, R. Y., & Scheerhorn, D. R. (1986). Communication in faulty group decision making. In R. Y. Hirokawa & M. S. Poole (Eds.), *Communication and group decision making* (pp. 63–80). Beverly Hills, CA: Sage.

Hirst, R. (1993, March). *Training in risk communication: The art of environmental oratory.* Paper presented at the Conference on College Composition and Communication, Washington, DC.

Hochberg, L. (Segment producer). (1993, April 2). Timber talk. In Robert MacNeil (Executive producer), *MacNeil/Lehrer News Hour.* New York: PBS.

Horkheimer, M. (1947). *Eclipse of reason.* New York: Oxford University Press.

Horkheimer, M., & Adorno, T. (1972). *Dialectic of enlightenment.* New York: Herder.

Hornsby, B. (1992, September 22). Can environmentalism help the economy? *Denver Post,* p. 6B.

Hughes, J. (1992, November/December). Greens and Socialists seek harmonic convergence. *Democratic Left, 20*(6), 3–5.

Hughey, J., et al. (1987, November). *Insidious metaphors and the changing meaning of AIDS.* Paper presented at the annual convention of the Speech Communication Association, Boston, MA.

Hummel, S. (1988, October 21). Mohawks detail how PCBs changed Akwesasne lifestyle. *Watertown (New York) Daily Times,* pp. 20, 32.

Hunter, R. (1971). *The storming of the mind.* Garden City, NY: Doubleday.

Hunter, R. (1979). *Warriors of the Rainbow: A chronicle of the Greenpeace movement.* New York: Holt, Rinehart, and Winston.

Ihde, D. (1979). *Technics and praxis.* Holland: Reidal.

Ihde, D. (1983). *Existential technics.* Albany: State University of New York Press.

Ihde, D. (1990). *Technology and the lifeworld: From garden to earth.* Bloomington: Indiana University Press.

Innis, H. A. (1950). *Empire and communications.* London: Oxford University Press.

In skimpy environment fund, find cash for Woodlawn Beach. (1993, July 13). *Buffalo News,* p. C2.

Interior official chides environmental nuts. (1991, March 23). *New York Times,* p. I6.

Jacoby, R. (1989). The decline of American intellectuals. In I. Angus & S. Jhally (Eds.), *Cultural politics in contemporary America* (pp. 271–382). New York: Routledge.

Jamieson, K. H. (1980). The metaphoric cluster in the rhetoric of Pope Paul VI and Edmund G. Brown, Jr. *Quarterly Journal of Speech, 66*, 51–72.

Jamieson, K. H. (1988). *Eloquence in an electronic age: The transformation of political speechmaking.* Oxford: Oxford University Press.

Jeffco quarry showdown. (1991, October 21). *Rocky Mountain News*, p. 17.

Jones, J. (1993, November). The politics of land. *Empire State Report*, pp. 33–35.

Kammen, M. (1991). *Mystic chords of memory: The transformation of tradition in American culture.* New York: Alfred A. Knopf.

Kasperson, R., & Stallen, P. (Eds.). (1990). *Communicating risks to the public.* Dordrecht, Netherlands: Kluwer Academic Publishers.

Katz, S. (1992). The ethic of expediency: Classical rhetoric, technology, and the Holocaust. *College English, 54*, 375–386.

Kerr, R. A. (1988). Report urges greenhouse action now. *Science, 241*, 23–24.

Killingsworth, J., & Steffens, D. (1989). Effectiveness in the environmental impact statement: A study in public rhetoric. *Written Communication, 6*, 155–180.

Killingsworth, M. J., & Palmer, J. S. (1992). *Ecospeak: Rhetoric and environmental politics in America.* Carbondale: Southern Illinois University Press.

Kimball, D.(1992). *Recycling in America.* Santa Barbara, CA: ABC-Clio.

Klapp, M. (1992). *Bargaining with uncertainty: Decision-making in public health, technological safety, and environmental quality.* New York: Auburn House.

Kleiner, A. (1991, July/August). The three faces of Dow. *Garbage*, pp. 52–58.

Klumpp, J., & Hollihan, T. (1989). Rhetorical criticism as moral action. *Quarterly Journal of Speech, 75*, 84–97.

Knickerbocker, B. (1993, January 12). The United States goes green: A special report. *Christian Science Monitor*, pp. 1, 11.

Kohak, E. (1984). *The embers and the stars: A philosophical inquiry into the moral sense of nature.* Chicago: University of Chicago Press.

Kohlberg, L. (1981). *Essays on moral development: Vol. 1. The philosophy of moral development.* San Francisco: Harper & Row.

Kohlberg, L. (1984). *Essays on moral development: Vol 2. The psychology of moral development.* San Francisco: Harper & Row.

Krimsky, S., & Plough, A. (1988). *Environmental hazards: Communicating risk as a social process.* New York: Auburn House.

Krippendorf, K. (1980). *Content analysis: An introduction to its methodology.* Newbury Park, CA: Sage.

Kumar, K. (1991). *Utopianism.* Minneapolis: University of Minnesota Press.

Kunreuther, H., Kleindorfer, P., Knez, P., & Yaksick, R. (1987). A compensation mechanism for siting noxious facilities: Theory and experimental design. *Journal of Environmental Economics and Management, 14*, 371–383.

Laird, F. N. (1989). The decline of deference: The political context of risk communication. *Risk Analysis, 9*, 543–549.

Lakoff, G. (1990, November). *Metaphor and war: The metaphor system used to justify war in the Gulf.* Paper presented at the annual convention of the Speech Communication Association, Chicago, IL.

Lakoff, G., & Johnson, M. (1980). *Metaphors we live by.* Chicago: University of Chicago Press.

Lamonick, M. (1991, December 9). Whose woods are these? *Time*, pp. 70–75.

Lanphear, M. (1993a, April 7). Landfill fight teams rival Mohawks. *Watertown (New York) Daily Times*, p. 32.

Lanphear, M. (1993b, April 9). Mohawks to battle landfill at session. *Watertown (New York) Daily Times*, p. 25.

Lanphear, M. (1993c, June 22). Tribal council's attorney says county violated state rules. *Watertown (New York) Daily Times*, p. 27.

Lansana, F. (1992). Distinguishing potential recyclers from nonrecyclers: A basis for developing recycling strategies. *Journal of Environmental Education, 23*, 16–23.

Leiss, W. (1972). *The domination of nature.* Boston: Beacon Press.

Lentricchia, F. (1983). *Criticism and social change.* Chicago: University of Chicago Press.

Leopold, A. (1968). *A Sand County almanac.* Oxford: Oxford University Press.

Levitas, R. (1991). *The concept of utopia.* Syracuse, NY: Syracuse University Press.

Lewis, J. (1983). The encoding/decoding model: Criticisms and redevelopments for research on decoding. *Media, Culture and Society, 5*, 179–197.

Lewis, J. (1991). *The ideological octopus: An exploration of television and its audience.* New York: Routledge.

Lewis, M. (1992). *Green delusions: An environmentalist critique of radical environmentalism.* Durham, NC: Duke University Press.

Lichtenberg, J., & MacLean, D. (1990). The role of the media in risk communication. In R. Kasperson & P. Stallen (Eds.), *Communicating risks to the public* (pp. 157–173). Dordrecht, Netherlands: Kluwer Academic Publishers.

Likert, R. (1971). The principle of supportive relationships. In D. S. Pugh (Ed.), *Organization theory* (pp. 279–304). Baltimore: Penguin.

List, P. (1993). *Radical environmentalism: Philosophy and tactics.* Belmont, CA: Wadsworth.

Logsdon, J. M. (1991). Interests and interdependence in the formation of social problem-solving collaborations. *Journal of Applied Behavioral Science, 27*, 23–37.

Lowe, P., & Morrison, D. (1984). Bad news or good news: Environmental politics and the mass media. *Sociological Review, 32*, 75–90.

Lyons, O. (1992). Land of the free, home of the brave. In J. Barreiro (Ed.), *Indian roots of American democracy* (pp. 30–35). Ithaca, NY: Akwekon.

Lyotard, J. (1984). *The post-modern condition: A report on knowledge.* Minneapolis: University of Minnesota Press.

Mackie, J. (1977). *Ethics: Inventing right and wrong.* Harmondsworth, England: Penguin.

Mailloux, S. (1985). Rhetorical hermeneutics. *Critical Inquiry, 11*, 620–641.

Manes, C. (1990). *Green rage: Radical environmentalism and the unmaking of civilization.* Boston: Little, Brown.

Mannheim, K. (1936). *Ideology and utopia.* New York: Harcourt Brace Jovanovich.

Marcuse, H. (1969). *An essay on liberation.* Boston: Beacon Press.

Marino, R. (1993, June 28). Senate passes environmental trust fund legislation [New York senate memo].

Marshall, E. (1989). Science advisers need advice. *Science, 245*, 21.

Martin, R. (1992, May 14). Mohawk breast milk said safe. *Potsdam (New York) Daily Courier-Observer*, pp. 1–2.

Martin, R. (1993, April 8). Local woman speaking out to protect river. *Potsdam (New York) Daily Courier-Observer*, p. 1.

Mathews, J. (1994, December 18). Green sweep. *Washington Post*, p. C7.

Mattessich, P. W., & Monsey, B. R. (1992). *Collaboration: What makes it work.* St. Paul, MN: Amherst H. Wilder Foundation.

Matthews, C. (1989). *The elements of the Celtic tradition.* Longmead, England: Element Books.

McCoy, W. J. (1991). Building coalitions for the future in Charlotte-Mecklenburg. *National Civic Review, 80*, 120–134.

McGee, M. (1980). "Social movement": Phenomenon or meaning? *Central States Speech Journal, 31*, 233–244.

McGee, M. C. (1980). The "ideograph": A link between rhetoric and ideology. *Quarterly Journal of Speech, 66*, 1–16.

McKee, D. (1991). *Energy, the environment, and public policy.* New York: Praeger.

McKerrow, R. (1989). Critical rhetoric: Theory and praxis. *Communication Monographs, 56*, 91–111.

McKibben, B. (1992, November). Wild thoughts: Is there a workable future for the Adirondack Park? *Adirondack Life, 23*, 40–45, 59–60.

McLuhan, M. (1962). *The Gutenberg galaxy: The making of typographic man.* Toronto: University of Toronto Press.

McLuhan, M. (1964). *Understanding media: The extensions of man.* New York: McGraw-Hill.

McMartin, B. (1994, January). The thin Blue Line. *Adirondack Life, 24*, 16–21.

McQuail, D. (1984). With the benefit of hindsight: Reflections on uses and gratifications research. *Critical Studies in Mass Communication, 1*, 177–193.

Meadows, D. (1972). *The limits to growth: A report for the Club of Rome's project on the predicament of mankind.* New York: New American Library.

Medici, M. (1988). *Good magic.* New York: Prentice-Hall.

Meier, R. (1991, March 30). Products that are wrapped in messages. *New York Times*, p. I36.

Mende, S. (1993a, April 6). Landfill war begins. *Potsdam (New York) Daily Courier-Observer*, p. 1.

Mende, S. (1993b, April 11). Brasher site faces quick OK Monday. *Ogdensburg (New York) Advance News*, pp. 13–14.

Mende, S. (1993c, June 17). Director: Deal is "win-win" situation. *Potsdam (New York) Daily Courier-Observer*, p. 2.

Mende, S. (1993d, July 21). County landfill cheaper than Rodman. *Potsdam (New York) Daily Courier-Observer*, p. 1.

Merchant, C. (1992). *Radical ecology: The search for a livable world.* New York: Routledge.

Metzler, M. (1993, April). *When laws are not enough: Ethical criteria for environmental risk communication.* Paper presented at the Eastern Communication Convention, New Haven, CT.

Michaels, P. (1992). *Sound and fury.* Washington, DC: CATO Institute.

Milburn, T. A. (1992). *Organizational construction of self identity in technological society.* Unpublished master's thesis, Texas A & M University, College Station, TX.

Miller, C. (1981). Environmental impact statements and some modern traditions of communication. *International Technical Communication Conference Proceedings, 28*, E–67–69.

Miller, C. (1984). Genre as social action. *Quarterly Journal of Speech, 70*, 151–167.

Miller, J. (1993, April). The wrong shade of green. *Dollars & Sense*, pp. 6–9.

Miller, K. (1995, March 31). The environmental movement after a quarter-century of Earth Days. *Gannett News Service*, p. 1.

Mink, L. (1987). *Historical understanding.* Ithaca, NY: Cornell University Press.

Mitchell, J. (1970). *Ecotactics: The Sierra Club handbook for environmental activists.* New York: Pocketbooks.

Mohawk, J. (1992). The Indian way is a thinking tradition. In J. Barreiro (Ed.), *Indian roots of American democracy* (pp. 20–29). Ithaca, NY: Akwekon.

Moncrief, L. (1973). The cultural basis of our environmental crisis. In I. Barbour (Ed.), *Western man and environmental ethics: Attitudes towards nature and technology* (pp. 31–42). Reading, MA: Addison-Wesley.

Moore, C. (1988). Effective governance by cooperation: Negotiated investment strategy. *National Civic Review, 77*, 298–314.

Moos, R., & Brownstein, R. (1977). *Environment and utopia.* New York: Plenum Press.

Morgan, G. (1983). *Beyond method.* Beverly Hills, CA: Sage.

Morley, D. (1986). *Family television.* New York: Comedia.

Morris, D. B. (1995). *Earth warrior.* Golden, CO: Fulcrum.

Mumby, D. (1987). The political function of narrative in organizations. *Communication Monographs, 54,* 113–127.

Mumford, L. (1934). *Technics and civilization.* New York: Harcourt, Brace.

Murphy, M. (1995, March 25). Environmental battle heats up: "Angry" group targetting "radicals." *Phoenix Gazette,* p. B1.

Murray, F. X., & Curran, C. (1983). *Why they agreed.* Washington, DC: Georgetown University, Center for Strategic and International Studies.

Naar, J. (1990). *Design for a livable planet.* New York: Harper & Row.

National Research Council. (1989). *Improving risk communication.* Washington, DC.: National Academy Press.

New York State Department of Health. (1993). *Public health assessment General Motors/Central Foundry division* [Public comment draft]. Massena: New York State Department of Health.

Nixon, W. (1995, April). Making Earth Day count. *Environmental Magazine,* pp. 31–36.

Norris, T. (1993). *The healthy communities handbook.* Denver, CO: National Civic League.

Norton, B. G. (1991). *Toward unity among environmentalists.* New York: Oxford University Press.

Null, G. (1990). *Cleaner, cleaner, safer, greener.* New York: Villard.

Oelschlaeger, M. (1991). *The idea of wilderness.* New Haven, CT: Yale University Press.

O'Hare, M., Bacow, L., & Sanderson, D. (1983). *Facility siting.* New York: Van Nostrand.

O'Keefe, D. (1975). Logical empiricism and the study of human communication. *Speech Monographs, 42,* 169–183.

Olds, L. E. (1992). *Metaphors of interrelatedness.* Albany: State University of New York Press.

Ong, W. J. (1982). *Orality and literacy: The technologizing of the word.* London: Methuen.

O'Riordan, T. (1981). Environmentalism and education. *Journal of Geography in Higher Education, 5,* 3–18.

Osborn, M. (1967). Archetypal metaphor in rhetoric: The light-dark family. *Quarterly Journal of Speech, 53,* 115–126.

Oskamp, S., Harrington, M., Edwards, T., Sherwood, D., Okuda, S., & Swanson, D. (1991). Factors influencing household recycling behavior. *Environment and Behavior, 23,* 494–519.

Pacey, A. (1983). *The culture of technology.* Cambridge, MA: MIT Press.

Pasquero, J. (1991). Supraorganizational collaboration: The Canadian environmental experiment. *Journal of Applied Behavioral Science, 27,* 38–64.

Pell, E. (1991, November/December). Stop the Greens. *Environmental Magazine,* pp. 33–36.

Pepper, D. (1990). *The roots of modern environmentalism.* New York: Routledge.

Pepper, D. (1993). *Eco-socialism: From deep ecology to social justice.* New York: Routledge.

Perrecone, J. (1992). *Incineration: Too hot to handle? Westinghouse Superfund sites, Bloomington, Indiana, a case study.* Paper presented at Superfund 1992 Conference, Chicago, IL.

Perry, S. (1983). Rhetorical functions of the infestation metaphor in Hitler's rhetoric. *Central States Speech Journal, 34,* 229–235.

Petty, R. E., & Cacioppo, J. T. (1986). *Communication and persuasion: Central and peripheral routes to attitude change.* New York: Springer-Verlag.

Petulla, J. (1978). *American environmental history.* San Francisco: Boyd & Fraser.

Petulla, J. (1980). *American environmentalism: Values, tactics, priorities.* College Station, TX: Texas A & M University Press.

Petulla, J. (1987). *Environmental protection in the United States: Industry, agencies, environmentalists.* San Francisco: Boyd & Fraser.

Piasecki, B., & Asmus, P. (1990). *In search of environmental excellence.* New York: Simon and Schuster.

Pinchot, G. (1968). The fight for conservation. In R. Nash (Ed.), *The American environment: Readings in the history of conservation* (pp. 59–61). Reading, MA: Addison-Wesley.

Plattel, M. (1972). *Utopian and critical thinking.* Pittsburgh, PA: Duquesne University Press.

Plough, A., & Krimsky, S. (1987). The emergence of risk communication studies: Social and political context. *Science, Technology and Human Values, 12,* 4–10.

Pollan, M. (1991). *Second nature: A gardener's education.* New York: Dell.

Poore, P. (1993, May). Enviro-education. *Garbage,* pp. 26–31.

Pope, C. (1995, March/April). To a former Sierra Club member. *Sierra,* p. 20.

Porritt, J. (1985). *Seeing green: The politics of ecology explained.* Oxford: Basil Blackwell.

Porter, T. (1992). Men who are of the good mind. In J. Barreiro (Ed.), *Indian roots of American democracy* (pp. 12–19). Ithaca, NY: Akwekon.

Portney, K. E. (1991). *Siting hazardous waste treatment facilities: The NIMBY syndrome.* New York: Auburn House.

Posner, R. (1992). *Economic analysis of law* (4th ed.). Boston: Little, Brown.

Potapchuk, W. R. (1991). New approaches to citizen participation: Building consent. *National Civic Review, 80,* 158–168.

Purdue, R. B. (1990, November 16). It's not about the environment: Issue in Adirondacks is power. *Rochester Democrat and Chronicle,* p. A1.

Raskin, F. (1990, January). Undermined. *Friends of the Earth,* pp. 15–23.

Ray, D. (1990). *Trashing the planet.* Washington, DC: Regnery Gateway.

Reagen, J. (1993, April 6). Too close to St. Regis River: Mohawks angry, vow to fight site. *Potsdam (New York) Daily Courier-Observer,* p. 1.

Regenstein, L. (1982). *America the poisoned.* Washington, DC: Acropolis Books.

Reinfeld, N. (1992). *Community recycling: System design to management.* Englewood Cliffs, NJ: Prentice-Hall.

Report warns of environmental crisis. (1992, April 14). *New York Times,* p. A8.

Rifkin, J. (1983). *Algeny.* New York: Viking.

Robbins, M. (1995, March/April). Earth Day and clear days [Editorial]. *Audubon,* p. 6.

Robinson, K. S. (1988). *Pacific Edge.* New York: Orb.

Robinson, K. S. (1993). *Red Mars.* New York: Bantam.

Robinson, K. S. (1994). *Green Mars.* New York: Bantam.

Roberts, N. C., & Bradley, R. T. (1991). Stakeholder collaboration and innovation: A study of public policy initiation at the state level. *Journal of Applied Behavioral Science, 27,* 209–227.

Robles v. Environmental Protection Agency, 484 F.2d 843 [C.A. Md. 1973].

Rogers, E. M. (1983). *Diffusion of innovations* (3rd ed.). New York: Free Press.

Rosenbaum, W. A. (1991). *Environmental politics and policy.* Washington, DC: Congressional Quarterly Press.

Ross, S. (1992). High risk technologies, ethical argument, and engineers-in-training. In J. Jaksa & M. Pritchard (Eds.), *Discussion group proceedings of the Second National Communication Ethics Conference* (pp. 327–355). Rochester, MI: Hampton.

Ross, S. (1994). A feminist perspective on technical communicative action: Exploring how alternative world views affect environmental remediation efforts. *Technical Communications Quarterly, 3,* 325–342.

Ross, S., & Karis, B. (1991). Communicating in public policy matters: Addressing the problem of non-congruent sites of discourse. *IEEE Transactions in Professional Communication, 34,* 247–254.

Royce, J. R. (1964). *The encapsulated man.* Princeton, NJ: D. Van Nostrand.

Rubin, C., & Landy, M. (1993, February/March). Global warming. *Garbage,* p. 24.

Russell, D., & deLong, O. (1991, November/December). Can business save the environment? *Environmental Magazine,* pp. 28–37.

Russell, M., Colglazier, W. E., & English, M. R. (1991, December). *Hazardous waste remediation: The task ahead.* Knoxville: University of Tennessee, Waste Management Research and Education Institute.

Sale, K. (1993). *The green revolution: The American environmental movement 1962–1992.* New York: Hill and Wang.

Samdahl, D., & Robertson, R. (1989). Social determinants of environmental concern: Specification and test of the model. *Environment and Behavior, 21,* 57–81.

Sandman, P. (1986). *Explaining environmental risk.* Washington, DC: U.S. Environmental Protection Agency, Office of Toxic Substances.

Sandman, P. (1988). Risk communication: Facing public outrage. *Management Communication Quarterly, 2,* 235–238.

Sandman, P. (Producer) (1991). *A formula for effective risk communication* [Video]. Fairfax, VA: American Industrial Hygiene Association.

Sarup, M. (1993). *An introductory guide to post-structuralism and postmodernism.* Athens: University of Georgia Press.

Scarce, R. (1990). *Eco-warriors.* Chicago: Noble Press.

Scheffer, V. (1991). *The shaping of American environmentalism.* Seattle: University of Washington Press.

Schneider, K. (1992, February 16). When the bad guy is seen as the one in the green hat. *New York Times,* p. E3.

Schwichtenberg, C. (1989). The "Mother Lode" of feminist research: Congruent paradigms in the analysis of beauty culture. *Rethinking Communication, 2,* 291–306.

Scott, R. L. (1967). On viewing rhetoric as epistemic. *Central States Speech Journal, 18,* 9–16.

Scott, R. L. (1976). On viewing rhetoric as epistemic: Ten years later. *Central States Speech Journal, 27,* 258–266.

Scott, R. L., & Smith, D. K. (1969). The rhetoric of confrontation. *Quarterly Journal of Speech, 55,* 1–8.

Selsky, J. W. (1991). Lessons in community development: An activist approach to stimulating interorganizational collaboration. *Journal of Applied Behavioral Science, 27,* 91–115.

Severson, G. J. (1993). *Gaining community acceptance.* Golden, CO: Waste-Tech Services.

Shabecoff, P. (1993). *A fierce green fire: The American environmental movement.* New York: Hill and Wang.

Sharfman, M. P., Gray, B., & Yan, A. (1991). The context of interorganizational collaboration in the garment industry: An institutional perspective. *Journal of Applied Behavioral Science, 27,* 181–208.

Shenandoah, A. (1992). Everything has to be in balance. In J. Barreiro (Ed.), *Indian roots of American democracy* (pp. 36–42). Ithaca, NY: Akwekon.

Short, B. (1991). Earth First! and the rhetoric of moral confrontation. *Communication Studies, 42,* 172–188.

Sierra Club targets Shaefer, Allard. (1995, March 24). *Denver Post,* p. 7A.

Simon, J. (1980). Resources, population, environment: An oversupply of false bad news. *Science, 208,* 1431–1437.

Simons, H. (1972). Persuasion in social conflicts. *Speech Monographs, 39,* 227–247.

Sjoo, M., & Mor, B. (1987). *The great cosmic mother: Rediscovering the religion of the earth.* San Francisco: Harper & Row.

Sloan, R. J., & Jock, K. (1990). *Chemical contaminants in fish from the St. Lawrence River drainage on lands of the Mohawk Nation at Akwesasne and near the General Motors Corporation/Central Foundry Division, Massena, New York.* Albany: New York State Department of Environmental Conservation.

Slovic, P. (1991). Perceptions of risk: Paradox and challenge. In S. Friedman & L. Rogers (Eds.), *Environmental risk reporting: The science and the coverage* (pp. 7–12). Bethlehem, PA: Lehigh University Press.

Slovic, P., Layman, M., & Flynn, O. (1991). Lessons from Yucca Mountain. *Environment, 33,* 7–11, 28–30.

Smith, R. (1993a, July 8). Site work on cleanup of GM property starts. *Watertown (New York) Daily Times,* pp. 34, 40.

Smith, R. (1993b, July 19). Review raps RAP's report on pollution. *Watertown (New York) Daily Times,* p. 27.

Spangle, M., & Germann, C. (1994). Saving our cousins, the chimps: A dramatistic analysis of the environmental rhetoric of Jane Goodall. *New York Communication Annual, 8,* 5–23.

Spretnak, C., & Capra, F. (1985). *Green politics.* London: Paladin.

Stamato, L. (1988). Land-use and siting conflicts: New roles for community organizations. *National Civic Review, 77,* 315–322.

Starhawk. (1979). *The spiral dance: A rebirth of the ancient religion of the great goddess.* San Francisco: Harper & Row.

Starhawk. (1982). *Dreaming in the dark: Magic, sex and politics.* Boston: Beacon Press.

Starhawk. (1993). *The fifth sacred thing.* New York: Bantam.

Stern, P. C. (1991). Learning through conflict: A realistic strategy for risk communication. *Policy Sciences, 24,* 65–119.

Stewart, C., Smith, C., & Denton, R., Jr. (1984). *Persuasion and social movements.* Prospect Heights, IL: Waveland Press.

Stewart, C., Smith, C., & Denton, R., Jr. (1994). *Persuasion and social movements* (3rd ed.). Prospect Heights, IL: Waveland Press.

Stone, W. B., Jock, K., & Gradoni, P. B. (1991). *Draft: Chemical contaminants in wildlife from the Mohawk Nation at Akwesasne and the vicinity of the General Motors Corporation/Central Foundry Division, Massena, New York.* Albany: New York State Department of Environmental Conservation.

Swanson, D. (1991). Factors influencing household recycling behavior. *Environment and Behavior, 23,* 494–519.

Taylor, C. (1980). Understanding in human science. *Review of Metaphysics, 34,* 3–23.

Tedesco, R. (Segment producer). (1992, September 20). Clean air, clean water, dirty fight. In D. Hewitt (Executive producer), *60 Minutes.* Denver: KMGH (CBS).

Television offensive launched by environmentalists. (1995, April 5). *U.S. Newswire,* p. 1.

Terrie, P. (1985). *Forever wild: Environmental aesthetics and the Adirondack forest preserve.* Philadelphia: Temple University Press.

Terrie, P. (1992). Behind the Blue Line. *Adirondack Life, 23,* 46–51, 60, 62.

Therborn, G. (1980). *The ideology of power and the power of ideology.* London: Verso.

Thomas, J. (1992a). The Great Law takes a long time to understand. In J. Barreiro (Ed.), *Indian roots of American democracy* (pp. 43–46). Ithaca, NY: Akwekon.

Thomas, J. (1992b). Words that come before all. In J. Barreiro (Ed.), *Indian roots of American democracy* (pp. 10–11). Ithaca, NY: Akwekon.

Tokar, B. (1987). *The green alternative: Creating an ecological future.* San Pedro, CA: R. & E. Miles.

Tokar, B. (1992). *The green alternative: Creating an ecological future* (2nd ed.). San Pedro, CA: R. & E. Miles.

Tokar, B. (1994, April). The Clinton forest plan. *Z Magazine*, pp. 25–30.

Tomsho, R. (1990, November 29). Dumping grounds: Indian tribes contend with some of worst of America's pollution. *Wall Street Journal*, pp. A1, A6.

Toulmin, S. (1982). The construal of reality: Criticism in modern and postmodern science. In W. Mitchell (Ed.), *The politics of interpretation* (pp. 99–117). Chicago, IL: University of Chicago Press.

Treichler, P. A. (1993). AIDS, gender, & biomedical discourse: Current contests for meaning. In L. S. Kauffman (Ed.), *American Feminist Thought at Century's End: A Reader* (pp. 281–354). Cambridge, MA: Blackwell.

U.S. v. J. B. Williams Co. Inc., 402 F. Supp. 796 (D.C.N.Y. 1975).

Van Gelder, L. (1992, January/February). Saving the homeplace: How Kentucky's most powerful environmental group gets what it wants. *Audubon*, pp. 62–67.

Van Liere, K., & Dunlap, R. (1981). Environmental concern: Does it make a difference how it's measured? *Environment and Behavior, 13*, 651–676.

Wagner, S. (1992). The Iroquois influence on women's rights. In J. Barreiro (Ed.), *Indian roots of American democracy* (pp. 115–134). Ithaca, NY: Akwekon.

Wald, M. (1990, April 22). Guarding environment: A world of challenges. *New York Times*, p. 1.

Warning on "risk-o-phobia." (1990, May 2). *New York Times*, p. A22.

Wartella, E. (1994). Challenge to the profession. *Communication Education, 43*, 54–62.

Watzlawick, P., Beavin, J., & Jackson, D. (1967). *Pragmatics of human communication: A study of interactional patterns, pathologies, and paradoxes*. New York: Norton.

Ways, M. (1970, February). How to think about the environment. *Fortune*, pp. 98–101.

Weaver, R. (1953). *The ethics of rhetoric*. Chicago: Regnery.

Webb, S. (1993a, May 13). Mohawks make move in challenging landfill. *Watertown (New York) Daily Times*, pp. 30, 34.

Webb, S. (1993b, July 18). Estimates from St. Lawrence using DANC landfill unchanged. *Watertown (New York) Daily Times*, p. B2.

Wehrwein, P. (1993, July 9). Legislature approves environmental fund. *Albany (New York) Times Union*, p. A1.

Wellford v. Hardin, 315 F. Supp. 768 (D.C.D.C. 1970).

Westley, F., & Vredenburg, H. (1991). Strategic bridging: The collaboration between environmentalists and business in the marketing of green products. *Journal of Applied Behavioral Science, 27*, 65–90.

Whalen, E. (1993). *Toxic terror* (2nd ed.). Ottawa, IL: Jameson Books.

White, L. (1973). The historical roots of our ecological crisis. In I. Barbour (Ed.), *Western man and environmental ethics: Attitudes towards nature and technology* (pp. 18–30). Reading, MA: Addison-Wesley.

White, S. (1988). *The recent work of Jurgen Habermas: Reason, justice and modernity*. Cambridge: Cambridge University Press.

Williams, D. C. (1989). Under the sign of (an)nihilation: Burke in the age of nuclear destruction and critical deconstruction. In H. W. Simons & Trevor Melia (Eds.), *The legacy of Kenneth Burke* (pp. 196–223). Madison: University of Wisconsin Press.

Williams, R. (1977). *Marxism and literature*. Oxford: Oxford University Press.

Wilson, A. (1992). *The culture of nature: North American landscape from Disney to the Exxon Valdez*. Cambridge, MA: Blackwell.

Wise use group targets environmental movement. (1991, December 29). *Denver Post*, p. 4A.

Wittgenstein, L. (1988). *Wittgenstein's lectures on philosophical psychology, 1946–47*, trans. P. T. Geach. Brighton, England: Harvester.

Wood, D. J., & Gray, B. (1991). Toward a comprehensive theory of collaboration. *Journal of Applied Behavioral Science, 27*, 139–162.

World Resources Institute. (1992). *The 1992 environmental almanac.* New York: Houghton-Mifflin.

Worster, D. (1993). *The wealth of nature: Environmental history and the ecological imagination.* New York: Oxford University Press.

Year of the deal. (1991, February). *National Wildlife*, pp. 33–40.

INDEX

ABOUT THE EDITORS AND CONTRIBUTORS

EDITORS

Star A. Muir is Associate Professor of Communication at George Mason University in Virginia where he has taught Public Communication and Environmental Communication for seven years. He has authored articles and chapters critically assessing cultural and social elements of environmental discourse and is coauthor (with J. Muir) of *Foundations in Public Communication* (1992). He has served as president of the national Policy Caucus and is Conference Planner for the 1996 triennial meeting of the *Kenneth Burke Society*.

Thomas L. Veenendall is Program Coordinator and Professor of Communication Studies at Montclair State College in New Jersey where he has taught for fifteen years. He has authored or coauthored eleven textbooks and instructor's manuals focusing on effective communication and empowerment including *Let's Talk About Relationships* (1994) (with M. Feinstein). He is a past officer of the Eastern Communication Association for which he recently coordinated a conference to bring together environmental advocates and communication specialists.

CONTRIBUTORS

Laura A. Belsten is the Director of Health and Environmental Programs at the University of Denver, where she teaches courses in negotiation, mediation, conflict resolution, facilitation, leadership, teambuilding, and community collaboration. She was recently awarded a $100,000 grant from the Colorado Center for Environmental Management and the U.S. Department of Energy to research community involvement and public participation in environmental decision making. She has published articles in the *Journal of Environmental Systems* and *Rivers* and published a book on *Renewable Resources in Colorado.*

Rod Carveth is Assistant Professor and Chair of the Department of Mass Communication at the University of Bridgeport. Coeditor of *Media Economics: Theory and Practice,* he has authored articles for *Communication Research,* the *Journal of Applied Communication Research,* the *Journal of Business Communication,* the *Journal of Communication,* and the *Journal of Broadcasting and Electronic Media.*

John W. Delicath has presented papers at national and regional conferences on critical theory, radical ecology, environmental philosophy, conservation biology, and cultural studies. His research interests lie in bringing rhetorical and media studies into a critical ecological theory.

Kevin DeLuca is Assistant Professor in the Department of Communication at Penn State University. His primary research focus is on human/nature relations and how they are mediated by technology. He has presented papers at national conferences and is currently working on the tactics of radical environmental groups as they attempt to change public consciousness with respect to the ideographs "nature" and "progress." He has published articles in the *Western Journal of Communication* and *Crosscurrents.*

Roger Desmond is Professor of Communication at the University of Hartford. He has published over twenty-five research articles in professional journals and has contributed to five books. His research has addressed such topics as how children understand and respond to advertising, the development of thinking and language in children, and how adults process television programs. He was a visiting research fellow at Yale University, was awarded a fellowship in media literacy at the Annenberg School of Communication, and has been a consultant for both PBS and CBS.

David Easter is Lecturer in the Department of Communication at Ohio State University at Lima. He has presented several papers at national communication conferences on his continuing interest in cultural studies and environmental persuasion. His most recent publications have been in *Advances in Telematics* and *CommOddities: The Journal of Communication and Culture.*

Thomas R. Flynn is Assistant Professor of Communication at Slippery Rock University. His research reflects an interest in the rhetoric of history, viewing historical discourse as a window on cultural struggle. His paper "Principles of

Governance for Historical Discourse: The Rhetoric of Vietnam Revisionism" received the award for best paper from the Kenneth Burke Society at the 1993 Speech Communication Association Convention. Prior to joining Slippery Rock, he taught technical communications at Clarkson University.

David Knapp is Instructor in the Environmental Management and Policy Division at the University of Denver. President of Clear Ideas Communication Consultants, he is also a free-lance writer. He has published in such publications as *Speaker and Gavel, The Covenant Companion,* and *The Colorado Guide to Sports & Gaming.*

Trudy Milburn has taught courses on interpersonal communication, cultural codes in communication, and public speaking and has made several conference presentations. Her current research focuses on culturally situated ways of constructing identity.

Susan Mallon Ross is Assistant Professor at Clarkson University. She has published articles on environmental topics in *IEEE Transactions on Professional Communication* and *Technical Communication Quarterly.* In 1994 she participated in a speech communication seminar called "The Discourse(s) of 'Environmental Justice': Dilemmas of Race, Class, and Political Voice."

Warren Sandmann is Assistant Professor in the Department of Communication at the State University of New York at Geneseo. His major research interests are in rhetorical theory and criticism, law and rhetoric, and communication pedagogy. He has published in *Basic Communication Course Annual, Communication Studies, Iowa Journal of Communication Studies,* and the *Journal of the Communication and Theatre Association of Minnesota* and presented papers at a number of national and regional conferences.

Susan Senecah is Assistant Professor in the Environmental Studies Department at the State University of New York's College of Environmental Science and Forestry in Syracuse, New York. She researches environmental conflict and citizen groups, inclusive structures of public participation in decision making, environmental justice, rhetorical strategies of environmental campaigns, and women as leaders of grass-roots groups. She also does policy analysis in the New York state senate.

Michael Spangle is Acting Director of the bachelor's degree in Environmental Science and Instructor in the Departments of Applied Communication and Environmental Policy at the University of Denver. He has presented papers on environmental communication at a variety of regional and national conferences and has published in *The New York Communication Annual, Speaker and Gavel,* and the *Florida Communication Journal.*